An Uncomfortable Paradise

A history of dispossession and slavery in Simon's Town

BY

Joline Young

NagsPro Multimedia
Cape Town
2023

©Joline Young

No parts of this publication may be reproduced, stored in a retrieval system, or transmitted in any form or by any means, electronic, mechanical, photocopying, recording or otherwise, without the prior written permission of the copyright owner.

ISBN: 978-0-7961-2539-2

Printed by Bidvest Data

Design and layout:

Sandra Rowoldt Shell
NagsPro Multimedia
7 Gordon Street, Gardens, 8001
Cape Town

"Slavery considered in itself I acknowledge to be contrary to the principles of the Law of Nature, and an evil in Society, but it is an evil which has crept into this and other Colonies by the acquiescence of the Sovereign."

—*Fiscal Denyssen to Sir John Cradock, Fiscal's Office, 16 March 1813*

At the Old Burying Ground in Seaforth, Simon's Town rests Alethica who lived 99 years and is described as having been "an old slave of Lord Charles Somerset's time."

What happens to people when they are historically wrought by cruelty?

—*Joline Young*

This book is dedicated to:

Blanche, Nicole (1982-2004), Colin, Kyle, Ocean, Nick and Charlie

Table of Contents

Introduction 1

Part 1

Isolation 11

Part 2

1751 to 1795: Significant Change 47

Part 3

The Period Of Transition 1795 To 1814 55

Part 4

Simon's Town During Batavian Rule 1803 To 1806 73

Part 5

Simon's Town During The 2nd British Occupation 1806 ..81

Part 6

Amelioration 1816-1834 119

Part 7

Emancipation & the "Apprenticeship" Period: 1834-38 ...187

Part 8

From Emancipation to Working Class Community 203

CLOSING WORDS	239
MESSAGE TO MY ENSLAVED MOTHER	240
ACKNOWLEDGEMENTS	243
SELECTED SOURCES	245

List of Figures

Fig.0-1: Map of the Dutch East India Company's sea routes to Asia... 4

Fig. 0-2: Simon van der Stel & son Willem Adriaan on horseback 9

Fig.1-1: Waterfall near Block House, Simon's Town ca.1838........... 14

Fig. 1-2: Admiralty House, Simon's Town..16

Fig. 1-3: Thomas Lane, Simon's Town... 21

Fig. 1-4: Notebook of Jan Smiesing, schoolmaster, Slave Lodge..... 25

Fig. 1-5: "Teresa the wet-nurse" 29

Fig. 1-6: "Vue de la Baie Fals" Simon's Bay, 1776-1777................. 30

Fig. 1-7: Drostdy Steps, Simon's Town 34

Fig. 1-8: Map of eighteenth-century Malabar district, India 36

Fig. 1-9: Panorama of Simon's Town 43

Fig. 2-1: Simon's Town, Naval Port 52

Fig. 3-1: Battery at Simon's Town circa 1838 62

Fig. 3-2: Mother and child 66

Fig. 3-3: Dock Gates, Simon's Town 70

Fig. 4-1: Simon's Bay circa 1803 to 1806 73

Fig. 5-1: Simon's Town from Kalk Bay, circa 1838 89

Fig. 5-2: Mary and Percy Kindo in Simon's Town 94

Fig. 5-3: Fishermen in Simon's Bay, circa 1860 101

Fig. 5-4: A street plan showing Black Town in Simon's Town 113

Fig. 5-5: Untitled portrait by Lionel Davis.......................................116

Fig. 6-1: From the Hills above Simon's Bay, 1838 133

Fig. 6-2: Osmond's home "The Palace" 134

Fig. 6-3: Simon's Town circa 1866 144

Fig. 6-4: Zilvermyn Farm, Noordhoek............................ 150

Fig. 6-5: Cottage and mosque in Simon's Town, circa 1902 157

Fig. 6-6: The Malay Quarter, Simon's Town 164

Fig. 6-7: Watercolour of Rocklands Farm 178

Fig. 7-1: Untitled portrait by Lionel Davis.........................193

Fig. 7-2: Imhoff's Farm, Kommetjie, 1925 196

Fig. 8-1: Admiralty House, entrance to Simon's Town, ca 1854..... 203

Fig. 8-2: Washerwomen at the Waterfall, Simon's Town 204

Fig. 8-3: The Kru believed in Obeah (or fetish) 209

Fig. 8-4: The Kru dominated the palm trade 211

Fig. 8-5: A young Kru boy 214

Fig. 8-6: Smith's Lane, Simon's Town, 1975............................... 235

Fig. 8-7: Rectory Lane, Simonstown 236

INTRODUCTION

For many years, before I started on an extensive archival journey into the history of slavery in Cape Town, I wondered how it was that people, including some of my ancestors, came to be enslaved. Who were these people and how was it that they ended up enslaved at the Cape? Research shows that people in South Asia and South East Asia most often became enslaved because of severe poverty and not being able to pay their debts. In some countries, like Bali for instance, cockfight gambling was a huge trend and people who incurred gambling debts that they could not repay were forced to relinquish themselves to their creditors. In short, if you owed somebody money that you could not repay, you would be ceded to that person who would be entitled to either personally hold you as a "slave" until the debt was repaid, a concept known as "debt slavery," or to sell you on to a third party.

In Africa, people became enslaved because of warfare between villages. In this way, people from Africa who were enslaved at the Cape experienced what Cape slavery historian the late Robert Shell described as a "double trauma" as not only were they natally-alienated from their homes and families; they were also physically injured. Many people from Africa arrived at the Cape only to die of the injuries they sustained during warfare. Still others died on board while the ships were coasting, waiting for additional "supplies" of enslaved people.

Slavery is a phenomenon that has occurred throughout the ages and throughout the world including, of course, Europe. In these scenarios, when people were enslaved by their fellow countrymen, they were physically mutilated in order to set them apart as "slaves."[1]

At the Cape the burden of slavery did not end with the emancipation of enslaved people. Instead its legacy has travelled as a silent shame through the lives of subsequent generations in the same way that the legacy of domina-

---

[1] Robert Carl-Heinz Shell, *Children of Bondage: A Social History of the Slave Society at the Cape of Good Hope 1652-1838* (Johannesburg: Witwatersrand University Press, 1994), xxxv.

tion did. It was something not spoken about. Something considered better forgotten.

An Intersection of People and Cultures

The history of enslaved people in the Simon's Town district does not exist in isolation and cannot be told without also telling the story of the people whose lives intersected with their own. These were not only the European settlers who enslaved them, but pertinently the indigenous people who had inhabited this landscape for millennia before the Dutch East India Company/Verenigde Oostindische Compagnie (hereafter VOC) created firstly, a refreshment station and finally a settlement at the Cape: hence the term the Cape Colony.

This book is inspired by research done for my Masters degree completed at UCT at the end of 2013. My motivation for doing this work began after a lengthy oral history project of many people who were forcibly removed from Simon's Town during the Apartheid forced removals. Many, but not all of them, are descendants of people who were enslaved in the town during the period 1725 and 1838. Still others arrived in Simon's Town post emancipation of slavery. These were migrant workers from West Africa since 1838, amaXhosa from the Eastern Cape who arrived to build the Simon's Town Railway Station in the 1890s and Indian merchants who set up businesses in the town in the late 1800s. This book deals with the earlier history of Simon's Town from the time of indigenous dispossession to the period post Emancipation of enslaved people in the town.

My interest in the "slave" history of Simon's Town is invested in the role that slavery played in re-shaping this landscape, which has never been adequately acknowledged. Nor has the presence of the indigenous people of this area. While most of the later histories have been covered in some form or another, this early history of Simon's Town has been an historical omission for many years, and my Master's thesis was an attempt to fill this historical gap.

This book, on the other hand, tells the human stories of people whose neglected histories were begging to be resurrected from anonymity, while also giving historical context. It is my greatest hope that this book will open a window for people who may find their ancestors surfacing in this book. As importantly, I hope that this book will help the reader to understand how Simon's Town was shaped by this early history.

Most people date the formation of Simon's Town to the year 1743 when Baron von Imhoff declared Simon's Town a winter anchorage for the VOC. Still others date it to the year 1687 when Governor Simon van der Stel did a survey of the area and re-named the area Simon's Bay. However, the first physical change to the landscape began in 1725 when Anthonij Visser arrived and set up a household here. We will get to this later.

Long before the arrival of Jan van Riebeeck and his crew, European ships were stopping at the Cape. The people they traded with are commonly described as the Watermen or *Strandlopers* (beachcombers). These men negotiated with travellers on the beachfront and acted as middle men between the Khoe and the Europeans. The most notable middleman in this region was known as Autshumato or Harry, who was abducted by English mariners circa 1631 and taken to Batavia, where he learnt their language.[2] There was also the Khoe Captain Coree who was similarly abducted by English mariners in 1613 and taken to London, where he learnt English. His homesickness seemed to perplex the Chaplain Edward Terry, who felt he should be grateful for the food and lodging he was provided by the principal merchant of the English East India Company, Sir Thomas Smythe.[3]

Of course the key protagonists of change on the Cape landscape were a group of businessmen who, in 1602, were given permission by their government to form a business co-operative in order to strengthen their mercantile dealings against their European contemporaries. This co-operative was named the Dutch East India Company (DEIC) or in Dutch the *Verenigde Oostindische Compagnie* (VOC), which operated under the control of seventeen directors, who were referred to in Dutch as the *Heeren XVII*.

---

[2]Hedley Twidle, Prison and Garden: Cape Town, Natural History and the Literary Imagination. Thesis (PhD), University of York, 2010, 55.
[3]Twidle, Prison and Garden, 53.

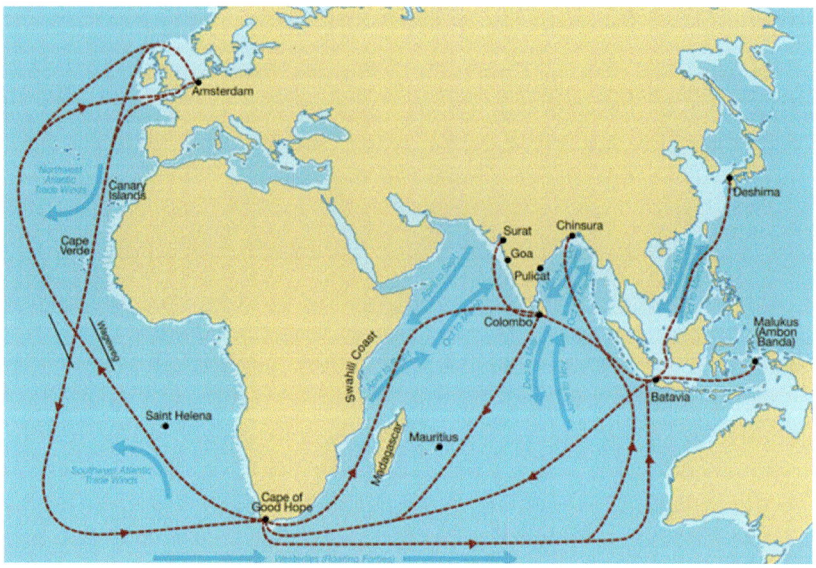

Fig. 0-1. Map of the Dutch East India Company's sea routes to Asia[4]

The VOC ships sailed along the coast of Africa, making their way towards South Asia and South East Asia, carrying with them cargoes of gold, silver, textiles, wine and mercury. On the coast, ivory was among the commodities for which they bartered. By the time they reached Asia they carried a diverse range of products representing both Africa and Europe. This in turn was traded for a variety of products including

> cloves and nutmeg from the Moluccas, pepper from Sumatra and west Java, textiles from India, silk from Persia and China, tea, sugar, and coffee from China and Java, porcelain from China and Japan, and indigo, sandalwood, benzoin, and musk from tropical forests in the regions between Arabia and Indochina.[5]

---

[4]Map drawn by Susan Reese for Laura Jane Mitchell, *Belongings: Property, Family, and Identity in Colonial South Africa (an Exploration of Frontiers, 1725-circa 1830)* (New York: Columbia University Press, 2009), 17.

[5]Ashley Brenner, The "Dutch Have Made Slaves of Them All, and… They Are Called Free": Slavery and Khoisan Indentured Servitude in the Eighteenth-Century Dutch Cape Colony. Thesis (MA), Emory University, 2009, 21.

The decision to set up a refreshment station at Table Bay at the Cape in 1652 was made to provide fresh fruit and vegetables for the crews of the VOC ships who were battling with scurvy due to the lack of fresh fruit and vegetables in their diet while at sea. This prompted the arrival of Jan van Riebeeck and his hapless crew at Table Bay in 1652, an event that would forever change the course of history at the Cape and destroy a way of life that existed here for thousands of years. Jan van Riebeeck's journals give abundant insights into his double-handed dealings with the indigenous people, most notably the chiefs, whom he charmingly entertained in his tent while at the same time he was writing back to the VOC in the Netherlands, requesting permission to enslave them. This request was not granted as the VOC considered the indigenous Khoe people to be important trading partners for livestock and did not want to antagonise them, at least not initially.[6]

Contrary to their original plan, which was to establish a refreshment station in Table Bay and not a permanent settlement, the Heeren Seventien were motivated by positive reports from Jan van Riebeeck about the abundant landscape and a decision was taken by the VOC to form a permanent settlement at the Cape. By 1657 the VOC offered land grants to company employees who wished to engage in agriculture.[7] Ironically this was also the year that the young Goringhaiqua warrior Doman[8] was "abducted and taken to Batavia."[9]

The conversion of the landscape from a hunter-gatherer/herder environment to an agricultural environment proved catastrophic to the nomadic lifestyle of the indigenous hunter-gatherers and herders, who were effectively cut off from their water courses.

The fencing in of land and ownership of land was a foreign concept to the indigenous people for whom, like all aboriginal people of their time, land

---

[6]For an insight into this period see Richard Elphick, *Kraal and Castle: Khoikhoi and the Founding of White South Africa* (New Haven and London: Yale University Press, 1977).

[7]Brenner, The "Dutch Have Made Slaves of Them All," 25.

[8]Willa Boezak, "The Cultural Heritage of South Africa's Khoisan" in *Indigenous Peoples' Cultural Heritage: Rights, Debates and Challenges*; edited by Alexandra Xanthaki, Sanna Valkonen, Leena Heinämäki, and Piia Kristiina Nuorgam (Leiden: Brill/Nijhoff, 2017), 254.

[9]Twidle, Prison and Garden, 61.

was communally shared and not individually owned.[10] This precipitated the first Dutch/Khoe war of 1659 led by Doman on his return.[11]

The Dutch writer Olfert Dapper recorded this war as follows:

> In 1659 there arose between the Goringhaiquas or Capemen and our countrymen who were there a violent struggle over the occupation and ownership of the land about the Cape. The Capemen attempted to expel us, alleging that they had held this land from time immemorial.[12]

Following this war in which Dapper described the Khoe as having fought "valiantly" for nearly a year, they lost more land to the Dutch East India Company and their movement on their natal land was restricted to "designated footpaths and to use designated gates when entering the fortified area."

With the second Dutch/Khoe war of 1673 the Khoe were summarily dispossessed as the VOC claimed the land by conquest.[13] The destruction of the Khoe way of life by the Dutch VOC was well-articulated by the dying Khoe fighter Eykamma at the time of the first Dutch/Khoe war, as follows:

> The reason for all their attacks, he continued, was nothing else than to revenge themselves for the harm and injustice done to them: since they not only were commanded to keep away from certain of their grazing grounds, which they had always possessed undisturbed and only allowed us at first to use as a refreshment station, but they always saw their lands divided out amongst us without their knowledge by the heads of the settlement, and boundaries put up

---

[10] Leonard Guelke and Robert Shell, "Landscape of Conquest: Frontier Water Alienation and Khoikhoi Strategies of Survival, 1652-1780" *Journal of Southern African Studies* 18, 4 (December 1992): 803.

[11] Olfert Dapper, Willem Ten Rhyne and Johannes Gulielmus de Grevenbroek, *The Early Cape Hottentots Described in the Writings of Olfert Dapper [1668], Willem Ten Rhyne [1686] and Johannes Gulielmus de Grevenbroek [1695]*; edited by Isaac Schapera (Cape Town: The Van Riebeeck Society, 1933), xiv.

[12] Dapper, Ten Rhyne, Grevenbroek, *Early Cape Hottentots*, 13.

[13] "Establishment of the Cape and its Impact on Khoikhoi and Dutch" [online resource] *South African History Online* (SAHO) https://www.sahistory.org.za/article/establishment-cape-and-its-impact-khoikhoi-and-dutch (accessed 31 August 2023).

within which they might not pasture. He asked finally what we would have done had the same thing happened to us.[14]

The weapons of the indigenous people were traditional poisoned arrows; however, the Europeans had the advantage of superior ammunition.[15] By 1676 an official commando was formed against the Cochoqua KhoeKhoe of the Western Cape and by 1699 their dispossessed status was solidified.[16] With the loss of their land and herds to the VOC, many indigenous people were forced to accept work on farms or face starvation.[17] However, it was the people who held the longest occupation of this landscape, those who the Khoe referred to as "San" who "increasingly coalesced to fight off colonial intrusion."[18]

While this book is primarily about slavery and about Simon's Town in particular, it is important to consider the historical landscape into which enslaved people were brought or born into. This was a landscape where indigenous people, hostile at their dispossession, were attacking the Dutch settlers with bows and arrows. This was also a landscape where the majority of the landed settlers were not from the upper stratum of European society, but from what was considered in Europe to be the peasant class of very poor people.

The scholar Ashley Brenner gives a fascinating account of the early Europeans who arrived at the Cape as employees of the VOC. With the exception of the VOC high ranking officials, the majority of the Europeans who arrived at the Cape were in fact from the area known today as Germany. These were people who had emerged from the 30 year religious war, which ended in 1648, many of whom had migrated to the Netherlands for reasons of extreme poverty. Many were coerced into VOC employment through deceitful means, which Ashley Brenner describes in the following way:

---

[14]Dapper, Ten Rhyne, Grevenbroek, Early Cape Hottentots, 15.

[15]For an insight into San and Khoi resistance see Shula Marks, "Khoisan Resistance to the Dutch in the Seventeenth and Eighteenth Centuries" *Journal of African History* 13, 1 (1972): 55-80.

[16]Mohamed Adhikari, *The Anatomy of a South African Genocide: The Extermination of the Cape San Peoples* (Claremont: UCT Press, 2010), 10.

[17]Dapper, Ten Rhyne, Grevenbroek, *Early Cape Hottentots*, xiv.

[18]Adhikari, *Anatomy of a South African Genocide*, 39.

Company sailors and soldiers were generally drawn from the lowest caste of European society. Several of the VOC's so-called recruits were actually the victims of *seelenverkäufers* (soul-sellers). These pariahs were boarding-house keepers who gave impoverished migrants to the city food and lodging only to turn a profit from their naïve guests by selling their labour to the VOC for a finder's fee.[19]

These were people who themselves had likely experienced trauma at the hands of the European gentry. As is found to be the case with people who have experienced trauma, many would later play out this trauma on a group of people who were in a weaker social position than themselves in what came to be known as the Cape Colony. Unused to holding power in their native countries, they suddenly found themselves in positions of power in a newly formed society of people where social hierarchies were constructed racially.

With the encroachment of VOC burgher settlement onto indigenous communal land, and as land was cleared for agriculture, foraging societies came to know hunger for the first time in their existence. As a result, their status altered from that of being the original inhabitants, livestock herders and traders to either that of landless starving people or people who were enserfed. However, technically they were never enslaved.

Simon's Bay was an isolated place of which the VOC had sparse knowledge initially. It was also very difficult to access by land as there was quicksand in Fish Hoek. However, in 1687 Simon van der Stel in his capacity as commander of the Cape, did a survey of the False Bay area. At the time he was so impressed by this abundant and beautiful landscape that he re-named the area, then referred to as Yzelstein's Bay, to Simon's Bay.

Within the context of slavery, Van der Stel himself cut a curious historical figure as his grandmother Monica was a formerly enslaved Indian woman from the Coromandel Coast in India. This heritage was rarely acknowledged during the apartheid period in South Africa.

---

[19]Brenner, The "Dutch Have Made Slaves of Them All," 77.

Fig. 0-2. Simon van der Stel and his son Willem Adriaan on horseback
Source: Attributed to Jan Weenix, original destroyed by fire, (Ireland, 1962)

Notwithstanding his maternal family links to slavery and the fact that on his death his will instructed the freedom of his personal "slaves," Simon van der Stel was first and foremost a representative of the VOC, firstly as commander of the Cape and from 1691, Governor of the Cape. He was also the head of the High Court. A powerful man who ran the Cape with military precision,[20] he introduced the nightly *"ratel wacht"* system. This was a system whereby three burghers would patrol the streets of Cape Town on a

---

[20] Marius Diemont, *Rogues to Riches: The Fortunes of Olof Bergh and the Van Der Stels* (Hermanus: Penstock Publishing, 2012), 24.

rotation basis and use their rattles to report deviant behaviour in an effort to ensure that in the City "silence, rest and peace should prevail."[21] As with all such forms of social control and military discipline, there is always the danger of abuse of power. Under his command young boys of European ancestry aged nine to thirteen years were co-opted into the Boys Brigade from which they would graduate into the Burgher Militia by the age of sixteen.[22] Van der Stel also introduced the *veldwagter* system at the Cape. The *veldwagters* or field cornets were ordinary men who were given the power to arrest "criminals" for which they were rewarded by being exempted from paying tax.[23] In all these ways, a society upheld by European masculine hegemony was being entrenched. The Van der Stel family themselves formed a mighty dynasty at the Cape for many years before falling out of favour with the VOC, mainly due to the actions of Simon van der Stel's son, Willem Adriaan van der Stel. In 1687 Simon van der Stel recommended to the VOC that Simon's Bay be used as a winter anchorage to avoid the devastating shipwrecks caused by weather conditions in the Table Bay. However, this recommendation was not acted upon at the time and as such the False Bay area remained untouched by European settlement for many decades thereafter.

This changed in 1725 when a Dutchman named Anthonij Visser was granted a loan farm in Simon's Bay by the VOC, where he established himself as a livestock farmer. The date is significant as it was by 1725 that the historian Nigel Penn reports there being a shortage of meat at the Cape.[24] Thus by settling in the False Bay region Anthonij Visser was locating himself in a prime area from which to trade for livestock with the indigenous Khoe herders. The year 1725 is also significant in terms of slavery, being the year when the first enslaved people arrived in the town.

---

[21]Margaret Whiting Spilhaus, *Company's Men* (Cape Town: John Malherbe, 1973), 148.
[22] Spilhaus, *Company's Men*, 144.
[23] Spilhaus, *Company's Men*, 145.
[24]See Nigel Penn, *The Forgotten Frontier: Colonist and Khoisan on the Cape's Northern Frontier in the 18th Century* (Athens: Ohio University Press; Cape Town: Double Storey: 2005), 52-55.

PART 1

ISOLATION

Susanna van Bengal—5 April 1725

When Susanna van Bengal arrived in Simon's Bay by boat on an autumn day in April 1725, the land before her was covered in thick vegetation and at first glance there was no sign of human life. On closer inspection, however, she would have seen human eyes watching her motley group—and the tips of poisoned arrows at the ready. If she had glanced up at the mountain she might have seen (as would another traveller a few years later) a "small species of stag and a race of very large monkies."[1] Overhead, seagulls may have screamed a warning of what was to come. On the land she might have heard noises that some travellers wrongly described as the unwelcoming sounds of "wolves."[2] Around her, she and her group of five enslaved people may have glanced at each other nervously as they pondered their fellow travellers, a commando of grim-faced European men armed with muskets, taking orders from the Dutchman Anthonij Visser, who had bought all five of them from the widow of Governor Mauriz Pasques de Chavonnes in Table Bay.[3] There was only one other female in this expedition. She was named Jolanda of the Cape.

---

[1] "In his excursions he frequently saw a small species of stag, and a race of very large monkies." Pierre-Marie-François de Pagès, "Voyage of M. de Pagès towards the South Pole in 1773 and 1774" in William Mavór, *An Historical Account of the Most Celebrated Voyages,* … Volume 12 (Philadelphia: Samuel F. Bradford, 1802), 123.

[2] A number of travellers in their journals mentioned hearing the sound of wolves. However in all probability they were hearing the calls of hyenas or African wild dogs. The *Dictionary of South African English* gives multiple examples of such usages [online resource] https://www.dsae.co.za/entry/wolf/e07923?q=wolves (accessed 20 May 2023).

[3] Saledeed, a database of "slave" transactions compiled by Robert Shell (Unpublished, 2014).

If Jolanda needed extra comfort to face a fear of the unknown, this may have been provided by Susanna. This was not the first time that Susanna would find herself ripped away from a familiar world. Her life had been a long journey of ruptured experiences, starting from when she was a child born into the Barkers caste in an area in India known as Nagamaij Palim. At the time of her birth her mother Moeslaaij named her Polo. By the time Polo reached her ninth or tenth year of life, her mother sold her due to severe poverty.[4] In subsequent years her name was changed from Polo to Amarenta, Amarenta to Dafnie van Bengalen and by the time of her arrival to the Cape, she was named Susanna van Bengalen. On 11 March 1723, Susanna van Bengalen was sold to Governor Mauriz Pasques de Chavonnes by Jan van Strijen, a VOC employee listed as a "fiscal [slave officer]" who was in transit at sea.[5]

By this time she would have changed hands at least four times, the curse of poverty overshadowing her life as she went from one "slave-holder" to the next. When Anthonij Visser settled in Simon's Bay, the ownership of Susanna would pass to him, the purchase registered on 5 April 1725.[6] To understand the Simon's Bay into which Susanna van Bengal arrived in 1725, one has to imagine indigenous hunter-gatherers moving through the thicket of bushes with a familiarity that could only come from an ancestral legacy that stretched back in time for thousands of years. One also has to imagine Khoe herders moving purposefully as they ushered their cattle along luscious grazing sites within earshot of the rippling sounds of water cascading down the waterfall, a sacred site for shamanic ceremonies: a site of healing.

One wonders about her thoughts as she landed ashore and gazed at this dense green landscape and heard the sounds of animals interspersed with the regular cracking of waves in the sea beneath a brilliant sun. Certainly she would have regarded Visser with some trepidation, wondering what her life would be like as his "slave" and if he was cruel.

The landing group consisting of mainly German-speaking men and five enslaved people would camp on a section of land close to the shore. This

---

[4]*Cape Transcripts 1673-1834*; transcribed by TEPC team [CD-ROM]: *Inventories of the Master of the Orphan Chamber*, MOOC 14, Volume1-85.
[5]Saledeed; compiled by Robert Shell.
[6]Saledeed; compiled by Robert Shell.

land was given to Anthonij Visser on loan by the Here XVII, of the VOC. That this "gift" would potentially cause hostility with the indigenous Khoe and "San" people was not lost on Visser, which is why he was accompanied by an armed commando. However, he was also eager not to antagonise the people on whose land he was trespassing, as he needed their cooperation to obtain livestock.

Once landed, Susanna and her group of five "slaves" would have busied themselves, following orders to collect wood for fires and to prepare tents. She and Jolanda would prepare the evening meal. If she feared the Europeans, Susanna would have viewed the other enslaved people in her group of five with a degree of familiarity, as they had all been part of the household "slaves" belonging to the De Chavonnes family. There was December van Malabar, a countryman; Jochem from Madagascar, a far-off island of which she would have known little, as well as Alexander and Jolanda, who were born at the Cape. Certainly the latter two would have been more accepting of their circumstances as, having been born into slavery at the Cape, they would have had nothing against which to compare their situation. What was certain on landing was that their work was cut out for them. For the males there was land to be cleared and a homestead to be built (as well as a kraal and other outbuildings),[7] vegetable gardens to be laid out, fish to be caught and hunted, game to be slaughtered.

What is significant to the history of Simon's Town[8] is that the arrival of this diverse group of people formed a pivotal intersection of people and cultures that would re-shape the history of the False Bay in a way that would have been unimaginable to the cast in this historical drama. Through this settlement a connection of unequal, often cruel, multifaceted and complex relationships began.[9] Thus it was that Anthony Visser, a bachelor from Utrecht in the Netherlands, would establish himself as a single European "slaveholder" and livestock farmer on a landscape which, for the "San" and Khoe,

---

[7] Hendrik Carel Vos Leibbrandt, *Precis of the Archives of the Cape of Good Hope: Requesten (Memorials) Volume IV, 1715-1806* (1743): T-Z (Anthony Visser, no. 77). (Cape Town: South African Library, 1989), page 1280.

[8] The small town was initially named Simon's Bay and today is known as Simon's Town.

[9] Shula Marks, "Khoisan Resistance to the Dutch in the Seventeenth and Eighteenth Centuries," *Journal of African History* 13, 1 (1972): 61-64.

was their birthright. Historical records show that during this period the Khoe were not as amenable to trading their livestock as they had been at the time of Jan van Riebeeck's settlement. This leaves it to speculation as to whether Visser traded peacefully with the Khoe or whether he used violent coercion to obtain livestock, as had occurred with *trekboers* in the interior.[10]

Fig. 1-1. Waterfall near Block House, Simon's Town ca. 1838
Source: Christopher Webb Smith (artist): 19359 (xix), Library of Parliament

---

[10] Mohamed Adhikari, *The Anatomy of a South African Genocide: The Extermination of the Cape San Peoples* (Claremont: UCT Press, 2010), passim.

A slight interruption in Visser's newly-created world and a further interruption in the lives of the indigenous people were caused by the arrival of the English contraband ship the *Grooten Alexander* in August 1725. However, following a few days of high tension and military assistance by fifty soldiers despatched to Simon's Bay by the Council of Policy, the *Grooten Alexander* "left for the open sea" on 22 August 1725.[11]

The norm at the Cape during this historical period was that enslaved males worked and slept outside the house in a shed whereas enslaved females worked inside the home and slept in the kitchen at night. Levels of sexual exploitation of enslaved females by "slave-holding" males within the home environment have been extensively documented by the late Robert Shell.[12]

Early in 1727, Visser married a widow named Maria Brons, with whom he fathered a daughter, Elizabeth Theresa Visser, born towards the end of that year. Their home was the shell that in later years grew into Admiralty House, which still exists in Simon's Town today and belongs to the South African Navy. By this time Visser had developed the reputation of being a very hospitable host, particularly to captains and crews of ships wrecked on the Bay.

The birth of his daughter seemed to have occurred during a period when Visser was experiencing economic prosperity, as it coincided with further "slave"[13] purchasing with another of Susanna's countrymen joining the Visser "slave-holding" in Simon's Town. This was Domingo van Bengal, who arrived at the Cape on the *Yarmnik* on 24 May 1727, as the "slave" of Johannes Needer, an employee of the VOC.

Two years later, two more males arrived on this male-dominated "slave-holding." They were Mangorij van Macassar, formerly the "slave" of Pieter G Noordt a VOC employee, whose ownership was transferred to Anthonij

---

[11] Helena Liebenberg, "Introduction to the Resolutions of the Council of Policy of Cape of Good Hope," page 53 [online resource] https://www.academia.edu/48793365/Resolutions_Introduction_English p1_p27. Regrettably, the online TANAP database of transcriptions has been hacked and is no longer accessible.

[12] For an insight into the sexual exploitation of enslaved women, see Robert Shell, *Children of Bondage: A Social History of the Slave Society at the Cape of Good Hope, 1652-1838* (Johannesburg: Witwatersrand University Press, 1994).

[13] The use of inverted commas around the demeaning word "slave" throughout this publication is to emphasise the fact that this was an identity imposed upon people in the same way that the later identity "Coloured" has been imposed on people.

Visser on 1 July 1729; and Coridon van Madagascar whom Visser bought from the widow of Dirk Gijsbert Noodt on 14 December 1729.[14]

Fig. 1-2. Admiralty House, Simon's Town

Although the VOC held the monopoly on the "slave-trade" at the Cape, many VOC employees made hefty profits for themselves through private trading when their ships docked in port. The treatment of enslaved people at the Cape during this period of Dutch colonial settlement, particularly in remote areas such as Simon's Bay, suggests that early on in their experiences all these people would have been exposed to violence—or the threat of violence. If running away was considered an option, this would have had to be viewed against the threat of capture by Visser's private commando of armed Europeans.[15]

---

[14]Saledeed database; compiled by Robert Shell

[15]Donna Corns, Offended Shadows: Marronage in the Cape Hanglip 1720s-1730s. Thesis, (BA Hons), University of Cape Town, 2011, 100.

As this household grew, so too did the number of its outbuildings, including a kraal that was filled at various times with cattle. Children were born into slavery in this household, although with the high infant mortality rate of enslaved children at the Cape during this historical period, many would die before reaching the age of three. Robert Shell has argued that the primary aim of "slave-holders" was to secure strong male labour. Their crude reasoning was that it was considered cheaper to buy an adult who could perform hard manual labour than to bear the cost of raising a child to adulthood. However, through this settlement a new phenomenon began on the landscape of Simon's Bay: the birth of mixed-race children. Some children were the offspring of Khoe women and European men, some were the offspring of Asian or African enslaved men and Khoe women and others the offspring of Asian women and European men. These children carried a variety of racial mixes, but the VOC administrators had disparaging names for them all. The children of Khoe women and European men were called "Bastards"; the children of enslaved men and Khoe women were called "Bastard Hottentots." The indigenous hunter-gatherers and their children were called "boesman" and the indigenous herders and their children were called "Hottentotten." In this way they became exposed to trauma–induced identity transformation in a manner that was arguably not dissimilar to that experienced by refugees today.[16] As history unfolded on this landscape, this "identity distress"[17] would continue to affect subsequent generations as new, but consistently disparaging, identities were assigned to them through the colonial census and transported into the fabric of their daily lives.

The Dutch naming system for the children of European men and enslaved women hinged on the outcomes of their fate. If the fathers married the mothers, the child would make the transition from "*slaaf*" to burgher. As a result a number of Afrikaner families are able to trace their ancestral mothers to formerly enslaved women.

---

[16]Jessica Guler, The Relationship among Previous Exposure to War and Conflict, Acculturation, and Identity Formation among Adolescent Refugees. Thesis (BA Hons), University of Central Florida, 2014, 12. University of Central Florida STARS [online resource] https://stars.library.ucf.edu/honorstheses1990-2015/1573/ (accessed 29 July 2023).

[17]Guler, Relationship among Previous Exposure to War and Conflict, 25.

If the father did not acknowledge the child or marry the mother, the status of the child would remain that of *slaaf*. Although by VOC decree children born of European fathers were ordered to be freed on the death of their fathers, this did not always happen.[18]

Simon's Bay becomes a Winter Anchorage for the Dutch East India Company (VOC)—1743

In 1743, after eighteen years of single settlement in the Simon's Bay by the Visser household, Baron von Imhoff stopped off at the Cape to declare Simon's Bay the winter anchorage for the VOC. This declaration sounded the death-knell for the indigenous people who were summarily dispossessed of their land in the False Bay region; and was a defining factor in irrevocably altering the natural landscape and changing relations between indigenous people and Europeans in this area. Anthonij Visser was granted the land that he had previously occupied on loan from the VOC.[19] The land he occupied was described as "a cattle farm on which he has built a house, kraal and other buildings."[20]

In 1745 Anthonij Visser died. For Susanna van Bengal his death brought freedom, which suggests that she bore some of his children. This would have been in line with the VOC ruling that enslaved women who bore the children of "slave-holders" should be freed at the death of the respective "slave-holder." Furthermore, her absorption into this complex society would see Susanna herself become listed as a "slave-owner."

Other recipients of land grants in the Simon's Town District at this time included Christina Diemer, the widow of Fredrik Russouw, who was granted land that became known as the farm De Goede Gift.[21] There was also a

---

[18]Shell, *Children of Bondage*, 342. George McCall Theal, *Records of the Cape Colony from October 1812 to April 1814* ... (London: William Clowes for the Government of the Cape Colony, 1901): volume 9, 131 ff.

[19]Anthony Visser in Leibbrandt, *Precis of the Archives of the Cape of Good Hope Requesten (Memorials), volume 4, 1715-1806: T-Z* (No. 77), 1743 (Cape Town: South African Library, 1989), 1280.

[20]Leibbrandt, *Precis of the Archives of the Cape of Good Hope Requesten (Memorials), volume 4, T-Z,* 1743, 1280.

[21]Western Cape Archives & Records Service (hereafter WCARS), C121 (20 February 1743), 169.

request by Carel Wieser for freehold of a farm held in loan by him and Christina Diemer for some years, situated behind the Steenbergen, between the "Groote Slange Kop" and the "Poespaskraal"[22] namely Imhoff's Gift farm. Imhoff's Gift was granted to Christina Diemer on 27 May 1743.[23]

Christina Diemer's enslaved labour force included the following foreign-born people:

Table 1:-1:   CHRISTINA DIEMER'S ENSLAVED LABOUR FORCE

NAME	ORIGIN
Ismail van Bougies (Bugis)	Sulawesi, Indonesia
Alec van Bougies	Sulawesi, Indonesia
April van Bougies	Sulawesi, Indonesia
Rob van Bougies	Sulawesi, Indonesia
Maladie van Bougies	Sulawesi, Indonesia
Mandar van Bougies	Sulawesi, Indonesia
Tino van Batavia	Jakarta, Lesser Sunda Islands, Indonesia
Pieter van Bali	Lesser Sunda Islands, Indonesia
Tuan van Mozambique	Mozambique, Africa
Domingo van Rio de la Goa	Maputo, Mozambique, Africa
Francois van Rio de la Goa	Maputo Bay, Mozambique, Africa
Carel van Madagascar	Madagascar, Africa
Justinus van Malabar	Malabar, India
August van Malabar	Malabar, India
Secules van Malabar	Malabar, India
Fortuijn van Malabar	Malabar, India
Mathys van Bengal	Bengal, India

[22] Carel George Wieser in Leibbrandt, *Precis of the Archives of the Cape of Good Hope Requesten (Memorials) Volume IV, 1715-1806: T-Z*, no. 21, 1332.
[23] *Cape Freeholds*, Volume 2, part 3 (13. April 1717 to 10 August 1746): page 442 (27 May1743). Simon's Town Museum, The Willis Files.

Table 1:-1: CHRISTINA DIEMER'S ENSLAVED LABOUR FORCE

NAME	ORIGIN
Martha van Bengal	Bengal, India
July van Bengal	Bengal, India
Jacob van Malabar	Malabar, India
Pagtra van Nias	Nias Island, off Sumatra, Indonesia

On the death of Christina Diemer in 1765, a man named Ismail was listed in an inventory of her "assets." The story of Ismail—who is said to be one of the two *tuans* (teachers) buried in the *kramat* in Dolphin Street—was passed down in families who lived in the Malay Quarter of Simon's Town. Family stories are often conflicted as different people remember different aspects and tales change over time with each teller, but during an interview in 2009 with the ninety-one year old Kobera (known in the community as "Aunty Kobie") Manuel, former resident of Thomas Lane, Simon's Town and daughter of Hadji Bakaar Manuel, she mentioned as her ancestors, the South East Asian Ismail and his son Jaliludien:

> The two Tuans from Sumbawa, Indonesia were Ismail and his son Jaliludien. Ismail had another son in Indonesia who died as a child. His name was Zainab Abedien. Jaliludien fathered Abdul Gakien, Amina, Kobera, Fatima, Aisha, Abdul Kariem, Abdul Majied, Gadija, Mymoma.

A prized possession of "Aunty Kobie," who was the aunt of the late heritage activist Ebrahiem Manuel, was the *kitaab* of her ancestor Abdul Kariem, grandson of Ismail, which carried the following inscription:

> *Hierdie Kitaab ibin Imam Abdul Kariem, ibin Imam Abdul Jaliel Ibin Imam Ismail min Sumbawa.*[24]

---

[24] "This *kitaab* belongs to Imam Abdul Kariem, son of Imam Abdul Jaliel, son of Imam Ismail of Sumbawa."

Fig. 1-3. Thomas Lane, Simon's Town
Artist: Peter Clarke, courtesy of Muriel Rubin

Given that Islam, like all religions other than the Dutch Reformed religion, was banned until 1804, the names Ismail, Pagtra, Arij, Tuan, Mandaar and Malade are a glaring anomaly in the naming system of enslaved people at Imhoff's Gift.

In a survey done of the "Malay Quarter" in Simon's Town just before the apartheid forced removals during the 1960's, at least twelve Muslim families claimed they were descendants of Ismail, who hailed from the VOC era and is buried in the *kramat* in Dolphin Road, Simon's Town. The surnames of these families are Ismail, Solomon, Manuel and Baker.

The role of Imhoff's Farm as an incubator for Islam while under the ownership of the Widow Christina Diemer therefore deserves consideration.

Imhoff's Farm

As the VOC asserted their ownership of this landscape, the landscape itself became altered. This included the naval West Dockyard, which was commenced in 1743 as well as "the erection of a building to accommodate storehouses, a bakehouse, a smith's shop and quarters for the garrison and workmen."[25] The introduction of a commercial liquor house on this landscape soon followed, with the *pachter* Jan de Waal being given permission to open a *taphuis* in Simon's Bay.[26] A warehouse was erected for the storage of anchors, rope, wood and dry provisions and an elongated building erected, which stored ships goods and provided accommodation for postal officials, soldiers, medical officers and the infirm.

Viewed differently, through the intervention of the VOC—a mercantile company motivated by profit—indigenous people were dispossessed and their landscape irrevocably altered. It is incredible to consider that the former was achieved with the assistance of impoverished German-speaking people and the latter through the labour of people who were enslaved.

Hidden from the researcher's view is the toll that this alteration of the landscape had on the labour force. However, references in correspondence about enslaved men being tasked with carrying rocks from high up in the mountainside in Simon's Town gives one an indication of the taxing conditions enslaved men laboured under in the harsh climatic conditions of Simon's Town. In summer the area is extremely hot and in winter Simon's Town is a wet and windy place. A hint at high mortality rates among

---

[25]The Vernacular Architecture Society of South Africa, Sixth Annual General Meeting, Simon's Town, 1969, page 3.

[26]Dan Sleigh, *Die Buiteposte: VOC-Buiteposte onder Kaapse Bestuur, 1652-1795* (Pretoria: HAUM, 1993), 306.

enslaved people comes through a decree (or *placaat*) on 1 February 1747, when a Public Day of Prayer was ordered because of the "great mortality among the slaves." This was ostensibly done because of concern about loss of revenue rather than concern for the lives of the enslaved people.[27]

Through this labour force the VOC also created a wagon route linking Simon's Bay with Table Bay.[28] By March 1745 work was commenced on the construction "of a magazine, a hospital and quarters for people in charge." More lavish residences that were constructed were the Drostdy, which was the residence of the post-holder Justinus Blas and his successor Adriaan de Neys. These developments were public symbols of VOC power.

In 1749 a land grant was given to Hendrik Versen[29] whose farm in Simon's Bay was named Constantia and situated in the area that houses the Heritage Museum and East Dockyard. His original homestead is now used as Naval offices. On his death the enslaved people linked to his estate were listed as Onrust of Malabar (India) and three locally born people, namely Adam, Hanna and Rachel of the Cape.

While the VOC and their staff most likely believed that through this alteration of the landscape they were adding to progress, the indigenous people must have looked on with shock and horror as their ancestral land and sacred sites became permanently altered. For the indigenous "San" hunter-gatherers who foraged from the land and the Khoe who were transhumant pastoralists/herders moving in a clear seasonal pattern to ensure availability of grazing for their herds;[30] the establishment of VOC buildings and private farms would have proved catastrophic. Unsurprisingly, the response of the indigenous "San" and Khoe people was to resist this threat to their way of life. As a result, constant attacks on the settlement occurred requiring the formation of a sentry guard system by both the Dutch and British colonial

---

[27] See Kaapse Argiefstukke. *Kaapse Plakkaatboek: deel 2: 1707-1753* (Cape Town: Cape Times, 1948), C. 683, (1 February 1747), 223-224.
[28] Enid Helen Robinson, Beyond the City Limits, People and Property at Wynberg 1795 to 1927. Thesis (PhD), University of Cape Town, 1995, 32.
[29] Simon's Town Museum: The Willis Files. Cape Old Freeholds, 6.10.1746-27.08.1782, Volume 3 Deeds Registry, No. 608, Simon's Town (15 October 1749).
[30] I am grateful to Professor Mohamed Adhikari for providing clarity on this issue (personal email, 16 October 2019).

settlements to ward off attacks by the indigenous people trying to remove these strangers from their land.

The indigenous people had a valuable history and culture that was unique to themselves. They were an animist society who had a strong spiritual connection to their natural environment and lived in harmony with nature.[31] Because of VOC dispossession, their lifestyle, free movement and the survival of their economy was destroyed.

The indigenous "San" and Khoe people had cultural norms and standards that the Europeans and the enslaved did not understand and on either side of this historical divide there were people who believed themselves to be superior to "the other." Whereas some Europeans referred to the Khoe and "San" as "savages" the Khoe had similar thoughts about the Europeans.

Johannes Gulielmus de Grevenbroek, Secretary of the Council of Policy at the Cape during the seventeenth century, recorded the following angry utterance by an indigenous person to the European settlers in 1695:

> You eaters of grass and lettuce, feed it to your oxen. Personally we would rather fast. Your habits disgust and sicken us … With your foolish values you treasure a woman's necklace of tiny beads above sheep. You have no gods: you have none. Like savages you disburden your bowels on the graves of our ancestor Heitsi Abib.[32]

With the loss of land, free movement and an altered landscape taken captive by a foreign conqueror, the indigenous people and their descendants were reduced to poverty, powerlessness and a consequent loss of self-esteem. Pertinently too, along with the alteration of the landscape came an alteration of the people themselves due to miscegenation. Creolisation took a variety of forms and racial identity constructions were designed by administrative staff of the VOC in unique and peculiar ways. Fair-skinned people of either total European or mixed racial origin were categorised in the census as "white." For the latter this was dependent on whether they were enslaved or free.

---

[31] Adhikari, *Anatomy of a South African Genocide*, 38.
[32] Johannes Gulielmus de Grevenbroek, "A Very Brief History: People and Places in the Western Cape" in Carohn Cornell and Antonia Malan, *Places at the Cape: A Guidebook for Beginner Researchers* (Cape Town: Department of Historical Studies, University of Cape Town, 2008), 5.

Through these identity constructions came notions of superiority where "whiteness" or a fair skin was constructed as being superior and worthy of privilege and respect. To this end the culture and world-view of the conquerors was privileged over the cultures of people they had either enslaved or dispossessed. The irony is that among the people from the conquering class were those who were illiterate and from very poor backgrounds, while among the enslaved there were people who were literate in their native languages.

The Heritage Museum in Simon's Town houses many *kitaabs* written in beautiful Arabic script that attest to this. Another example is the archival notebook of Jan Smiesing, an enslaved man who was the schoolmaster in the Slave Lodge, which contained health remedies written in Tamil.

Fig. 1-4. Notebook of Jan Smiesing, enslaved person and schoolmaster at the Slave Lodge, Cape Town
Source: Photograph by Robert C-H Shell

If the indigenous people, quite rightly, experienced the alteration of their natural habitat as a form of psychological subjugation, the subjugation of the minds of enslaved people was also taking place.

Natally alienated, traumatised, humiliated and fearful, elements of low self worth may have been psychologically introduced into the minds of enslaved people and even more so to their offspring, who would have been born into a society where their enslavement was normalised. The negative social status of "slaves" became formalised through Governor Ryk Tulbagh's "Tulbagh Code" of 1754[33] whereby the treatment of enslaved people became mandated by law. In terms of the Code, enslaved people were tightly controlled. The regulations included that enslaved people:

- had to be indoors after 10 pm; if they were out, they had to carry a lantern
- could not ride horses or wagons in the streets
- could not sing, whistle or make any other sound at night
- could not meet in bars, buy alcohol or form groups on public holidays
- could not gather near the entrance of a church during a church service
- who stopped in the street to talk to other [enslaved people] could be driven off with canes if necessary
- who insulted or falsely accused a freeman were to be flogged and chained
- who struck a "slave-holder" were to be shown no mercy and put to death
- were not permitted to own or carry guns
- who accused their "master" falsely with any disgraceful act should be scourged, put in irons or punished according to the circumstances of the case.

During the period 1743 to 1795 the ethnicities of the foreign-born enslaved people in Simon's Town appeared to be largely Asian. A database of enslaved people in Simon's Town compiled by the author from archival research, reveals that a tenth of the enslaved people in Simon's Town were Madagascan and about 6% were Mozambican. These low figures may be due to the fact that Madagascan and Mozambican people were more likely to escape during this period than Asian people, who found themselves on a different continent to their natal homes.[34] It is notable that during the period

---

[33]Kaapse Argiefstukke. *Kaapse Plakkaatboek: deel 3: 1754-1786* (Cape Town: *Cape Times,* 1949), C. 684 (3/5 September 1754), 1-6.

of VOC colonial control at the Cape, escapes were always undertaken by foreign-born enslaved people. Some of these escapes were well organised and took place in large groups of mainly Madagascan and Mozambican people.[35] In 1758 seven people escaped in the boat of the Simon's Town post-holder.[36]

In 1761 ten Madagascan people escaped by sea and in 1763 twenty two Mozambican people attempted a sea escape and when this proved unsuccessful, they escaped inland. Whether these groups of people survived is not known, however, they were certainly never found.

By 1775 Simon's Town had in fact gained the reputation of being the one outpost of the VOC where there were the most "daring" escapes by enslaved people.[37] This was despite the fact that a financial reward was paid to people for apprehending "deserters."[38]

The high ratio of Asian people during this period should also be considered within a background that apart from the settlement of Anthonij Visser in 1725, the formalised VOC settlement in the False Bay occurred in 1743, nearly a hundred years after their initial settlement in Table Bay in 1652. This happened at a time when the VOC slaving expeditions had turned East. The demographics of enslaved people during this period strongly favoured the practice and growth of Islam in Simon's Town, which is still in evident in the built environment today through the Simon's Town mosque, the Malay Quarter and the *kramats* in Dolphin Street, Simon's Town.

Escape

For people born into slavery, there would have been nothing with which to contrast their life experiences. However, foreign-born enslaved people would have experienced their lives as free people, which is why they were more

---

[34]"Origin and Gender of Privately-Owned Enslaved People in Simon's Town during the Period 1743-1795" in appendix to Joline Young, The Enslaved People Of Simon's Town, 1743 to 1843, Thesis (MA), University of Cape Town, 2013.

[35]WCARS, Verbatim Copies, VC 30, (2 May 1767), 178.

[36]WCARS, Verbatim Copies, VC 28 daghregister, (30 November 1758), as cited in Sleigh, *Die Buiteposte*, 327.

[37] Sleigh, *Die Buiteposte*, 327.

[38]See Kaapse Argiefstukke. *Kaapse Plakkaatboek: deel 2: 1707-1753* (Cape Town: *Cape Times*, 1948), C. 683 (7 August 1743).

likely to try to escape. Throughout the period of slavery at the Cape there was also a community of people who had escaped from slavery, living in caves in Hanglip.[39] Known as the Hanglip Maroons, they were secretly aided by "Malay [fishermen] 'slaves' and even among the free community" in Simon's Town.[40] However, running away came at huge penalty for those who were caught. Punishments for running away included being brutally flogged, having one's nose cut off, being kept in chains and even death. Running away thus carried its own casualties to the psyche as it carried the risks of extremely violent punishment if caught by the special commandos who were paid per head for each "run-away" enslaved person caught. To survive as a "run-away" where the threat of capture, violent punishment and possible death loomed large, would have either required or created a certain type of persona.

The Hanglip maroons were perhaps the most successful resisters of enslavement, but this was a brutal existence where the dynamics of power played themselves out between the enslavers and those who were prepared to fight enslavement by any means possible. It is an unfortunate fact that the violence that was meted out to enslaved people, particularly the men, created a mirror image of itself within some of these men. Leander Bugis, the early leader of the Hanglip maroons was an extremely violent man and a number of callous and cruel murders were attributed to him.[41]

For those enslaved people with a fair skin, opportunities arose for more innovative escapes, such as was the case with an enslaved man named Joseph. Owned by Mathias Bergstedt of the Burgher Council of the VOC, Joseph managed to pass himself off as a Dutchman and escaped to the Netherlands where he incredibly found himself employment on a ship owned by the VOC.

Unfortunately when the *Duijnenberg* docked in Simon's Bay, Bergstedt became aware of his presence, had him removed from the vessel and

---

[39] The spelling "Hanglip" ("drooping lip") has been used throughout this text following the lead of scholars Robert Shell and Robert Ross. The author is aware of the alternative spelling of Hangklip ("hanging stone").

[40] Robert Ross, *Cape of Torments: Slavery and Resistance in South Africa* (London: Routledge and Kegan Paul, 1983), 69.

[41] Corns, "Offended Shadows," 60.

"instructed the Fiscal to take action against him" so that he could be returned to him as a "slave."[42]

Fig. 1-5. "Teresa the wet-nurse"
Source: Watercolour by Lady Anne Barnard. Courtesy of Koos Bekker

---

[42]Leibbrandt, *Precis of the Archives of the Cape of Good Hope Requesten (Memorials), 1715-1806]: Volume 1: A-E*: 1742 (Cape Town: Government Printers, 1905), 73.

For enslaved people who arrived here as very young children, and for enslaved children who were born into this society, the negative social value imposed upon them would have been more difficult to combat.

Pertinently, this would have been internalised as being quite normal. In much the same way, in this society that was structured on a pedestal of European dominance, the offspring of the Europeans would have internalised a sense of superiority.

Fig. 1-6. "Vue de la Baie Fals" Simon's Bay, 1776-1777
Source: Print engraved by Jean Herman Schneider, Library of Parliament

The presence of "Company slaves" in Simon's Town was linked to specific and fluctuating labour requirements in the town. Their more permanent "home" would have been the Slave Lodge in Cape Town.[43] However, a few enslaved people resided in Simon's Town on a more permanent basis, serving the labour requirements of the various VOC post-holders who were permanently stationed in Simon's Town over this time.

In 1767 a "Slave Lodge" was built in the Company vegetable garden in Simon's Town.[44] It is likely that this "Slave Lodge" would have been situated at Groot Tuin. This Lodge would have had to accommodate a complement

---

[43] As the Slave Lodge in Cape Town was and is the official name of the building, it has not been italicised in this text.

[44] WCARS, (Council of Policy) C 566, Inkomende Brieven: C. Brand to van de Graaff, (15.5.1787), page 11. (Verbatim Copies) VC 30, Daghregister (12.7.1767), as cited in Sleigh, *Die Buiteposte*, 101.

of "Government Slaves," whose numbers grew during the busy winter months when the demand for labour increased. After winter the bulk of enslaved people returned to the Slave Lodge in Cape Town.

The winter months saw an increased presence of VOC officials as well as the migration of junior VOC officials and enslaved people "who regularly assisted the Post-holder." These periods also saw the arrival of chandling and shipping clerks, artisans and tradesmen who swelled the population of Simon's Town during the bustling winter months. Enslaved people were also tasked with loading and unloading ships as they anchored.

The "Company slaves" performed a multitude of tasks which included assisting with boats or nets that needed to be hauled in, collecting water and wood and carrying stones from high up in the mountains to the awaiting *waens* or wagons that then delivered them to Cape Town.[45] There is no record of fatalities for enslaved people during this historical period, but certainly this arduous task in the summer heat would have exacted a price. Other health-threatening tasks assigned to enslaved people were the indelicate tasks of patient care in the VOC hospital. In addition they performed a multitude of other duties at the hospital such as cooking, washing clothes, scrubbing floors and cleaning toilets. Enslaved people owned by the VOC were also assigned to care for people with infectious diseases, which may have proved fatal to themselves. The historian Dan Sleigh mentions that the arrival of the Wurtemberg Regiment in 1788 placed a huge burden on the hospital and an even greater burden on the five enslaved people who had the odious task of having to wash and take care of 380 patients, a ratio of one carer for seventy-six patients.

Enslaved people also prepared and tended the Company vegetable gardens where carrots, turnips, red cabbage, cabbage, lettuce and legumes were typically grown. They were responsible for the slaughtering of animals in the slaughter house and could be seen taking animals out to graze beyond the Steenbergen mountains.[46]

Whatever sense of satisfaction the VOC officials may have felt at the progress of their establishment in Simon's Town this development, as already

---

[45] Sleigh, *Die Buiteposte*, p. 991 (translations by Jean Redelinghuys).
[46] WCARS, Resolusies van die Politieke Raad, C 12 (23.2.1751), page 61-66; Ibid, 25.1.1751, page 53, as cited in Sleigh, *Die Buiteposte*, 304-305.

discussed, came at huge cost—both physical and psychological—to indigenous and enslaved people. Historians have already argued that the loss of their water courses and exposure to diseases brought by foreigners caused the destruction of the indigenous people.

In addition to this I believe that the insertion of foreign structures onto their pristine landscape was equally destructive to their mental and physical well-being. At this time the enslaved work force in Simon's Town were people who came from a variety of places, namely Bali, Batavia, Bengal, Bougies, Cheribon, Macassar, Madagascar, Malabar, Mozambique (including from Rio de la Goa—now Maputo), Nias, Siam (now Thailand) and Timor.

The unusually strong Asian component that my research has revealed for enslaved people in Simon's Town during the VOC period is also alluded to in a statement by a visitor to the town in 1775, when he wrote that in Simon's Bay "French, English, Portuguese, and Malay languages are very commonly spoken."[47]

Although in 1787 the Society for Effecting the Abolition of the Slave Trade was established in Britain[48] this held little comfort for people enslaved at the Cape, which fell under the control of the VOC.

Enslaved men in Simon's Bay during the period of VOC control

Because privately owned enslaved males were mostly housed outside in fenced-in enclosures, this placed them at even greater health risks because of their exposure to the elements, especially in inclement weather. By contrast the six permanent enslaved males belonging to the VOC were housed in a large storeroom belonging to the VOC that also served as a garrison.

A number of methods were used by "slave-holders" and VOC officials to control enslaved men, which ranged from physical violence to public humiliation. Enslaved men were not able to protect their "wives" or children. I have mentioned wives in inverted commas, as until 1824, enslaved people

---

[47] George Forster, *A Voyage Round the World: In his Britannic Majesty's Sloop, Resolution ...* (London: printed for B White, 1777) Volume 2: 74.

[48] Kirsten McKenzie, *The Making of an English Slave-Owner: Samuel Eusebius Hudson at the Cape of Good Hope 1796-1807* (Rondebosch: UCT Press, 1993). 53.

were not allowed to marry legally.[49] Control was in the hands of European males, both private individuals and representatives of the VOC.

In Simon's Town, VOC control was represented by the post-holder.[50] Burghers who held the position of post-holder in Simon's Town during this era were Justinus Blass from 1743, who was replaced by Adriaan de Neijs in 1747, Johan Friedrich Kirsten in 1761 and finally, Christoffel Brand. All had a vested interest in slavery as they were all "slave-holders."[51]

September van Malabar—8 April, 1753

It was after 10 p.m. on a winter's evening on the night of 8 April 1753 when the sound of a commotion echoed along the cobbled steps of Drostdy Lane in Simon's Town. The noise was coming from the Drostdy, the home of the VOC post-holder, Adriaan de Neijs.

The sounds were of a lashing *sjambok* cutting through human flesh, cries of pain and anger and accusations of supposed wrongdoing. The story that emerges from the court records is that September of Malabar was a "slave" of Adriaan de Neijs. In court it was stated by Sergeant Marks that he was informed by Corporal Wolraad, "also stationed at Simon's Bay, at about ten o'clock in the evening" on the night of 8 April 1753, that he was warned by Abraham van Banten that there was "another one of the Post Holder's slaves with the men at the Watch." This "Watch" was the VOC equivalent of the British sentry guard system, used to protect the area from attacks by indigenous people who were resisting VOC settlement.

According to Sergeant Marks, Adriaan de Nijs was away and had left him in charge of "the Honourable Company's houses in the bay" and of his "slaves." It must have been a cold night as Sergeant Marks describes putting on his coat before heading for the home of de Nijs, where he found September of Malabar in the kitchen, making a fire. Confronting September of Malabar for being at the Watch "against the express orders of his Master"

---

[49] Nigel Worden, *The Chains That Bind Us* (Cape Town: Juta, 1996). 73.

[50] Sleigh, *Die Buiteposte*, 321.

[51] WCARS, C.123 Resolusies van die Politieke Raad (22.6.1745), pages 229-230; ZK1/190, Uitgaande Brieven: H Swellengrebel to Here XVII (18.6.1749), page 296; C.152 Resolusies van die Politieke Raad: (25.4.1774), page 171 as cited in Sleigh, *Die Buiteposte*, 321-323.

and simultaneously asking what he wanted with a fire "at this late hour," in court records he stated that he "gave him six or seven lashes with the sjambok that he had in his hand."

Fig. 1-7. Drostdy Steps, Simon's Town; Watercolour by Terence John McCaw
Source: SAHRIS, AVM 4152

As an enslaved person within this historical setting, September of Malabar was meant to accept the painful lashing that would have torn his flesh and left him with open bloodied wounds, without reprisal. However, he reacted not as a "slave" but as a man. In the court he was accused of attacking the sergeant bodily, stabbing him with a knife, he "jumped through the open kitchen window and from outside swore violently at the Sergeant ... and thereupon ran away."[52]

A month later, September of Malabar would appear in court to hear his fate. He was "accused of opposition against Sergeant Valentijn Marks."[53] The case was presided over by "the Honourable Sergius Swellengrebel." The prosecutor in the case was "the Independent Fiscal Pieter Reede van Oudtshoorn." September of Malabar was not provided with any defence. Of one thing the law was clear: "any 'slave' who struck a 'slave-holder' was to be shown no mercy and be put to death."[54] A gruesome feature of capital punishment for the enslaved during this historical period was the breaking of the prisoner's body alive on the wheel. The place of execution was situated in what is today known as Wharf Street in Simon's Town.

September of Malabar was likely one of many Indian children who were sold as "slaves" to the VOC. Indian children were generally sold at a "slave station" in Cochin, India and distributed by the VOC between Batavia and the Cape.[55] On arrival at the Cape his identity as a young Indian boy from a village in India who had a name, a family and was part of the community and tradition would have been wiped away.

Once declared a "slave" his true identity would have been submerged forever except in his own memory and through hidden stories told out of the earshot of the "slave-holders."

The case of September of Malabar offers an illuminating insight into the emasculating treatment meted out to enslaved males by their free counterparts and the dangers of attempting to retain their manhood by resisting.

To be an enslaved male meant to always be referred to as a boy and never a man. It meant watching your wife or child being beaten and not having the power to prevent it. It meant being beaten and humiliated in front of your

---

[52]WCARS, Court of Justice, CJ 361, Ref. 18 (April 1753).
[53]WCARS, Court of Justice, CJ 361, Ref. 18 (April 1753).
[54]WCARS, Court of Justice, CJ 361, Ref. 18 (April 1753).
[55]Adoor K K Ramachandran Nair, *Slavery in Kerala* (Delhi: Mittal Publications, 1986), 16.

family and being prevented by law from defending them. Certainly it meant not having access to guns.

Laws and restrictions affecting the behaviour of the enslaved in public during the Dutch colonial period seemed designed to affect particularly the males as they were more likely to be occupied outside the home.[56] In this unnatural setting enslaved men were navigating their lives and trying to hold onto their sense of masculinity within the context of a dominating society that strove to emasculate them.

Fig. 1-8. Map of eighteenth-century Malabar district, Kerala, India
Source: Wikimedia [online resource] https://commons.wikimedia.org/wiki/File:Malabar_district_Map.jpg

---

[56] See the Tulbagh Code, Kaapse Argiefstukke. *Kaapse Plakkaatboek: deel 3: 1754-1786* (Cape Town: Cape Times, 1949), C. 684, 3/5 September 1754, 1-6.

Enslaved Women during the Period of VOC rule

Enslaved women generally slept on a blanket on the floor in the kitchen, close to the hearth. This came with its own problems as enslaved women and girls were vulnerable to sexual exploitation. Conversely there were enslaved women like Anna van Jacoba van de Kaap who married or partnered with men of the "slave-holding" class and as such were able to traverse slavery to become burgher wives.

There were also "favoured slaves" such as Rosetta van Bengal, who were manumitted either during the lifetimes of their "slave-holders" or on their deaths.

The People Described as "Free Blacks" during the Period of VOC Rule

A certain category of people came into being in this society of social constructions, who were called "Free Blacks." The term referred either to formerly enslaved people who had been manumitted from slavery or to Asian political exiles or "convicts" who had completed their sentences and chose to remain at the Cape.

In the 1760s the stylish attire of "Free Black" women, many of whom were likely skilled seamstresses, caused consternation in the dominant society, leading to legislation being passed in 1765 that all women who held "Free Black" status were confined in terms of their dress. They were no longer allowed to appear in public in "coloured silk clothing, hoop skirts, fine laces, adorned bonnets, curled hair or even earrings. Formerly enslaved women who had been manumitted from slavery were ordered to wear no material other than chintz and striped cotton" and in church, a habit (*kledje*) of black silk.[57] One of the local women who would have been affected by this law was Cartche Rooy. She fitted into the social construction of a Free Black woman in Simon's Town, having been born to "Free Black" parents Jan Rooy and Flora Rooy in 1786 at "her father's erf near Simon's Town."[58] The said erf was in fact Koperfontein in Noordhoek where her father made a living

---

[57] *Kledje* is a derivative of the Dutch word *kleden*. Shell, *Children of Bondage*, 323.

[58] Cartche Rooy, Death Certificate, 2320 (November 1846). *Family Search* [online resource] https://www.familysearch.org/ark:/61903/3:1:3Q9M-CSQF-V997-V?i=1675&cc=2517051.

through gardening.[59] Widowed young with one child, she supported herself and her daughter as a washerwoman and though she didn't own property of her own, at the time of her death she was noted as living "at her sister's house in Simon's Town." A "Free Black" neighbour to the Rooy family was Abdul of the Cape who was a fisherman.[60]

On the death of Anna Margaretha van der Heijde on 10 June 1783, her will stipulated that her "slave" Rosetta van Bengal should be released into freedom, but under the care of Christoffel Brand, the VOC resident who was also her son in law.[61] In this way Rosetta van Bengal would have become known as a "Free Black."

Anna van Jacoba van de Caab—1765

The couple who, in 1765, moved into the De Goede Gift residence (the former home of "slave-holder" Christina Diemer) were registered as Johan Volraad and Anna Volraad. Johan Volraad was a German mercenary who arrived at the Cape as a soldier in 1752. By 1758 he rose to the rank of corporal and later, in 1762 he became a sergeant. The year 1765 was an eventful year for Johan Volraad. It was the year that he was able to break free from his employment with the VOC and obtain burgher status. In 1765 he also entered the liquor trade, selling brandy and wine in Rondebosch, regarded as a sure way to achieve wealth in VOC-dominated Cape society. Most significantly, 1765 was the year that he got married and he and his wife moved into their new home, De Goede Gift in Simon's Town.

For Anna Volraad, 1765 was a significant year not only because it was the year of her marriage; but also because it was the year that her official status changed. Born to Jacoba van der Kaap in the Slave Lodge in Cape Town, as a little girl she might have been one of the children whose task it was to weave

---

[59] WCARS, Opgaafrolle, J181, 1826: Field Cornetcy of Noord Hoek in the Residency of Simon's Town, 1826.

[60] Owen Pryce Lewis, *When First We Practice, or The Life of Jan Michiel Endres* (Simon's Town: The Simon's Town Historical Society, 1989), 35.

[61] *Cape Melting Pot*; translated by Delia Robertson from Hans F Heese, Groep Sonder Grense, ... (Bellville: University of the Western Cape, 1985). *Cape Melting Pot* [online resource] http://www.e-family.co.za/ffy/RemarkableWriting/CapeMeltingPot-FFY.pdf (accessed 23.05.2023).

the silk thread, for which purpose Governor de Chavonnes imported silk-worm eggs from Persia.

She would have trudged daily, along with other "slave" children, up the path that became known as Spin Street, to a building on the East side of the Slave Lodge, where the weaving was done. As a child growing up in the Slave Lodge, its dismal living conditions notwithstanding, she would have had the benefit of receiving some schooling at the "Slave" School, as opposed to the children of enslaved people owned privately, who received no schooling during this period. Sitting at her school desk, she would have been taught the alphabet and arithmetic, carefully practising her writing on a slate board. Although her mother, Jacoba van der Kaap, also resided at the "Slave Lodge," at night, Anna would have slept in separate quarters reserved for children at the Lodge.[62] Whether she knew the identity of her European father and whether he had contact with her is open to conjecture. However, her biological link to him afforded her certain privileges.

By 1762 Anna rose to the ranks of Matron of the Slave Lodge. This was a "privilege" reserved for enslaved women whose fathers were European. As a matron, the other female "slaves" at the Lodge would have been under the overall control of Anna. Besides being in charge of maintaining discipline, she would have also served as a schoolmistress. This status ensured that her lodgings were superior to, and separate from, the other enslaved people at the Lodge.

It was in 1762, with her rise to becoming matron, that she requested that her two children, Elisabeth (four years) and Jan (ten months) be manumitted. For their freedom she offered 200 guilders.[63] Two years later she sent a request to Governor Ryk Tulbagh, asking for her own manumission and in line with the laws at the time, offered in exchange for herself an enslaved man named Cupido van Bengal. The request was granted and on 18 August

---

[62] We learn from the Court of Justice records that after 1732 there were married quarters in the Lodge where children could eat with their parents, but presumably this did not apply to single mothers with their children. WCARS: Court of Justice: CJ: 329: folios 365 to 372; Court of Justice: CJ: 9: 58 to 60 cited in Robert Carl-Heinz Shell, *From Diaspora to Diorama* (Cape Town: NagsPro, 2012), pages 2021-2022.

[63] Hendrik Carel Vos Leibbrandt, *Requesten*, 1: pages 10 to 11 number 190 of 1762; Pama; *Geslagregisters*; 1074.

1765 Anna married Johan Volraad and took his name. Elizabeth and Jan accompanied their mother to Volraad's newly acquired property, namely De Goede Gift at Simon's Bay. Among Anna's neighbours in Simon's Town were the Elshoud family who lived on the farm Constantia headed by Hendrik Elshoud and the Hurter family headed by Johan Wilhelm Hurter. His father, Johan Wilhelm Hurter (Senior) was himself no stranger to the Slave Lodge, having manumitted Sophia of the Cape from the Lodge in 1761. Beyond the mountain lived the Post-holder of Simon's Town, the Swiss Johannes David Soublet, with his Khoe wife, Esther.[64]

Still further beyond lived the family of Frederik Kirsten at Imhoff's farm. He became the owner of the farm following the death of Christina Diemer in 1765.

The relationship that Johan and Anna Volraad had with their neighbours is impossible to speculate, although certainly the events of the night of Saturday 2 May 1767 may have resulted in them rallying together with the Munnik and Elshoud families through a common cause. On this night, as dusk settled on the town, the sails were removed from the VOC "Company" storeroom. In addition, three muids of flour were removed from the Volraad household as well as muskets and lead from the Munnik household. This done, a group of enslaved people made their way towards the ocean where they made good their escape in the "flat-bottomed boat belonging to the Bay." When their escape had been discovered, the post-holder said he was convinced that "if the wind had at this time come from the west" the "absconders would have set a course with the stolen boat to Hanglip or the beaches of Hottentots Holland." The response of the

> Lord Governor was to send written notice to the landdrost of Stellenbosch and Drakenstein, Mr Jacobus Johannes le Seuer, to send some men to track down as swiftly as possible the perpetrators of this plot, and to give such further orders as he would find necessary.[65]

---

[64] Adolphe Linder, *The Swiss at the Cape of Good Hope, 1652-1971* (Basel: Basler Afrika-Bibliographien, 1997, 126-127. Alternative spellings of Soublet are known to have been Soeblee, Souble and Sublet.
[65] WCARS, Verbatim Copies, VC 30 (2 May 1767), 178.

However, there is no evidence to suggest that this group of people were found.

Escaping from slavery was a huge risk and the stakes were high. Special commandos were paid per head for arresting people deemed to be "escaped slaves."[66]

On 2 October 1768 Johan Volraad (Volraath) died. At this time Anna Volraad was five months pregnant with their last-born child, who would be named Anna Adriana Volraad. Another daughter, named Maria Petronella Volraad, was also born at De Goede Gift in Simon's Town in 1766. Johannes Roep bought the property when, after her husband's death, Anna was forced to sell De Goede Gift on 7 January 1769.

The money from the sale of the estate also afforded Anna the opportunity to be reunited with her son, Nicolaas, who was aged five at the time. For the privilege of having her child, the Widow Volraad would pay 100 Rixdollars, an amount that she paid willingly so that Nicolaas could join the rest of his family. The reason for Anna only requesting Nicolaas's manumission after the death of her husband raises many questions. However, Nicolaas assumed the name of Volraad and went on to marry Adriana Patinger (Pattenger) on 15 March 1789 with whom he had three sons and two daughters[67].

Anna van Jacoba van de Kaap—Mrs Anna Volraath/Volraad—undoubtedly met Johannes Volraad at the Slave Lodge in Cape Town where she had spent her entire life up to the point of their marriage.

Robert Shell describes how enslaved men in the Slave Lodge were made to empty the town's latrine buckets while the Lodge was turned into a brothel at night from 8 p.m until 9 p.m. The patrons of this brothel were VOC employees and European seamen who would queue up outside the Lodge.

The sexual exploitation of enslaved women in this patriarchal society dominated by males from Europe is one of the sinister legacies of slavery. For the most part, the women had no choice as they were enslaved and as such their bodies were "owned" by the "slave-holders," in this case the VOC. This came at huge psychological cost.

---

[66]Sleigh, *Die Buiteposte*, 327.
[67]Marriage record, Dutch Reformed Church, Cape Town *Family Search* [online resource] https://www.familysearch.org/ark:/61903/1:1:6KYN-3TSG.

Enslaved children in Simon's Town during the Dutch Colonial Period

The VOC era was a particularly harsh time for enslaved people at the Cape and mortality rates were high. Nutrition was poor, people were overworked, medical attention was limited to non-existent, and, as already mentioned, "slave-holders" unashamedly expressed their preference for strong male adults whose labour could be maximally exploited rather than to carry the cost of raising children, from whose labour they would not benefit in the short-term.

During the VOC era the birth rates of children born to enslaved women were extremely low. The historian Nigel Worden has suggested self-induced abortions as being a major contributing factor.[68] When one ponders the terrible cruelty of slavery, with the possibilities of the child being separated from the mother into some unknown fate, as well as the possibilities of the child being raped, tortured or maimed, then it might have seemed a kindness to enslaved women to end that life of hell before it began. Notwithstanding all these factors, of the children who were born in Simon's Town some did survive in the period of VOC settlement.

At Imhoff's farm, Rebecca of the Cape gave birth to her son Jan van de Caab, Sarah from Mozambique gave birth to her son Africa, Dina from Batavia gave birth to her daughter Rakina and Aletta of Cheribon gave birth to her son Samuel.

Enslaved children at Imhoff's Farm whose mothers were not recorded were Hester of the Cape, Aletta of the Cape, Aaron of the Cape and Moses of the Cape. Abraham van de Caab was born at the Hurter Lodging House (Admiralty House).

A baby girl named Carin was born at the Constantia homestead in Simon's Town belonging to Hendrik Elshoud. At Poespaskraal farm Dina van de Caab was recorded as being the mother of five children named Abraham, Frederik, Hannetje, Jeannet and Leentje. Julia, Carolina and Albert were the children of Rosina of the Cape at the Oliphant's Bosch farm. Also located there were Charlotta and April, whose mother "Peggy" was Mozambican.[69]

---

[68] Nigel Worden, *Slavery in Dutch South Africa* (Cambridge: Cambridge University Press, 1985), 59.

Fig. 1-9. Panorama of Simon's Town
Source: Christopher Webb Smith (artist). Library of Parliament, 19349 (xvi)

The tragedy for children born into slavery was that they were children without childhoods. By virtue of their mothers being enslaved, they were born into a state of slavery and owned by the "slave-holders" who "owned" their mothers.

The primary expectation of their mothers by the dominating class was to follow the instructions of "slave-holders." Care for their children would have been secondary. Enslaved women were challenged with mothering their children in a state of economic and psychological disempowerment and trauma, where the will of the dominant power took precedence over natural maternal

---

[69]Joline Young, Database of enslaved children in Simon's Town during the Dutch colonial era (unpublished), (December 2013).

instincts. There was simply very little time left in their day to care for and nurture their children. One enslaved woman expressed this tragic state of affairs with great sadness, saying "we slaves had no time to watch our children properly. They were left to themselves."[70]

Enslaved children would have grown up with the notion that their needs were secondary to the needs and desires of the children of "slave-holders." This would have been apparent to them in the amount and quality of time their parents were able to give them.

It would have also been visible to them materially, through the shelters they lived in, access to soap and water, the food they ate and the clothes they wore as well as through the interactions of their parents with the dominant class. Privately-owned enslaved children received no education during this period. Pertinently, for enslaved mothers and children, there was always the knowledge that their time together may be short.

Many children were sold off separately from their parents by the age of ten. Sometimes this happened at the death of the "slave-holder" and sometimes while he was alive.

For example, when Jan Fredrick Kirsten (ensign and post-holder in Simon's Bay from January 1756) died in 1783, his will stated that the child Aaron van der Caab was to be left to Anna Catherina Kirsten, wife of Johannes Gie. Africa van der Caab was to be sold jointly with his mother, Sarah van Mozambique, to Johannes Kirsten; Aletta van der Caab was left to Jan Pieter Kirsten. Hester van der Caab was left to Geesje Kirsten.

Jan van der Caab's mother, Rebecca of the Cape was allowed to purchase his freedom if she could raise the purchase price of 150 Rixdollars. Moses van der Caab was left to Jan Frederik Kirsten.[71] Rakina of the Cape was to be sold together with her Batavian mother. They were sold jointly to Jan Look for 520 Rixdollars on 21.05.1783[72] while Samuel van der Caab was left to Jan Frederik van Reede van Oudtshoorn.

---

[70]Emilie Lehn in Jackie Loos, *Echoes of Slavery: Voices from South Africa's Past* (Cape Town: David Philip, 2004), 92.

[71]Names were often repeated in families or with variant spellings, as with Jan Fredrick Kirsten and Jan Fredrick Kirsten.

[72]*Cape Transcripts*, M8/18.52 (21.05.1783).

Conversely, in some cases enslaved families were not sold, but were passed down as intact parallel families of "slave-holding" families. This was more likely to occur in the case of enslaved children whose mothers were born at the Cape.

For example Dina van der Caab was listed as living on the farm Poespaskraal with her five children. Admittedly, the data shows this to be a rare case during the Dutch colonial period, and it was probably no accident that this occurred at a time when Poespaskraal was under the charge of Maria Smith, the widow of Nicolaas Sertyn.[73] Some, but by no means all, Dutch widows were known to have used their social power to shield enslaved women from the excesses of slavery.[74]

There also seemed to have been favoured "slaves" and those who were not favoured, which resulted in differential treatment and outcomes for enslaved people and their children.

For enslaved people, the value of European blood as a means to escape the excesses of slavery was held out like a nugget of gold in this society where hierarchies were racially inspired. On 20 January, 1766 it was proclaimed that:

> No child procreated by Christians by their female slaves should be sold, the Estate being solvent or not, authorising to give such children to persons requesting to maintain these unfortunates and to instruct them in the Doctrine of the reformed church.[75]

Though this law was not strictly followed, the following extract from Jan Willem Hurter's will requesting that Abraham of the Cape be "put into a state of freedom" after Hurter's death should be viewed in light of this law:

> *Abraham van de Caab mits nog thans dat denselven na overlyden van den langst, levender van hug beyden in vrijdom zals moeten worden gesteld.*[76]

---

[73] *Cape Transcripts*, MOOC, 8/21.44 (29.08.1796).

[74] Shell, *Children of Bondage*, 293.

[75] See Article 8 in George McCall Theal, *Records of the Cape Colony from October 1812 to April 1814 …* (London: William Clowes for the Government of the Cape Colony), 1901, Vol. 9: 130-131.

In 1758 when the ship the *Grantham* was captured by the French and landed in Simon's Bay, two influential passengers named Nicholas Vincent and Charles Boddam, the one a naval captain and the other a member of the Madras Council, petitioned to take with them to Europe a group of servants and two young "slave" children named Frank and Rosa.[77] There is no mention of their parents and no record of what became of Frank and Rosa in Europe.

---

[76]Will of Jan Willem Hurter, WCARS, Master of the Orphan Chamber, MOOC 7/1/29, Reference 71 (23 February 1783).

[77]Leibbrandt, *Precis of the Archives of the Cape of Good Hope Requesten (Memorials), 1715-1806: T-Z*: No. 82 (1758), page 1287.

PART 2

1751 TO 1795: SIGNIFICANT CHANGE

The period 1751 to 1795 saw significant change in Simon's Bay. During the preceding years, Simon's Bay was as an isolated place obscured by mountains "before proper roads could be cleared."[1] There were also few ships arriving in Simon's Bay before this time as most ships continued to anchor in Table Bay.[2] This all changed from 1751 onwards when Simon's Bay became a fully operational winter anchorage for the VOC. As a consequence to this the population grew exponentially, particularly during the winter months, as traders from Cape Town moved into Simon's Bay in order to derive economic benefits from the increased activity in the Bay.

There was also a great deal of building work taking place during this time as the population of farmers in Simon's Bay began to grow. Local farmers also sought to benefit from the increased arrival of ships in the Bay by sending enslaved people from ship to ship to sell fresh fruit and milk. From the perspective of the "slave-holders," this had the unintended consequence of heralding a surge of escapes by enslaved people from the Bay.[3]

Johannes David Soublet and Esther of the Cape

During apartheid in South Africa, we were brainwashed into believing the myth of racial purity. However, during these early years, miscegenation and racial integration were being written into the fabric of this evolving society. The Swiss national Johannes David Soublet, (baptised in Perroy, Berne, Switzerland on 25 March 1734) signed a five-year contract with the Dutch East India Company in 1757 and worked as the VOC postholder of Simon's Bay from 1760 to 1762 (the end of his contract) before returning to Switzer-

---

[1] Janet-Anne Cladingbowl, A Study in the Development of Simon's Town 1898-1910. Thesis (BA Hons), University of Cape Town, 1984, 8.
[2] Dan Sleigh, *Die Buiteposte* (Pretoria: Protea, 2004), 303-304.
[3] WCARS, Verbatim Copies, VC 30, page 178 (2 May, 1767).

land. However, he decided to return to the Cape in 1764 and resumed his post in Simon's Bay until 1786, when he retired at the age of fifty-two years.[4] At that time he was described as a gardener on his "Company farm Wildschuts Brandt."[5] Although Soublet was far from his native home, his wife Esther had the distinction of being a descendant of the indigenous Khoe of this land.[6] The couple had a large family of mostly daughters[7] and lived simply in a little cottage hidden between the mountains in Simon's Town, where they grew a variety of vegetables. Their daughters would have been able to play freely and carefree amongst the mountainous hills and garden patches, while their mother earned an extra income from home as a washerwoman for the crews of ships arriving in the Bay,[8] soaking up soap-suds and rubbing clothing against a washing-board. When they became older they would be inducted into this laundry service industry. It was an honest living, if not a glamorous life.

In 1792 the Dutch travel writer Cornelius de Jongh visited Soublet and his family on his way back from going to view a Dutch shipwreck nearby. He described the family as living quite reclusively in a cabin-style home or "hut," which was comfortably furnished "with simplicity and taste." Having already had lunch at a nearby farm, De Jongh and his companions were served a simple refreshment of bread and wine.[9]

Some nine years later, in October 1801, Soublet finalised his Will, which was presented to the Orphan Chamber after his death in April 1802. Soublet's wife Esther was the sole beneficiary of his estate.

For the next six years after the death of Soublet, Esther continued to live in this abode, but a resident of Simon's Town named Barend Muller, who considered her to be a frail old woman, would "enter into a bargain with her"

---

[4]Adolphe Linder, *The Swiss at the Cape of Good Hope, 1652-1971* (Basle: Basler Afrika Bibliogaphien, 1997), 126.

[5]Linder, *The Swiss at the Cape of Good Hope*, 126.

[6]*Cape Melting Pot*; translated by Delia Robertson from Hans F Heese, *Groep Sonder Grense*, ... (Bellville: University of the Western Cape, 1985). Downloadable from *Cape Melting Pot* [online resource] http://www.e-family.co.za/ffy/Remarkable-Writing/CapeMeltingPot-FFY.pdf (accessed 23.05.2023).

[7]Linder, *The Swiss at the Cape of Good Hope*, 126.

[8]Linder, *The Swiss at the Cape of Good Hope*, 127.

[9]Linder, *The Swiss at the Cape of Good Hope*, 127.

whereby she would only be compensated for the buildings and not the land.[10] Socially vulnerable until her marriage to Soublet, her social vulnerability would have returned after his death and become exacerbated as she advanced in age. This social vulnerability would have extended to her children.

Children of European fathers and indigenous mothers were given the disparaging title of "Bastards" while children of enslaved fathers and indigenous mothers were described as "Bastard Hottentots." In 1775 it was decreed that the latter children be absorbed into the labour pool of the "slave-holders" until they were twenty-five years old.[11]

Jean Michiel of the Cape 1783

Although Jean Michiel of the Cape was most likely born at the Slave Lodge in Cape Town, his link to Simon's Town through his father makes him worth a mention, for the very different outcome his life had compared to most of his contemporaries. Jean Michiel was the son of Sophia of the Cape and Joseph Dempfle, the junior surgeon in False Bay. Although Joseph Dempfle did not marry Jean's mother, he took full paternal responsibility for Jean. In 1783 Joseph Dempfle bought his son from "slave-owner" Sieur Johannes Steijn for 100 Rixdollars and immediately manumitted him.[12] Through his father's actions, Michiel was able to transcend slavery and enter the world of the dominant class, both culturally and materially, as he was also appointed his father's sole heir in 1784.[13] Most enslaved children were not as fortunate as Michiel. In the main, European fathers did not publicly acknowledge offspring who were enslaved and in cases where the fathers were themselves enslaved persons, they did not have access to the type of economic and social power that Joseph Dempfle was able to exercise.

---

[10]WCARS, Records of the Magistrate of Simon's Town (1/SMT 2/5), Letters received, Simonstown 1/SMT 10/2, Ref. 99 and 100 (11 April 1808).
[11]WCARS, Dagregister: Stellenbosch en Drakenstein, 1729-1784, C. 655 (4 September 1775) resolution cited in Nigel Penn, The Northern Cape Frontier Zone, 1700-c.1815. Thesis (PhD), University of Cape Town, 1995, 255.
[12]Hendrik Carel Vos Leibbrandt, *Precis of the Archives of the Cape of Good Hope: Requesten (Memorials): vol. 1, A-E* (Number 116), page 395.
[13]John Hoge, *Personalia of the Germans at the Cape, 1652-1806* (Cape Town: Archives Year Book, 1946), 448 (where Joseph Dempfle is recorded as Joseph Demphle).

Hendrik Elshoud's Will: 1783

In the same year that Jean Michiel of the Cape was manumitted, Hendrik Elshoud, owner of the farm Constantia in Simon's Town, died. He left what appears to be a very carefully thought out Will that suggests a somewhat paternal interest in the people who formed his small "slave-holding."

TABLE 2:-1: INSTRUCTIONS IN THE WILL OF HENDRIK ELSHOUD

Name	Origin	Sex	Instructions
Aletta van Bougies	Bougies	F	To hire her services out until she has earned the 200 Rds to pay to the Estate to secure her freedom.
Carin	Unknown	M	Not to be sold, but to live with Margaret Berning (Elshoud's sister's granddaughter)
Clara	Unknown	F	Is old and not to be sold, but to live with Margaretha Berning
Jan van de Caab	This colony	M	Left to Margaretha Berning
January	Unknown	M	To be allowed to purchase his freedom for the sum of 150 Rds, of which 50 Rds is to cover manumission costs and the balance to be shared between his sister's grandchildren, namely Abraham, Anna and Margaretha Berning, in equal parts.
Joseph van de Caab	This colony	M	Left to his sister's grandson, Abraham Berning
Leander van de Caab	This colony	M	Left to his sister's granddaughter, Anna Berning

For example, he said that the young "slave" Carin should not be sold, but was to live with his (Hendrik's) sister's granddaughter, Margaretha Berning. As for the enslaved woman Clara, he stated that "she is old and not to be sold, but to live with Margaretha Berning."

Conversely, Jan van de Caab was "left" to Margaretha Berning; Joseph van de Caab was "left" to his sister's grandson Abraham Berning; and Leander van de Caab was "left" to his sister's granddaughter, Anna Berning. By contrast "January" was allowed to buy his freedom for the price of 150 Rixdollars, from which 50 Rixdollars would be used to pay for his manumission costs and the remainder to be divided between Margaretha, Anna and Abraham Berning.[14]

Unlike the British ameliorative period where the "Slave Register" listed the names of parents and children, making it possible for the researcher to make the genealogical links, this is not always possible with the VOC period where wills and inventories have to be searched. However, it is likely that an enslaved man named Baatjoe van Macassar—listed in the Will of Fredrik [Frederik] Kirsten on 17 April 1783—was the grandfather of Isaac Felix, believed to have been born in Simon's Town around 1787 and whose parents were given as Batju and Mietje. Isaac and his life partner, Alima, had six children named Mietje, Isaac (junior), Willem, Sara, Cornelia and Samuel. Although Isaac Felix (junior) had moved to Tulbagh where he worked as a labourer, he died in Simon's Town at the home of his sister Cornelia Felix. Isaac Felix was also recorded as owning an erf and a building in Simon's Town. The Felix family would have been considered to be part of the "Free Black" society at this time.[15]

The Winter Months

Old habits die hard and although Baron van Imhoff declared Simon's Bay the official winter anchorage of the VOC in 1743, it was only by 1751 that the Bay became a fully functional winter port. However, in 1746 two new European arrivals to Simon's Bay were the Danes, Pieter Weydeman[16] and David Leeuw, both having arrived on the Danish ship *The King of Denmark* (*Kongen af Danemarken*), following which they requested the right to settle as burghers in Simon's Bay.[17]

---

[14]WCARS, Wills, 7/1/38, reference 50, (05.09.1783)

[15]Isaac Felix (junior) was buried on 2 April 1854, aged 50 years (born circa1804). See burial register, Church of St Francis of Assisi, Simonstown, page 19 [online resource] *Family Search* https://www.familysearch.org/ark:/61903/1:1:QP4Y-FKWS (accessed 23 May 2023). According to the transcription of the Old Seaforth Burying Ground record, Isaac was herdsman to P F Hugo at the time of his death.

[16]Leibbrandt, *Requesten, 1715-1806: vol. 4, T-Z*, 1340 (no. 50).

Being a commercial enterprise with the aim of gaining the greatest return for the least cost, the VOC controlled all transactions related to the Cape. This included controlling who was allowed to receive land grants, what they would be allowed to farm on this land and what they would be paid for their produce. The VOC also controlled, and derived a profit from, the sale of enslaved people.

Fig. 2-1. Simon's Town, Naval Port; painting by Thomas Bowler, 1845
Source: Library of Parliament, 6567 (5)

The winter months saw the port filling with visiting ships, which purged ship-weary crews who were eager to put their feet on solid ground again. Traders from Cape Town arrived at the Bay for the winter months, keen to relieve the visitors of their cash. During the period of VOC possession there were, on average, six permanent enslaved people owned by the Company who were stationed in Simon's Bay. However, their numbers also swelled during the winter months as labour needs increased.[18]

---

[17]Leibbrandt, *Requesten, 1715-1806: vol. 2, F-O*, 679 (no. 50).

Enslaved people owned by private individuals were sent to the port from local farms to go from ship to ship selling their produce. The wicker baskets they carried were laden with farm-grown fruit, fresh milk and meat. For enslaved people these port visits during the wet winter months offered priceless opportunities for communication outside their isolated world and most pertinently, opportunities for escape. It is no wonder that this period of the year was notable for a surge of escapes of enslaved people from Simon's Bay.[19] Conversely, in 1756 Hendrik Veersen (also spelt Fehrsen) of the farm Constantia, applied to manumit Rachel of the Cape.[20]

Ban on Asian people

Whereas enslaved people from Madagascar and Mozambique were more likely to escape, enslaved Asian males were considered more likely to retaliate against violence, to the extent that on 28 September 1767 the VOC instituted a ban on the importation of Eastern male "slaves."[21] However, this was a dead letter and on 2 September 1784 there was a further ban on the importation of Eastern male "slaves." On 16 August 1791 it was declared that Eastern "slaves" were only to be imported by special licence and on 3 February 1792 a fine of 300 Rixdollars was imposed and forfeiture of the "slave."[22] These bans notwithstanding, the character of Simon's Town had by then already been strongly shaped by people from the East.

Although the VOC had up until this time monopolised all trade, including the "slave-trade," in 1795 a Swede named Isaac Strombom, who resided at what is known as The Residency in Simon's Town (current day Simon's Town Museum), was given permission by the Dutch East India Company to bring enslaved people from Mozambique into Simon's Town using his own vessels.[23] Beneath the beautiful façade of The Residency lurks a stark and

---

[18]Anton Ettienne Bekker, *The History of False Bay up to 1795* (Simon's Town: Simon's Town Historical Society, [1991], 81.

[19]Sleigh, *Die Buiteposte*, 305.

[20]Leibbrandt, *Requesten, 1715-1806: vol. T-Z*, 1286 (no. 104).

[21]Kaapse Argiefstukke, *Kaapse Plakkaatboek: deel 3: 1754-1786* (Cape Town: Cape Times, 1949): (28 September 1767); A.G. 58 (2 September 1784), 164.

[22]*Kaapse Plakkaatboek: deel 4,* C. 687 (3 February/30 March 1792), 80.

[23]Michael Reidy, Admission and Re-admission of Slaves and Prize Slaves into the Cape. Thesis (MA), University of Cape Town, 2001, 96.

sinister dungeon, which is possibly where Strombom housed the people he enslaved. Auctions were held in the garden of this property where he advertised furniture, livestock and "slaves."[24] The VOC would still derive a profit as, from 1791, a tax of 10 Rixdollars was payable for every enslaved person imported.[25] In 1790 it was declared that

> Masters [were to be] held responsible for their slaves and servants if guilty of not keeping to the left side in the roads with their wagons or not having proper boards the penalty of the first is payment of damage Rds 20 and of the latter offence Rds 50.[26]

Among the daily activities in Simon's Town at this time, Azar from Madagascar could still be seen driving the ox-wagon owned by Frederik Kirsten, until he was re-sold to Jacobus Hurter when Kirsten died.[27]

There was also the traumatic event for Francina and her son Jacob after what was meant to be their joint manumission in accordance with the will of "the former Burger Council member Jan Daniel Wiesner with his deceased wife Anna Dorothea Hiebner in 1788." Jacob's manumission was reversed by Wiesner's son-in-law Olof Berg on the basis that he "lived a bad life."[28] How easy to retain the labour of a strong young male when the word of someone with social power went unchallenged! However, by 1795, events in history overtook them all, as an even more powerful entity arrived.

---

[24] *Cape Town Gazette and African Advertiser* (22 February 1806).

[25] "The capitation or "head" tax for slaves was 10 rijksdaalders during the first British occupation." Reidy, Admission and Re-admission of Slaves, 101 (footnote 56).

[26] WCARS, Slave Office, SO 17/1, "Notes collected from the Colonial Placcards" (30 April 1790).

[27] *Cape Transcripts*, MOOC 8/18.52 (21 May 1783).

[28] Leibbrandt, *Requesten*, Volume 4: 1715-1806: T-Z: Supplement, page 1478 (27.12.1793).

PART 3

THE PERIOD OF TRANSITION 1795 TO 1814

> I have the honor to acquaint you for the information of my Lords Commissioners of the Admiralty that on the 16th instant the Colony and Castle of the Cape of Good Hope surrendered by capitulation to the British Arms, in consequence of which I proceeded in the Monarch to this Bay.
>
> —Admiral Sir George Elphinstone, 23 September, 1795[1]

In 1795, within a background of war and political tension in Europe, Britain took occupation of the Cape, primarily to protect their trade route to the East Indies by preventing French occupation of the Cape. The arrival of several foreign ships on 11 June 1795 saw the beginning of the end of 143 years of Dutch rule at the Cape. It was on that morning that Simon's Town residents awoke to the sight of several foreign ships arriving in Simon's Bay. Christoffel Brand (then the fourth Resident postholder in Simon's Town) immediately conveyed this information to the authorities at the Castle in Cape Town. Captain Dekker, the commander of a Dutch warship lying in Simon's Bay, sent a representative in the form of Lieutenant van Vegezak to meet with the strangers and ascertain whether they were friendly. It became apparent that they were not and when van Vegezak did not return, Dekker sent a messenger to the Governor at the Castle in Cape Town. The messenger arrived there at 10 p.m. and by 11 p.m. reinforcements in the form of Lieutenant Colonel Carel M W De Lille with 200 infantry and 100 gunners were despatched to Simon's Town.[2]

---

[1] George McCall Theal, *Records of the Cape Colony: From February 1793 to December 1796.* (London: printed for the Government of the Cape Colony, 1897) volume 1, 159.

[2] Simon's Town. Municipal and Naval Regatta Committee: *Souvenir of Simon's Town: Van Riebeeck Tercentenary Souvenir* (Simon's Town: Committee of the Simon's Town Municipal and Naval Regatta, 1952), 9.

In the meantime, another messenger arrived at Cape Town, this time from the foreign ships, and the Council of Policy was informed that "the English Admiral, Sir George [Keith] Elphinstone and Major General James Henry Craig requested the presence of the Governor on board to receive an important message."[3] The arrival of Van Vegezak at that crucial moment, with the news that there were troops on board the foreign ships, led the Governor and the Council of Policy to refuse this request, suggesting rather that the foreigners send a despatch to Cape Town.

Christoffel Brand, on the other hand, was instructed to allow provisions to be taken by the strangers, but to refuse landing permission to any armed men.[4] This was an impossible instruction for Brand to obey as he did not have the military strength to oppose the force that faced him. Realising this, the VOC Council of Policy arranged for further reinforcements to strengthen the post at Muizenberg, in the form of 200 infantry and 140 artillerymen.

Three English officers arrived at the Castle in Cape Town on the afternoon of 13 June 1795 with a mandate from the Prince of Orange stating that the Cape Government should allow the British troops to land and be treated as allies. This was met with derision by the Council. Henceforth supplies to the ships were stopped. Hereinafter Admiral Elphinstone "enforced" protection "to prevent the Cape's falling into the hands of the French."[5]

Sir George Elphinstone noted the events in correspondence as follows:

> June 17, 1795. — Captn. Dekker proposed sailing, hoping for conciliatory measures. I did not refuse his sailing, but expressed great surprize. Dispatched the *Sphynx* to St. Helena and St. Salvador.
>
> June 18. — The Major General Craig went to the Cape. The *Sphynx* sailed.
>
> June 19. — The Resident Brandt and his family dined on board the *Monarch*, saluted him with 9 Guns.

---

[3]*Souvenir of Simon's Town*, 9.
[4]*Souvenir of Simon's Town*, 9.
[5]*Souvenir of Simon's Town*, 9.

> June 20. — In the night all the Troops withdrawn from Simons Town & the Women fled ...[6]

On 29 June 1795, following orders from the Council and no doubt fearing the inevitable, the residents from the dominating class along with the people they enslaved. fled Simon's Town, but not before destroying all provisions and ammunition that could not be carried away. The only residents recorded to have remained were Assistant Resident, Johannes Hendricus Brand and two people listed only as "slaves" as well as the widows Auret and Aspeling, along with their households. The indigenous people remained.

The troops amalgamated with the forces of Muizenberg, where 1140 burgher horsemen were already stationed. However, on 9 July the British appropriated the three Dutch ships in Simon's Bay and on 14 July 1795, 4,500 English troops invaded Simon's Town. The Residency was occupied by Major General James Henry Craig. At this time Simon's Town was still virtually deserted except for Christoffel Brand, "Mrs Aspeling," two enslaved people and of course the indigenous people. The following week a further 400 marines were landed in Simon's Town.[7]

The burghers did not capitulate without a fight, albeit a very short one and, by 17 August 1795, 200 men of the National Battalion, 120 artilleryman, 200 burgher cavalry and 150 *pandours*[8] were stationed at the Muizenberg Camp. In addition a small guard was stationed at Kalk Bay.

However, when the column of 1,600 men approached along the road from Simon's Town under General Craig, the burghers realised that they were in trouble. When a further 3,000 soldiers arrived in a large British fleet on 4 September 1795, it was obvious that the Burgher Militia were outnumbered.

On 12 September 1795 Admiral Elphinstone, writing to Henry Dundas from "His Majesty's Ship *Monarch*," described the scene around him as follows:

---

[6]Theal, *Records of the Cape Colony,* volume 1, 122.

[7]*Souvenir of Simon's Town,* 10.

[8]This unit, comprising Khoe and mixed-race soldiers, was also known as the *Corps Pandoeren*, raised in 1793 when France declared war on the Netherlands. Vertrees Candy Malherbe, "The Khoekhoe Soldier at the Cape of Good Hope: How the Khoekhoen were drawn into the Dutch and British Defensive Systems, to circa 1809" *South African Military History Journal* 12, 3 (June 2002).

> The Seas are infested with Americans, Danes, Genoese, Tuscans et cetera or in other terms, smuggling ships, mostly belonging to Britain and Bengal, entrenched with oaths and infamy, who trade to the French Islands, and all the ports in India, changing the flags as is most convenient to them.[9]

An enclosure to his letter stated:

> A list of India Ships which arrived in Simon's Bay the 3rd of September 1795 with General Clarke on board, and the Forces under his Command, viz. *Northumberland, Prince William Henry, Exeter, Worcester, Osterly, Kent, Brunswick, Bombay Castle, Earl Cornwallis, Earl Howe, Deptford, General Coote, Warren Hastings, Prince of Wales* armed Transport.[10]

By 14 September 1795 Britain took possession of the Cape, bringing about the end of VOC rule in the Cape. When the British troops disembarked in Simon's Town, most of the burghers "took flight and decamped with torch light and took all their cattle and other effects along with them."

Major General Craig reported being fired on by not only Burgher militia, but also by the Khoe who positioned their aim of poisoned arrows from the surrounding hills.[11]

Interestingly, too, is that the enslaved people at the residence of VOC Resident Christoffel Brand were left behind in his house to face the British, while he escaped. General Craig alluded to this in a letter to Henry Dundas on 27 December 1795:

> Major Orde who happened to be there, having sent to ask my permission to take a room in the Resident's house, I gave it to him, expressly pointing out that especial care must be taken of Mr. Brandt the former Resident's furniture, and that his slaves who I knew to be in the house, and

---

[9]Theal, *Records of the Cape Colony*, volume.1, 121.

[10]Theal, *Records of the Cape Colony*, volume 1, 121.

[11] Michael Whisson, "Group Areas: The End of the Hottentot Tradition in the Simon's Town District." Unpublished manuscript, 5.

who I imagined to be the only inhabitants in it, must have access to it whenever they thought necessary.[12]

Admiral Elphinstone described the VOC buildings in Simon's Town as follows:

> very large storehouses in which the Dutch Company kept a constant supply of articles for the use of ships, with a barrack at one end and adjacent cooperage, forge, carpenters shop and excellent wharf and crane ... There is also an hospital on a great scale.[13]

Notwithstanding the fact that the British opened free market trade that was not allowed by the VOC, the burghers in Simon's Town responded to British presence with resentment. Some people, like the Widow Martha Maria Hurter (née Munnik), refused to allow British soldiers to be billeted in their homes.[14] Angry burghers blamed the British for the neglect of the Company Garden in Simon's Town[15] as well as the destruction of vegetable gardens in private homes.[16] During this time some local burghers were openly ambivalent towards the British. For example, there were bakers who refused to supply bread to the British, which is probably why the British set about developing the public oven system.[17]

The indigenous "San" and Khoe people also expressed their anger at this additional encroachment on their land by firing at the British sentry guards at the flag staff with bows and arrows.[18]

---

[12]"Letter from General Craig to the Right Honourable Henry Dundas (27 December 1795)" in Theal, *Records of the Cape Colony*, volume 1, 286.

[13]"Letter from Admiral Elphinstone to Evan Nepean, Esq., ... (12 October 1795) in Theal, *Records of the Cape Colony*, volume 1: 194.

[14]WCARS, Records of the Magistrate of Simon's Town (1/SMT 2/5), Letters received (1808) Simonstown 1/SMT 10/2, Ref. 92 (8 March 1808).

[15]Robert Percival, *An Account of the Cape of Good Hope* ...(London: Baldwin, 1804), 49.

[16]WCARS, Records of the Magistrate of Simon's Town (1/SMT 2/5) Letters received (1809) Simonstown 1/SMT 10/2, folio 193A (20 September 1809).

[17]Lady Anne Barnard, *South Africa a Century Ago: Letters Written from the Cape of Good Hope (1797-1801)* (London: Smith Elder, 1901), 89.

[18]Robert Warden, "Extracts from the Journal of Robert Warden ..." *Quarterly Bulletin of the South African Library* 7, 3 (March) 1953: 73.

Simon's Bay under British Colonial Rule

With the dawn of British colonial rule in 1796, the settlement in Simon's Town consisted of white-washed houses built from stone and lime, which were situated at the foot of the mountains. Above the houses six British regiments were housed in tents, from where a new battery was set up. At this time a visitor described the inhabitants of Simon's Town as consisting of "Europeans, Dutch, Malays and Hottentots [Khoe]."[19]

The first British occupation of the Cape Colony saw an increased arrival of British settlers. Their numbers included soldiers, sailors, civil servants and missionaries who were sent for fixed periods, as well as those who arrived at their own volition for a quick visit, but "beguiled by what the Cape had to offer," settled permanently.[20]

On 25 June 1796 Admiral Elphinstone lamented that he was no longer allowed the use of the Resident's House where he had previously allotted himself an office and accommodation "at the time of Capitulation" as it had been "appropriated as a mess for the military at the Bay" and he was forced to conduct his business aboard a ship.[21] He also described how European countries were playing out their hostilities in False Bay in the following excerpt:

> on the 25th ultimo His Majesty's Ship *Sphynx* was chased about 9 leagues to the Eastward of Cape Falso by four French Frigates, which recaptured the American Ship *Eliza*. I had left to be convoyed to the Cape by the *Sphynx,* being very anxious to proceed to this Bay in the *Monarch* with all possible dispatch; in consequence of the arrival of the *Sphynx* and the Letter from Captain Brisac, a copy of which is enclosed, I directed Commodore Blankett to put to sea with the *America, Ruby, Crescent* and *Sphynx* in pursuit of the French Frigates; but the sudden appearance of several sail[s] in the offing on the same day, which proved to be the

---

[19] Warden, "Extracts from the Journal," 72.
[20] Peter Hugh Philip, "The Vicissitudes of the Early British Settlers at the Cape" *Quarterly Bulletin of the South African Library* 40, 4 (June 1986): 161.
[21] "Letter from Admiral Elphinstone to the Right Honourable Henry Dundas," (25 June 1796) in Theal, *Records of the Cape Colony,* volume 1: 395.

Spectre's convoy, obliged me to counterorder the Commodore's pursuit and to order all the ships to be moored in line and prepared to receive the Enemy in the event of the sails seen proving hostile.[22]

The British efforts to protect themselves from foreign hostilities was through the repair of the old Battery where new guns were installed, as well as through the "new Battery building opposite to Noah's Ark" where several guns were placed close to the battery. To protect themselves from indigenous hostilities they set up a Flag Staff just above the town, where a sentry guard of two soldiers was placed.[23]

In 1796, construction of a Martello Tower commenced under the supervision of Major General Craig. The British found it necessary to fortify themselves from both foreign hostilities and indigenous people hostile to further foreign encroachment. The British regiments were constantly fired at with arrows by indigenous Khoe, one of whom was apparently taken prisoner by the British in July 1796.

There were also complaints by the six Regiments encamped on the mountainside of being attacked by monkeys and baboons at night, who threw down "showers of stones" at their tents.[24]

A pertinent development at this time was that the British authorities outlawed the practice of torture engaged in by the VOC leadership at the Cape, whereby indigenous or enslaved people were broken alive on a wheel and left to die slow and agonisingly painful deaths. However, "corporal punishment" was sanctioned to take place either in the homes of "slave-holders" or at the local prisons. In the case of the latter, a note would be sent to the magistrate requesting the lashing of a particular enslaved or indigenous person and also stating the number of lashes requested. Whips described as the cat o' nine tails—which had the capacity to shred the flesh and cause extreme pain—were commonly used and regular supplies of these instruments of cruelty were issued by the Civil Commissioner's office to all the "Special Justice Divisions."[25] One of the earliest laws pertaining to indigenous and enslaved

---

[22]"Letter from Admiral Elphinstone to the Right Honourable Henry Dundas," (25 June 1796), 393-396.
[23]Warden, "Extracts from the Journal," 73.
[24]Warden, Extracts from the Journal," 73.

people during this time was that enslaved or indigenous people found "galloping through the streets or smacking their whips" were "to be detained by the 'watches' or policemen and punished by order of the Fiscal."[26]

Fig. 3-1. Battery at Simon's Town circa 1838
Source: Watercolour by Christopher Webb Smith. Library of Parliament, 19349 (v)

This was also a period when "slave-trading" became lucrative for certain private individuals. Isaac Strombom was granted further "slave-trading" licences by Earl Macartney of the British colonial government and up until 1808 he profited by actively engaging in the "slave-trade." Other "slave-traders" in the town were Alexander Tennant and Michael Hogan who brought enslaved people into the town from West Africa.[27]

An interesting visitor to Simon's Town in September 1797 was Lady Anne Barnard, who expressed her displeasure that the public oven where all the

---

[25] WCARS, Records of the Magistrate of Simon's Town, 1793-1985: 1/SMT 2/5, SMT 10/23 (1835) Ref. 39.
[26] WCARS, SO 17/1 "Notes collected from the Colonial Placcards," 1796.
[27] Reidy, Admission and Re-admission of Slaves, 8.

bread was baked was situated above the hospital, which she asserted was a health hazard.

She was also not taken with Simon's Town resident Donald Trail, whom she described as a "great rogue."[28] Lady Anne Barnard was deeply distressed by the VOC practice of mutilating the faces of enslaved people who had attempted to escape, and it was partly due to her instigation that this practice was stopped during the British Colonial period. On the death of her husband Andrew Barnard she would raise her stepdaughter Christine, the daughter of Andrew Barnard and an enslaved woman named Rachel of the Cape, at her home in London.[29]

The Sequestration Sale of the farm Diemerskraal

A year before Lady Anne Barnard's visit to Simon's Town, there arrived in the town a man for whom the description "rogue" would have been suitably apt, although in the opinion of Samuel Hudson, Simon's Town in general was a place where "depravity and wickedness abounded."[30]

The arrival of a confidence trickster in Simon's Town in 1796 would leave a trail of destruction in the lives of many people, both free and enslaved. The man in question was Jan Michiel Endres. Posing as a surgeon and hiding the fact that he was already married, he beguiled Christina Rosseau, the widow of Jeremias Auret, whom he "married" and left only after he had financially ruined her.[31] With the collapse of Christina Rosseau's estate due to Endres' mismanagement, her assets were forfeited to John David Piton. Endres had initially taken out a bond with Piton for which he put up twenty-eight enslaved people from this estate as collateral.[32] He then arranged a second bond with Piton, which included Christina Rossouw/Rosseau's farm Diemerskraal at Buffelsfontein as well as twenty enslaved people and two

---

[28] Barnard, *South Africa a Century Ago:* 80.

[29] For insights into this story read Stephen Taylor, *Defiance: The Extraordinary Life of Lady Anne Barnard* (New York: Norton, 2017).

[30] Samuel Eusebius Hudson, Essay on "Improvements," 1807 to 1814, WCARS, A 602/9.

[31] For an insight into the shenanigans of Jan Michiel Endres see Owen Pryce-Lewis, *When First we Practise or The Life of Jan Michiel Endres Surgeon* (Simon's Town: The Simon's Town Historical Society, 1989), 47.

[32] Pryce Lewis, *When First We Practice*, 53.

enslaved children.[33] Endres, by his own admission, was not kind in his treatment of the people in this "slave-holding," and he expected their submission to his will, even when he was breaking the law through smuggling.[34]

The *modus operandi* with sequestration sales was that the Insolvency Chamber would "dispose of the Goods, Chattels, Houses and Slaves" of all people who were unable to pay their debts.[35] The affected enslaved people would be "confiscated" and either placed in the custody of the messenger or in the town prison until the sale took place.[36] On 5 April 1799 the ownership of Appolis van Ternate, Mey van Ternate, Philander van Mosambique, Anthony van Nias, August van Timor and Jephtha van Mauritius was passed on to John David Piton in a cadastral transfer.

What this meant is that they were being transferred with the farm Diemerskraal at Buffelsfontein. To this end they would remain on the farm unless the new owner decided to sell them at a later stage. Still others were sold off individually at the outset.

Four men—two from Malabar and two from Mozambique—who were part of the initial cadastral transfer were sold on. Their names were Cupido of Malabar (a house-cleaner who was resold to P D Meyburg for 651 Rixdollars), July from Malabar (a cattle-herder who was resold to P D Meyburg for 602 Rixdollars), Philo of Mozambique (a general labourer was resold to Petrus Francois Rossouw for 201 Rixdollars) and Anthony of Mozambique (a wagoner and fisherman was resold to John Osmond for 1,000 Rixdollars).

The remaining people who included Jeptha, Louisa and Tobias, all of Mozambique, were sold individually as was the case for Rozetta and Salomon. Whatever community they may have all formed among themselves on the farm would be severed forever. Such was the cruelty of slavery. They were collateral damage in consequence of the dishonesty of Jan Michel Endres.

The sequestration case took years to conclude. Salomon was still a child when he was sold to Hamilton Ross, a British born merchant and former army captain[37] whose residence was the Sans Souci Estate in Newlands, now

---

[33]Pryce Lewis, *When First We Practice*, 54.
[34]Pryce-Lewis, *When First We Practise*, 35-39.
[35]Shell, *Children of Bondage*, 99-100.
[36]Shell, *Children of Bondage*, 100.

a school.[38] Rosetta was sold to a "Mr Meshaar" for whom little information is available. Though Rosetta and Salomon were not the only enslaved people affected by the liquidation of this estate, for this mother and child the hour of separation had come. The cruel irony of the situation is that Rosetta's occupation was listed as being that of a Nanny. She was entrusted with the care and development of the children belonging to the "slave-holding" class, but her own child was denied the gift of her maternal care. In these and many other ways, historical trauma was being woven into the fabric of this enslaved society and subsequent generations.

A Defining Year in the History of Simon's Town

In 1798 a cry rose up from the "slave-quarters" of the Rossouw family, signalling the birth of a baby boy, Abdol Gafiel [Gaviel], a "slave" child of the Mohamedan faith whose legacy to Simon's Town Muslims would be far-reaching. Incidentally, a year after his birth, the Batavian Republic abolished the Vereenigde Oostindische Compagnie (the VOC).[39] By this time the first British occupation of the Cape was in its fourth year.

All in all the first British occupation at the Cape was a time of high tension between the British and the Dutch[40] at the Cape and these tensions filtered through very strongly in Simon's Town. This dilemma would require diplomatic engagement by John Henry Roselt when he was appointed wardmaster of Simon's Town in 1799.[41]

It was into this tense environment that a working class British shipwright, named John Osmond, arrived on the HMS *Lancaster* in Simon's Town in 1799.[42] Born in Gosport, Hampshire in England he was considered to be of

---

[37] Eric H Bolsmann, *The Mount Nelson* (Pretoria: HAUM, 1978), 33.

[38] Bolsmann, *The Mount Nelson*, 47.

[39] TANAP transcripts, page 57.

[40] I use the term Dutch loosely, as the majority of Europeans at the Cape at that time carried German ancestry. In excess of 4,000 Germans immigrated to the Cape during the period of VOC rule so the term "Dutch" in this instance includes the many Germans who settled in Simon's Town. John Hoge, *Personalia of the Germans at the Cape, 1652-1806* (Cape Town: Archives Year Book, 1946).

[41] Theal, *Records of the Cape Colony*, volume 5, 356.

[42] Peter Philip, *British Residents at the Cape 1795-1819* (Claremont: David Philip, 1981), 311.

humble origin and described in at least one source as being a "mere carpenter." However, Osmond showed himself to be astute in political manoeuvring as well as in social elevation. Through his marriage to Margaretha Johanna Rossouw, a wealthy widow of the Rossouw family, he managed to rise above his economic and social station. In time, Abdol Gafiel[Gaviel] would become his "slave."

Fig. 3-2. Mother and child
Artist: Nicole Joy Young; in the possession of the Author

Osmond procured the most highly skilled enslaved people, most notably masons and carpenters, which made it possible for him to build a thriving ship-building business. As a result he became an extremely wealthy man in his own right, earning himself the nickname of "King John"[43] with his opulent home dubbed by residents as "the palace."[44] Like many of his contemporaries, Osmond fell into the category of "landed gentry" although his wealth was generated from two components—the ownership of land and the ownership of enslaved people of whom the majority were highly skilled artisans. Osmond was the beneficiary of many land grants in Simon's Town, granted to him by the British colonial government who claimed that he was of "great benefit to the town." [45]His influence in the town would impact on the lives of enslaved people in a myriad of ways. Of course he was not alone.

At this time "slave-traders" were cashing in on what had previously been the domain of the Dutch East India Company. Archival records show that 1799 was also a particularly active year for the auctioneer and "slave-trader" Alexander Tennant.

He benefited from enslaved people through trade and also by using enslaved people as security in business dealings. If Tennant kept a ledger of his sales, this ledger would have included the following of his dealings in slavery:

> The transfer of fourteen enslaved people from Mozambique to Mauritz Bartels.[46]
>
> The receipt of four enslaved people named Tjoepar, Primo, Tilis and Christina, all from Bougies, transferred from Michiel Endres.[47]
>
> The receipt of Jacqueau of Mozambique transferred from Donald Trail.[48]

---

[43]Philip, *British Residents*, 311.
[44]Judy Rowe, *The Story of Rocklands Farm Simon's Town, South Africa 1815-2010* (Simon's Town: the Author, 2010), 22.
[45]WCARS, Records of the Magistrate of Simon's Town 1/SMT 2/5, Volume number 1/SMT 10/2, folio 1, (8 January 1813).
[46]WCARS, NCD, Vol. 1/40, Ref. 444, Part 1, 1799.
[47]WCARS, NCD, Vol. 1/40, Ref. 435, Part 1, 1799.
[48]WCARS, NCD, Vol, 1/40, Ref. 459, Part 1, 1799.

The transfer of three Mozambicans named Jacob, Jephta and Esau to Pieter van der Byl.[49]

The transfer of two Mozambicans named "July" and "August" to Marthinus Keet.[50]

The transfer of Geduld of Mozambique to Coenraad Liebenberg.[51]

Seven unknown people described simply as "slaves" transferred to Siewert Wiid in 1799.[52]

Clarinda of Mozambique served as security in a business transaction with Louis Matthys Greeff.[53]

In 1799 Major General Francis Dundas issued a Proclamation declaring that all road repairs in Simon's Town[54] were to be undertaken by enslaved people owned by inhabitants of Simon's Town. This helps us to understand the contribution of enslaved people to the roadworks in the town.

By 1800 the influence of the British colonial presence became evident in the way there was a change in the nature of slavery, brought about through the labour needs of the Navy. Some enslaved people were absorbed by the British Navy with the offer of paid wages of three shillings per week "after five years service, if they were diligent and expert in their business... ." Therefore by 1805 there were at least some enslaved people in Simon's Town who were on the payroll of the British Navy. The Navy were also very vocal about what they considered to be the humane treatment of enslaved people, with heavy penalties in place for officers who were found guilty of ill-treatment.[55]

---

[49]WCARS, NCD, Vol. 1/40, Ref. 501, Part 1, 1799.
[50]WCARS, NCD, Vol. 1/40, Ref. 493, Part 1, 1799.
[51]WCARS, NCD, Vol. 1/40, Ref. 546, Part 1, 1799.
[52]WCARS, NCD, Vol. 1/40, Ref. 546, Part 1, 1799.
[53]WCARS, NCD, Vol. 1/26, Ref. 568, 1799.
[54]Major General Francis Dundas, Proclamation: Instructions for the Wardmaster in Simon's Town (27 May 1799) in Theal, *Records of the Cape Colony*, volume 2, 429-433 (article 15).
[55]ADM 123/39 of 01.01.1800 cited in Michael Whisson, "Water and Workers: Meeting the Needs of the Royal Navy in Simon's Town" *Simon's Town Historical Society Bulletin* 13, 4 (July 1985): 151-154.

However, for the most part the psychological damage of slavery continued. Unless needed for their labour, enslaved people were expected to disappear into the shadows.[56]

The British colonial government created possibilities for a select group of enslaved people to register with the Fiscal for permission to "ply for hire in the wharfs and in the streets."[57] Those who were allowed to benefit from this system would receive a numbered ticket that was worn around their necks.

This was a privilege that was rigorously monitored by the British colonial government who issued severe penalties for any deviation. The penalties for anyone working "illegally" was corporal punishment and being condemned to work at the Public Works for three months. There was also a penalty of corporal punishment and six months imprisonment for any person who lent his ticket to another. All corporal punishment took place at the Simon's Town prison, the site of the current Simon's Town Museum.

There were of course private "slave-holders," who also engaged in what was termed the "hiring out system." The people who benefited from this system were mostly men referred to as "Malays." Their "slave-holders" realised the economic benefit for themselves, by allowing highly skilled enslaved artisans to hire out their services on the condition that they paid a considerable portion of their income to the "slave-holder."

It is interesting that while both the Dutch and British colonial governments used the term "Malay," the people they were describing were not Malaysian, but rather people of South East Asian and South Asian ancestry. In 1802 a group of six Malaysian men did in fact arrive in Simon's Town. Their names were Potro, Renno, Blembang, Singo, Viso and Callem and they had jumped ship off the *Henry Dundas* on or around the 18 February 1802.[58]

Their arrival in Simon's Town mimics that of a number of people described as "Free Blacks" in the history of the town and although the ward-

---

[56] See the Tulbagh Code, Kaapse Argiefstukke. *Kaapse Plakkaatboek: deel 3: 1754-1786* (Cape Town: *Cape Times*, 1949), C. 684, 3/5 (September 1754), 1-6.

[57] George Yonge, Proclamation (19 February 1800) in Theal, *Records of the Cape Colony*, volume 3: 45-47.

[58] WCARS, Records of the Magistrate of Simon's Town (1/SMT 2/5), Letters received 69, (1810) Simonstown 1/SMT 10/1, Ref. 62 (18 February 1802).

master was urged to look out for them, the "Malay" community in Simon's Town were known to give refuge to many people escaping the authorities. This was a time when the rumblings of resistance were starting to stir in Simon's Town through acts of defiance, notably against "slave-traders," whose storehouses were the targets of break-ins. One such target was Alexander Tennant, an auctioneer, "slave-trader" and "slave owner" known to be extremely heavy handed in his treatment of enslaved people.[59]

Fig. 3-3. Dock Gates, Simon's Town
Source: Photograph from the collection of Martin Plaut, with permission

In 1800 Alexander Tennant and William Proctor Smith were also noted in correspondence to be the agents to the captors of the prize vessel *Drie Broeders*.[60]

---

[59]*Cape Town Gazette* (13 March 1802).
[60]WCARS, BO 117, Ref. 36, Part 1 (1800).

Rynessa of the Cape and Tennant's dealings in enslaved people

Were it not for Alexander Tennant, Rynessa of the Cape would have travelled back to Bengal as a free woman, with the assistance of Charlot Mary Bolder, the widow of John Richard Coster. However, on 26 January 1801 Tennant hastily arrived at the office of the Notary John James Frederick Wagner where he produced "a [sic] original Letter of a history of Ann Deane dated Calcutta 20th of March 1799 and also a Bill of Sale in date 10 January 1798."

His aim was to prove that Rynessa was "not a free woman but the real property of Captain Deane and that he, "the appearer as agent has power and authority to claim the said Slave Woman Rynessa and to do and act on this subject as is mentioned to him in the aforesaid Letter, being consequently impossible to Mrs Coster to send her back to Bengal."[61] The irony of the situation was likely not lost on Rynessa, that though she was born at the Cape, a foreigner from Scotland had curtailed her freedom.

In 1802 "the freed slave woman Eva Cornelis" took issue with Tennant, who was evidently disliked in certain quarters, regarding the sale of Mentor of the Cape.[62] Mentor was eventually transferred to Eva.[63]

Tennant's dealings in enslaved people included the transfer of fourteen enslaved people from Mozambique to Mauritz Bartels.[64] Then there was the coach driver named Jephta of the Cape, who was transferred to Tennant by Donald Campbell in 1802.[65] Another enslaved man also named Mentor of the Cape was transferred to Hercules Sandenberg by Tennant in 1802.[66] If Tennant saw enslaved people as mere chattel from whom to derive a profit, the silenced voices of the people so affected became audible through what can surely be interpreted as acts of "slave justice."

For example, on 13 March 1802, the *Cape Town Gazette* reported that the storehouse of Alexander Tennant was broken into and thirteen bales of cam-

---

[61] WCARS, NCD, 1/21, Ref. 642 (26 January, 1801).
[62] WCARS, NCD, 1/36, Ref. 975 (1802).
[63] WCARS, NCD, 1/42, Ref. 846, Part 1 (1801).
[64] WCARS, NCD, 1/40, Ref. 444.
[65] WCARS, NCD, 1/43, Ref. 974, Part 1 (1802).
[66] WCARS, NCD, 1/43, Ref. 986, Part 1 (1802).

phor stolen "notwithstanding the same was under His Majesty's locks and also the locks of the Marshall of the vice Admiralty Court" (at this time George Rex). One hundred guineas reward was offered for any information that would lead to the conviction of the offender(s)[67] however, no-one came forward.

---

[67] *Cape Town Gazette* (11 March 1802).

PART 4

SIMON'S TOWN DURING BATAVIAN RULE 1803 TO 1806

Fig. 4-1. Simon's Bay circa 1803 to 1806
Source: Gleanings of Africa, courtesy African Studies Library, UCT

On 21 February 1803 the Cape came under Dutch Batavian rule as part of an agreement reached by Britain, France, Spain and the Batavian Republic (the Netherlands) under the Treaty of Amiens.[1] This agreement, signed on 27 March 1802, ensured peace in Europe for fourteen months during the Napoleonic wars.[2] A significant change at the Cape under Dutch Batavian rule was that from 25 July 1804 religious freedom was proclaimed, lifting the monopoly of the Dutch Reformed Church under VOC rule.[3]

---

[1] Nigel Worden, *Slavery in Dutch South Africa* (Cambridge: Cambridge University Press, 1985), 39.

[2] "Treaty of Amiens" *Encyclopedia Britannica* [online resource] http://global.britannica.com/event/Treaty-of-Amiens-1802 (accessed 11 July 2023).

[3] Frank R Bradlow and Margaret Cairns, *The Early Cape Muslims: A Study of their Mosques, Genealogy and Origins* (Cape Town: Balkema, 1978), 19. It was not until 25 July 1804 that religious freedom was officially proclaimed at the Cape.

During this period there were many memorials by local burghers requesting work privileges from the Batavian government. In their memorials they were quick to assert their allegiance to the Netherlands and denounce those who co-operated with the British. In one such memorial despatched to the Batavian authorities by Abraham de Smidt, who had resided at the Cape Colony from 1791 he wrote that:

> with a heart that burned with pure love for the Fatherland, he, in silence, detested just as much, all such individuals who had lost sight of their oath and duty to the source of their prosperity, their old benefactress, (the blessed Netherlands) and so faithfully embraced the service of the Enemies of the Batavian Republic.[4]

On 5 March 1803, Hermanus van der Schyff of Simon's Bay sent the following memorial:

> Hermanus van der Schyff prays that commissioner General de Mist may be pleased to give him the appointment (as he flatters himself that he knows the Gardener's business) of Superintendent of the large vegetable garden near Simon's Bay, and that, as those before him he may be assisted with six Government slaves. He promises to have ready at all times fit vegetables for the ships of the Batavian Republic, and at such reasonable prices as may be fixed by your Honour.[5]

In terms of slavery, the historian Robert Shell has written that the new "Batavian authorities were determined to treat the slaves at the Cape well." They considered it one of the Council of Policy's "most sacred duties to guard over the fate of these unfortunates."[6] However, how does one evaluate what "good treatment" meant in those times when it came to enslaved and indigenous people?

---

[4] Hendrik Carel Vos Leibbrandt, *Precis of the Archives of the Cape of Good Hope, Requesten (Memorials), Volume 3 (1715-1806)*: P-S, 1172.

[5] Leibbrandt, *Requesten, Volume 3 (1715- 1806)*: P-S, 1170-1171.

[6] Ockert Geyser, *The History of the Old Supreme Court Building* (Cape Town: Africana Press, 1982) in Robert Carl-Heinz Shell, *From Diaspora to Diorama* (Cape Town: Nagspro Multimedia, 2012), volume 7, chapter 1, page 2811.

In Simon's Town during the Batavian period, everyday worries were about the shortage of firewood, which the locals blamed on the "parching S[outh] E[ast] winds," saying that this prevented the growth of timber. In general, life in this distant outpost moved along as slowly as the heavily laden ox wagons that meandered into the town. On occasion the wealthy would arrive and the locals would be captivated by "waggons drawn by fourteen or sixteen horses."[7]

Henry Roselt must have been relieved that the change in Government did not affect his job as wardmaster. In fact in 1803 he was as busy as ever, dealing with a number of matters referred to him by the attorney general at the Cape, one Gerard Beelaerts van Blokland. There was a letter asking him to apprehend a "deserter" referred to as a "Hottentot"[8] followed by a request to have the streets repaired. On 15 June 1803 there was a complaint from Hendrik Cloete about the "Bastard" Moses Pietersen apparently cutting back on Government land.[9] Arrangements also needed to be made to transport six enslaved men from the Slave Lodge in Cape Town, to form the labour force of Hermanus van der Schyff who was appointed Superintendent of the large vegetable garden near Simon's Bay, which would supply ships of the Batavian Republic.[10]

Much of Roselt's worries concerned finding "deserters," some who travelled by foot from over the mountains and others who arrived by sea and absconded into the town.[11] He also needed to keep abreast of Colonial Office placards, most notably in December 1803 when it was chillingly declared that emancipated, formerly enslaved women who were infected with venereal disease were to be "cared for in the Slave Lodge and corporally punished when released, but a second time taken in[to the] Hospital to be confined or punished more severely."[12]

---

[7] James Kingston Tuckey, *An Account of a Voyage to Establish a Colony at Port Phillip ... in the Years 1802-3-4* (London: Longman, Hurst, Rees and Orme, 1805), 134-135.

[8] WCARS, Records of the Magistrate of Simon's Town (1/SMT 2/5), Letters received (1810) Simonstown 1/SMT 10/1, Ref. 95 (5 February 1803).

[9] WCARS, Records of the Magistrate of Simon's Town (1/SMT 2/5), Letters received 1810) Simonstown 1/SMT 10/1, Ref. 110 (10 June 1803).

[10] Leibbrandt, *Requesten, Volume 3 (1715-1806)*: P-S, 1170-1171.

[11] WCARS, Records of the Magistrate of Simon's Town (1/SMT 2/5), Letters received 1810) Simonstown 1/SMT 10/1, Ref. 113 (12 July 1803).

Julij

The year 1804 started uneventfully for Roselt, but on 8 May 1804 he was asked to ensure the court attendance of Timothy Fulgar in connection with people who died on the French ship the Sara.[13] In June, there were also complaints about "beggars" interfering with the Marguerite[14] and complaints about the rowdy behaviour of sailors.[15] On 18 July 1804 a more urgent message was sent to Henry Roselt regarding the fisherman Julij. The note, hurriedly written at 8 o'clock in the evening, read:

> The Warden Roselt will, upon receiving this, apprehend and send as a prisoner the slave Julij, a fisherman, belonging to Jan Pieter Kirsten and once again search his possessions carefully. If said Julij should be absent, Warden Roselt must undertake the strictest possible investigation in order to lay hands on him.[16]

The case of Julij offers an intriguing insight into a clandestine criminal network between a group of enslaved men from Simon's Town and a Dutch trader who bought their stolen wares and re-sold them in Cape Town. The people mentioned in this case were July from Macassar ("slave" to Jan Pieter Kirsten), Apollos from Ternate ("slave" to Gerrit Croeser), Matjang from Bougies ("slave" to Jan Pieter Kirsten), Andries from Mauritius ("slave" to Jan Pieter Kirsten), Toon (origin unknown) ("slave" to Widow Hurter) and Johannes Josephus Jantson aged 41 of Delft, in the Netherlands.

It is notable that both the storehouses that had been broken into belonged to noted "slave-traders" residing in Simon's Town. The first burglary occurred at the storehouse belonging to the Scottish "slave-trader" mentioned earlier, Alexander Tennant. From it Matjang and Andries stole six

---

[12] WCARS, SO 17/1 (23 December 1803).

[13] WCARS, Records of the Magistrate of Simon's Town (1/SMT 2/5), Letters received 1810, Simonstown 1/SMT 10/1, Ref. 134 & 135 (8 May 1804).

[14] WCARS, Records of the Magistrate of Simon's Town (1/SMT 2/5), Letters received 1810, Simonstown 1/SMT 10/1, Ref. 145 (11 June 1804).

[15] WCARS, Records of the Magistrate of Simon's Town (1/SMT 2/5), Letters received 1810, Simonstown 1/SMT 10/1, Ref. 150 (15 June 1804).

[16] WCARS, Records of the Magistrate of Simon's Town (1/SMT 2/5), Letters received 1810, Simonstown 1/SMT 10/1, Ref. 156 (18 July 1804).

chests of tea and 1,040 pieces of nankeen cotton[17] that were packed into five crates. They immediately sold the tea to Johannes Josephus Jantson for six rix dollars per case and hid the nankeen in the sand behind the house of Jacobus Kirsten before finally removing it. After a few days Jantson also bought two crates of the nankeen. He paid for them in silver and paper money and afterwards sold the goods at a profit in Cape Town.

Although Matjang and Andries committed the actual theft, the sale of the goods was conducted by all members of the group and Jantson was not their only customer. July of Macassar had, with the assistance of Aron—"slave" to Captain Dunning—sold to the late Hendrik Kannemeyer (who later died in the public prison in Simon's Bay) and to Toon, eight packages of nankeen for which Toon had paid ninety Rix dollars in rupees and paper money. It seems, therefore, that Toon was a buyer and not involved in the actual thefts. In court records it emerges that the group had also broken into Tennant's storehouse on 17 June 1804 at which time July and Apollos stole a sack of flour. Not long afterwards they broke into this storehouse again, this time with the help of Andries. On this occasion they stole "more baskets of flour and another calabash of wine." Another storehouse in Simon's Town was also broken into by this group, this one belonging to the Swiss "slave-trader" Isaac Strombom. From this storehouse the group stole a roll of blue cloth, a piece of striped linen, two bushels of rice, six pieces of white linen, a quantity of needles and thread, as well as some biscuits.

Some of these goods were sold by Matjang who found a ready buyer in Jantson. With the authorities on high alert to find them, the group concealed themselves in a cave in the mountains above Simon's Town where they survived in part by stealing three sheep from a flock "grazing under the care of the little Hottentot boy behind the Government's Garden."[18]

Unlike the Hanglip maroons who were largely able to elude the authorities, this group were discovered soon after. It is ironic that the person who reported Julij was his own wife, Clarissa. It transpired that he "visited" Clarissa and "threw her a bundle of dirty clothing" and told her "you must wash that shirt." He then went off towards the side of the mountain behind

---

[17]Nankeen refers to a pale buff coloured cloth originally made in Nanking (or Nanjing) in China.

[18]WCARS, Council of Justice, CJ 801, 22 (1806).

Kirsten's house. Clarissa opened the bundle and "found inside it some silver and paper money so she immediately informed the widow Olthof," whose late husband was the harbourmaster in Simon's Town.

Their sentences were harsh: Julij and Apollos were sentenced to

> be hanged by the neck till they are dead and their dead bodies being transported to the Gibbet outside the Town to be hanged thereon and there to remain as an example till consumed by the birds of the air.

Matjang, Andries and Toon were to be bound to a stake, severely scourged with rods on their bare backs and thereafter Matjang and Andries were to be branded with a hot iron, then put in chains—Matjang for twenty-five years and Andries for a term of fifteen years—and in this condition to labour without wages in the public works. Toon, after his punishment, was to be "given up to his Mistress, the Widow Hurter" whose home was present-day Admiralty House. Finally, in a public display of shaming, Jantson was made to witness these punishments, following which he was banished from the Cape Colony for life thereafter.[19]

People of Khoe Descent in Simon's Town During the Dutch Batavian Period

Before Anthonij Visser settled on this landscape in 1725, and the later utilisation of this landscape as a winter anchorage for the Dutch East India Company in 1743, indigenous communities inhabited this space with a sense of familiarity and carefree abandon. However, in the ensuing years they and their descendants had undergone significant forms of historical trauma. Their lifestyle of free movement, which was as natural as the wind, became constrained by a strong military force from a foreign land.

No longer moving freely and being forced to carry "passes," their descendants coalesced in remote areas of the False Bay coast. On 15 July 1804 a meeting was held by the Commissioners of the Court of Justice at which they discussed an investigation entrusted to Henry Roselt, where he was to oversee a search to locate the habitation of all people of Khoe descent in

---

[19] WCARS, Council of Justice, CJ 801, Raad van Justitie Sententies, 22 (1806).

Simon's Town and to rummage through their belongings. Clearly something had gone missing and these communities were the targets of blame.

This report offers an insight as to the settlement patterns of the descendants of the dispossessed indigenous people, described in colonial documents as "Bastard Hottentots." These communities may have been shocked to learn that even the remote areas of the land their ancestors had occupied freely were no longer considered theirs. One such kraal site was considered to be part of the farm Buffelsfonteyn belonging to Jan Michiel Endres. At the meeting it was discussed that "on the farm called Buffelsfonteyn, belonging to Jan Michiel Endres as well as in the vicinity of said Simon's Bay, [there were] more dwellings belonging to Bastard Hottentots."[20]

Two families of partial Khoe ancestry lived at a *kraal* named Kleyne Buffelsfonteyn. The report particularly focuses on three men who lived there with their wives and children. These men were Willem, Hannes and Hannes's son named December. Willem and Hannes were referred to as "Bastards," a disparaging term used during the VOC era to describe people of mixed Khoe and European ancestry.

At Klaver Valley lived Moses and Marthinus with their wives. These men were also disparagingly described in official documents as "Bastards." Moses, who has also been referred to as Moses Pieterson in other documents, was noted in this investigation to have two sons, four daughters, a brother named Andries and a sister named Steyntje, all of whom lived together. He also had in his employ a "Free Black" person named Aladie; a "hired slave" namely a man known as Leendert belonging to the widow Jurgens in the Garden at the Cape, a "slave" named Daris, as well as a man named Adam, referred to as "an old Hottentot."

What this report did not acknowledge was that Moses Pietersen was in fact the legal owner of Klaver Valley as noted in his Will. "Married" to Helena of Batavia, Moses Pietersen cut an interesting figure and his father must have been a man of standing in this colonial dominated society as he had connections with powerful burgher families in the Simon's Town district. While part of his earnings was derived from agriculture, he made good use of his

---

[20] WCARS, Records of the Magistrate of Simon's Town (1/SMT 2/5), Letters received (1810); Simonstown 1/SMT 10/1, Ref. 155 (15 July 1804).

wagons by running a transport service.[21] The family also earned a living from gardening and collecting bark while the females in the family brought in an income as washerwomen. Their possessions were listed in the minutes of the meeting as being "26 draught oxen, one bull, 6 cows, 2 wagons and 3 horses." Whatever the searchers were seeking, they did not find it on this property as the report stated that they had "found nothing."[22] As the minutes of this meeting shows, in Simon's Town there were descendants of Khoe mothers who established themselves with some autonomy in settlements along the mountainside.[23] However, they were under constant surveillance and viewed with suspicion by the class of people who held state power on this land that for their ancestors was once only theirs.

Fears of an impending British invasion are said to have prompted Governor de Mist to declare freedom of religion on 25 July 1804. Through this policy change the Batavian Republic was able to enlist the services of many "Free Malays" and Chinese firemen in Simon's Town to serve in the Cape Mounted Riflemen on 24 October that year.[24] However, notwithstanding these measures, the Battle of Blaauwberg on 8 January 1806 brought about the demise of the Dutch Batavian Republic and heralded the second British occupation at the Cape.

---

[21]WCARS, Records of the Magistrate of Simon's Town 1/SMT 2/5, Volume number 1/SMT 10/1, Ref. 155 (15 July 1804).

[22]WCARS, Records of the Magistrate of Simon's Town (1/SMT 2/5), Letters received (1810) Simonstown 1/SMT 10/1, Ref. 155 (15 July 1804).

[23]WCARS, Records of the Magistrate of Simon's Town 1793-1985: 1/SMT 2/5, SMT 10/18, "Report of the Commission of Heemraad on the Visit to the Field Cornetcy of Wildschutsbrand" (18 October 1825).

[24]WCARS, Records of the Magistrate of Simon's Town (1/SMT 2/5), Letters received (1810) Simonstown 1/SMT 10/1, 175 (24 October 2016).

PART 5

SIMON'S TOWN DURING THE SECOND BRITISH OCCUPATION 1806

The period 1806 to 1814 is significant as being the latter part of the period of transition at the Cape, which began in 1795. During this time there was a rise in anti-slavery sentiment in Britain, which saw the British colonial government under great pressure to get rid of slavery. Much pressure was channelled through abolitionists like Granville Sharpe and William Wilberforce. However, at the Cape the British colonial governor was walking a tightrope between appeasing the abolitionists back home and keeping the peace with the Dutch,[1] particularly the farmers who were anti-British and whose economy depended on the labour of enslaved people.

This was also a period of simmering resentment between the Dutch and the British in Simon's Town, with local Widow Rossouw, Widow Martha Hurter, Jan Michiel Endres, Johannes Gustavus Aspeling and Nicolaas Sertyn signing a petition to protest about being made to accommodate British officers in their homes.[2] Resentment towards the British was also evident in a memorial by Frederik Rossouw of Slangekop when he recalled with clarity the economic impact of the British colonial troops marching over his ground, which he said caused him "important damages."[3]

The Swede Isaac Strombom also put an in application to have "fewer British billeted officers at his house."[4] A known "slave-trader," Isaac Strombom

---

[1] The term "Dutch" in this instance includes the many Germans who settled in Simon's Town. John Hoge, *Personalia of the Germans at the Cape, 1652-1806* (Cape Town: Archives Year Book, 1946).

[2] WCARS, Records of the Magistrate of Simon's Town (1/SMT 2/5), Letters received 1808) Simonstown 1/SMT 10/2, Ref. 92 (8 March 1808).

[3] WCARS, Records of the Magistrate of Simon's Town (1/SMT 2/5), Letters received 1809) Simonstown 1/SMT 10/2, Ref. 193A (20 September 1809).

[4] WCARS, CO 3868, Ref. 167, Part 1 (1808).

sold commodities and people without differentiation, from his home, The Residency, in Simon's Town. On 28 February 1806 he advertised a sale in the press that stated:

> Public Sale on Friday 28 Feb in Simons Bay at the house of Mr Stromboom [sic], the following goods will be sold: household furniture, porcelain, wine glasses, 2 boats, slaves, etc, etc. etc.[5]

In that same year the Scotsman and "slave-trader" Alexander Tennant took ownership of the farm Constantia located in Simon's Town.[6] By then the farm had changed hands four times, the previous owners being Arend Munnik, Hendrik Elshoud and Hendrik Veersen (Fehrsen).[7] However, the greatest landowner in Simon's Town by far was John Osmond, who in December 1806 petitioned for a further piece of land:

> to establish a private Dockyard in Simon's Town, for repairing vessels and supplying them with such articles as they may require. Several storehouses near the beach are absolutely necessary for such an establishment, the want of the latter having prevented many vessels from calling here for repairs, as the few naval stores existing here are most extravagant in their prices. It is his intention to lay in such a stock of stores as not only to be able to furnish all merchant ships, but also, in case of necessity, to supply the navy at a moderate profit.[8]

The land requested was "situated between the South Battery and the rocks projecting from the front of Mr. Roselt's house in which there is a small nook under the denomination of Steenbras Bay." This he requested "under such conditions and for such a sum as may be considered reasonable." After an inspection by Abraham Fleck, member of the Court of Justice; Ernst

---

[5] *Cape Town Gazette and African Advertiser* (22 February 1806): page 2, column 2.

[6] Simon's Town Museum: The Willis Files. Cape Old Freeholds, Volume 3, page 86, Number 127 (11 July 1806).

[7] Cape Old Freeholds, (6 October 1746 to 27 August 1782), Volume 3, Deeds Registry No. 608, Simon's Town (2 February 1761).

[8] Leibbrandt, *Requesten 1715-1806: volume 2: F-O*, 878.

Frederik Schrader, member of the Burgher Senate; George Francis Grant, Inspector of Lands and Jan Willem Wernich, sworn Land Surveyor, a conclusion was reached that the land "can be safely granted to Osmond without prejudicing anyone."[9]

Unlike John Osmond, for his dark-skinned counterparts—whether enslaved, indigenous or "free"—this society was a traumatic one within which to retain a healthy sense of self. Experiences of random beatings and daily humiliation formed scabs that would blister the futures of people for whom these experiences became a lived reality.

Institutionalised violence was a defining feature of the British colonial era. The local magistrate Johannes Hendricus Brand arranged that many enslaved men and women could be sent by "slave-holders" to be beaten at the Simon's Town Prison, the site of the Simon's Town Museum (once the home of "slave-trader" Isaac Strombom).[10] This became the norm and on 4 January 1809 an incredulous Captain Robertson penned a note to the Simon's Town magistrate about what he rightly stated was the unjust imprisonment and beating of an enslaved man (whom he refers to as a "boy"):

> I was totally ignorant that Mr Endres' boy was lodged in the Trunk. I did give orders to the Man who is in charge of the Government Garden that should any cattle be allowed to stray into that garden through the negligence of the keeper, that he should immediately take those cattle and put them into the Pound and also bring the keeper to me that I might enquire further into the matter, but thro' some mistake in my absence yesterday, it appears instead of bringing the Boy to me, or his Master, he has been put in the Trunk and punished, quite contrary to my wish or intention.[11]

Vasily Mikhailovich Golovnin, a Russian aristocrat and ship's captain who was detained at Simon's Bay in 1809, was equally appalled by the Simon's

---

[9] Leibbrandt, *Requesten 1715-1806: volume 2:* F-O, 877-878.

[10] WCARS, Records of the Magistrate of Simon's Town 1793-1985: 1/SMT 2/5 (Letters received, 1793-1932), 1/SMT 10/9, Ref. 60.

[11] WCARS, Records of the Magistrate of Simon's Town (1/SMT 2/5), Letters received 1809) Simonstown 1/SMT 10/2, Ref. 137 (4 January 1809).

Town "slave-holding" society. In his journal wherein he wrote of "their eagerness to do business, their intellectual dullness and generally boring lives and conversation," he stated that "their main vice is the cruelty with which many of them treat their slaves."[12]

Certainly the British colonial authorities also took a dim view of working class soldiers and when a case of robbery was reported they first searched all the soldiers in the barracks before deciding to search the homes of "all the coolies or any other that we may suspect."[13]

In one case a soldier was caught stealing fowls out of John Osmond's garden. According to Osmond he was "seen by our young slaves."[14] There was also the report of a "Grenadier Cobler of the 87 Regiment" having taken the life of a woman and burying her on the beach in August 1809.[15] However, there is no evidence that this case ever got to trial and a dark skin continued to be the greatest liability in this society where hierarchies were racially inspired.

However, a select group of families who formed the upper hierarchy of the "Free Black" society seemed to have operated with a certain level of autonomy, at least during this time. The most notable of these families was the one headed by Moses Pietersen and this becomes evident through the wording of his last will and testament.

---

[12] Michael Whisson, "Group Areas: The End of the Hottentot Tradition in the Simon's Town District." Unpublished manuscript" 27. Boris Gorelik (editor), "*An Entirely Different World": Russian Visitors to the Cape 1797-1870* (Cape Town: Van Riebeeck Society, 2015), VRS Series 2: 46, 34.

[13] WCARS, Records of the Magistrate of Simon's Town (1/SMT 2/5), Letters received (1810) Simonstown 1/SMT 10/1, Ref. 93 (19 October 1802).

[14] WCARS, Records of the Magistrate of Simon's Town (1/SMT 2/5), Letters received by Resident Magistrate (1810) Simonstown 1/SMT 10/3, Ref. 24 and 25 (22 March 1822).

[15] WCARS, Records of the Magistrate of Simon's Town (1/SMT 2/5), Letters received by Resident Magistrate (1810) Simonstown 1/SMT 10/3, Ref. 20 (9 March 1810).

Moses Pietersen[16]

On 18 June 1807 the Simon's Town resident notary, Petrus Stephanus Buissine, visited the home of Moses Pietersen at his request. The purpose of the visit was to draw up a will for Pietersen. It is likely that Moses Pietersen was ill at the time, given that his death occurred at some stage during the ensuing weeks. This may also explain why Buissine travelled to his home to draw up the will. However, Pietersen was described as being "in full possession of his mind, sense and understanding."

According to Moses Pietersen's will, Mentor of Mozambique was left to his daughter Silla, Maart of Mozambique to his son Hendrik and April of Mozambique to his daughter Martha. However, on 14 September 1807 these three people were manumitted by his children. In the case of Drammat of Batavia it was the instruction of Moses Pietersen that he was never to be sold, but to serve Hester of Batavia, the partner of Moses and following her death to choose which of their children he chose to live with. Pietersen was emphatic that he was never to live with any stranger as long as there was still one of his children alive. This wish was honoured.[17]

Moses Pietersen's connection to the powerful Rossouw family is interesting. According to his will he left the farm Klaver Valley to his partner Hester van Batavia and their children, namely Jan Moses, Antje Moses, Rachel Moses, Saartje Moses, Sila Moses, Hendrik Moses and Martha Moses[18]. However, Hester was affected by a "linguering [sic] disorder by which she was attacked immediate after the death of the said Moses Pietersen"[19] from which she died soon after. It was then that Frans Rossouw and Nicolas Sertyn petitioned the Earl of Caledon[20] for the land rights of the children, asking that they be allowed to grant this property to the children on quitrent. This is confusing as this petition refers to the land as a temporary grant obtained from the Batavian Government[21] whereas, according to the will of

---

[16] Moses Pietersen was recorded variously as Moses Pietersen, Moses Petersen and Mosis Pietersen.

[17] WCARS, MOOC, 7/1/54, Folio 46 (14 September 1807).

[18] WCARS, CO 3873, Ref. 365 (23 August 1809).

[19] WCARS, CO 3873, Ref. 365 (23 August 1809).

[20] Du Pré Alexander, 2nd Earl of Caledon (14 December 1777-8 April 1839), Governor of the Cape from 1806 to 1811.

Moses Pietersen, this property belonged to him. In 1816 Jan Moses, the son of Moses Pietersen, was noted to be raising a family in the vicinity of Klaver Valley.[22] In 1824 the Batavian enslaved man Drammat was residing with Johanna Catherina Moses, the daughter of Moses Pietersen and the wife of Johannes Petrus Bredeveld.[23]

The Will of Moses Pietersen:

> On this the eighteenth day of the month of June in the year of our Lord One Thousand Eight Hundred and Seven I, Petrus Stephanus Buissine, Notary admitted at the Government at the Cape of Good Hope, and residing in Simon's Town having been requested went with the hereafter mentioned witnesses to the home of the Bastard Hottentot Moses Pietersen, residing beyond Simonsberg, where appeared before me, Notary and witnesses the said Moses Pietersen, of competent age, known to me, Notary and witnesses, in full possession of his mind, sense and understanding as became clear in the drawing up of this document; and the Appearer indicated that he had decided of his own free will to dispose of his possessions and therefore wished to set out in writing his last will and testament, which is this:
>
> In the first place the Testator revokes and annuls all previous Testaments, Codicils or other Deeds of this nature that he, Testator may have made before this date, not wishing or desiring that any one of these may have the least effect or value.
>
> In the second place the Testator declares to bequeath to his Brother Andries Pietersen the sum of Three Hundred Cape

---

[21] WCARS, CO 3873, Ref. 365 (23 August 1809).
[22] WCARS, Records of the Magistrate of Simon's Town 1793-1985: 1/SMT 2/5 (Letters received, 1793-1932), SMT 10/8, Ref. 157 (20 July 1816).
[23] CAD SO 2/16 Slave Registry Department Correspondence (30 October 1824).

Rix Dollars at Forty-eight Stivers each which sum must be disbursed to him three months after the Testator's death.

In the third place the Testator desires that the farmstead Klavervalley must not be sold after his death but must remain in possession of his hereafter mentioned heirs, and after their deaths must go to their children and whom he, Testator, wishes to live together on the Farm.

In the fourth place the Testator declares that because his Parents are no longer alive, he nominates and appoints as heir, as he does hereby, the Free Black woman Hester of Batavia, on this express condition that she may not sell anything belonging to his Estate or alienate it in any way, as it must go to his children in equal shares after his death, and after the death of one or more of them, to their descendants.

In the fifth place the Testator nominates and appoints as his Executrix the aforesaid Free Black woman, Hester of Batavia, desiring that no one else should interfere with his Estate or Heirs, not even the Honourable Orphan Masters or any other qualified persons, hereby excluding all of them and thanking them courteously for any other trouble they may go to.

In the sixth place the Testator declares to reserve to himself the full effect of the *Clausule Reservatoir*, to make use of as he deems fit.

And I, Notary, reminded the Testator of the injunction regarding Slaves who have professed the Christian Religion as well as that regarding the immoveable property willed to his said heirs and changes to the appointment of heirs.

All the aforesaid having been read to the Testator word for word, clearly and distinctly, he declared to have understood everything and that this was his last Will and Testament, with the desire that it will be accepted according to the law, regarding any solemnity that may have been omitted as included.

The Testator finally answered to my, Notary's, question that the value of his Estate is less than six thousand Guilders.

Thus done and passed on the Farm Klavervalley in the presence of the Clerks Arend Wahl and Christiaan Lodewijk Wentzel as witnesses; the minutes of this were properly signed and written under a Seal of Forty-eight Stivers. To which I attest was signed

P S Buisinne, Notary

By virtue of the *Clausule Reservatoir* inserted in this my Testament, I declare to bequeath to Silla, Hendrik and Martha of the Cape, children of my Heiress Hester of Batavia, my three male Slaves named Mentor, Maart and April of Mozambique to wit, Mentor to Silla, Maart to Hendrik and April to Martha, to be regarded as their own property after my death.

Furthermore I desire that my male slave named Dramat of Batavia will never be sold, but must serve the much mentioned Free Black woman Hester of Batavia during her lifetime, but that after her death he must be allowed to choose which of her children he would prefer to serve, and he will not be able to choose to live with any stranger, unless there is still one of them alive.

Klavervalley beyond Simonsberg the nineteenth of June 1807.

This X is the signature of Moses Pietersen signed in the presence of me

Signed: *P S Buisinne, Notary.*

Exhibited at the Orphan Chamber at the Cape of Good Hope the 14th September 1807.

After the death of Moses Pietersen, Andries Pietersen put in an application for "1 or 2 duct acres on quitrent" in Kalk Bay where he was already making a living by gathering shells. In his application he stated that he wished to build a shelter for himself and his family and start a kitchen garden.[24] His neighbours would have been Abraham Kloppers and his wife Sara Elizabeth Arendse, who were also of partial Khoe ancestry. In 1807 Kloppers is on record as owning a fishery in Kalk Bay and his wife Sara was herself the "slaveholder" of a fisherman named Mey who came from Bougies.[25]

Fig. 5-1. Simon's Town from Kalk Bay, circa 1838
Source: Watercolour by Christopher Webb Smith

---

[24]WCARS, Records of the Magistrate of Simon's Town (1/SMT 2/5), Letters received (1809), Simonstown 1/SMT 10/2, Ref. 141 (6 February 1809).
[25]WCARS, MOOC, 7/1/54, Folio 46, (14 September 1807).

The people described as "Free Blacks" in the census of the Cape Colony included people who had been manumitted from slavery as well as people who had arrived at the Cape as political prisoners or convicts and who elected to stay after serving their sentences.

However, among the people disparagingly described as "Bastards" and "Bastard Hottentots," there seemed to have developed a class hierarchy wherein those who stood at the top of this hierarchy could easily have been described as "Free Blacks" though in the census they were not.

This group of people were also more likely to be landowners and "slaveholders," albeit on a small scale. However, no evidence of cruelty towards enslaved people was ever levelled against them. Given that the children of Moses Pietersen freed the few enslaved people in his household almost immediately after his death, it is ironic that Moses Pietersen died in the same year that the British Abolition of the Slave Trade Act 1807 was promulgated in Great Britain, and which became effective in the Cape Colony on 1 January 1808.[26]

Abolition

In 1808 the efforts of abolitionists like William Wilberforce, Thomas Clarkson and Granville Sharpe bore fruit when Britain abolished the "slave-trade," its participation ending with the last English slaver, the *Kitty's Amelia* in 1807.[27] This Parliamentary Act, effective from 1 January 1808, stipulated that Africans brought into British colonies as "slaves" were to be "forfeited to the Crown" and apprenticed for not more than fourteen years.[28] It was in terms of this purpose that a British naval squadron was established in Simon's Town to intercept "slave" ships on route to the Americas whose human cargoes of mainly East African people were claimed as "prizes."[29]

---

[26] Michael Charles Reidy, The Admission of Slaves and "Prize Slaves" into the Cape Colony, 1797-1818 (UCT: MA thesis, 1997), 26.

[27] Christopher Lloyd, *The Navy and the Slave Trade: The Suppression of the African Slave Trade in the Nineteenth Century* (London and New York: Routledge, 2012), 3.

[28] Saunders, "Liberated Africans in Cape Colony" *The International Journal of African Historical Studies* 18, 2 (1985): 224.

The location of Simon's Town was pivotal to the enactment of the abolition of the "slave-trade" with Britain setting up an anti-slavery squadron in Simon's Bay, as it was then known, and another in Table Bay. This heralded a new form of labour exploitation at the time, known as the "prize negro" indentureship system. In this way a number of people, ostensibly "liberated" off "slave" ships by the British anti-slavery squadron were brought into the town. The modus operandi was such that the anti-slavery squadron would patrol the sea and if they found a Portuguese or French ship with enslaved people aboard, the ship would be impounded as a "prize" ship and the people would be held at Customs House until they were assigned as "prize negroes" for indenture for a period of fourteen years.

The harshness of their experience was in many ways dependent on whether they were assigned to the Navy and the Army or whether they were assigned to private individuals. The man who decided their fate was Charles Blair, who took up the post of Collector of Customs on his arrival at the Cape in 1808. It was his job to travel to the Custom Houses at Table Bay and Simon's Bay, where he selected the strongest and fittest men to be assigned to the Navy and the Army, the rest being assigned to private individuals, for an "indentureship" period of fourteen years.

Under the guise of preparing these "liberated slaves" or "negro apprentices" with skills that would equip them to earn a living after their fourteen year apprenticeship, slavery was at once abolished and extended.[30]

Considering them as gifts to the Crown in as much as were the ships they were delivered from, these vulnerable people were named "prize negroes" and listed as such in the official census.[31] Within the first eight years following abolition, more than 2,100 East African people were landed in the colony, in

---

[29] *Encyclopedia of Antislavery and Abolition*; edited by Peter P Hinks, John R McKivigan and R Owen Williams; (Britain: Greenwood, 2007), Volume 2: J-Z, 427.

[30] The people described as "prize negroes" were sources of wealth generation for many prominent families in the Cape, who hired their "apprentices" out, the hiring fees of which by the 1820s averaged at a rate of one Rix dollar per day. WCARS, Slave Office, SO 2/12 (21 March 1831), 120, 6.

[31] Nigel Worden, Elizabeth van Heyningen and Vivian Bickford-Smith, *Cape Town: The Making of a City* (Cape Town: David Philip, 1998), 109.

either Simon's Bay or Table Bay, where their fate lay in the hands of the Collector of Customs, Charles Blair.[32]

Unpacking Abolition

The abolition of the "slave-trade" can be seen as a compromise to appease abolitionists on the one hand and to retain the labour force at the Cape on the other. However, the impact of the abolition of the "slave-trade" was varied. For example, for those people already enslaved at the Cape this promised a false hope of freedom, as essentially what the Act meant was that though the oceanic "slave-trade" was now illegal, for people already enslaved their status would remain unchanged.

For "slave-traders" resident in Simon's Town, such as Scottish Alexander Tennant and Swedish Isaac Strombom, this must have been perceived in terms of what they stood to lose financially. Just a year before abolition Alexander Tennant had applied to land a "cargo of slaves" who were on board the Portuguese vessel *Constantia*.[33] In 1808 Tennant tried to minimise the impact of abolition on his personal financial gain by hurriedly putting in an application to "retain slaves on Robben Island as his property."[34]

On 6 February 1808, a month after the abolition of the "slave-trade" became effective on 1 January 1808,[35] Isaac Strombom made preparations to leave the Cape for England. Before his departure he advertised for sale "about 20-30 of his slaves, amongst which [are] carpenters, coopers, an excellent cook, ox-wagon driver, stable boy and other workmen."[36]

The Impact of the Abolition of the Slave-Trade in Simon's Town—1808

With the abolition of the "slave-trade," private "slave-holders" sought to protect their economic interests by improving the diets and decreasing the working hours of enslaved people. However, these "benefits" did not extend

---

[32] Worden, van Heyningen and Bickford-Smith, *Cape Town*, 2.
[33] WCARS, CO 3866, Ref. 565, Part 1.
[34] WCARS, CO 3868, Ref. 114, Part 1 (1808).
[35] Anna Maria Rugarli, "Eyes on the Prize: The Story of the Prize Slave Present" *Quarterly Bulletin of the National Library of South Africa* 62, 4 (October-December 2008): 161.
[36] *Cape Town Gazette* 2, 58 (6 February 1808).

to people "liberated" off "slave" ships, who found themselves indentured to private individuals in the town. Although the latter group came from a variety of origins, they were collectively referred to as "prize negroes" by the British colonial authorities. For the people so named, a commonality amongst themselves was the experience of trauma. The trauma began when they were taken from their homes and held captive on "slave" ships where they were transported under extremely inhumane conditions.

The late naval historian Christopher Lloyd described the plight of people held on "slave" ships as follows:

> Reputable witnesses declared that no slave was allowed more than a space measuring 5 ft 6 in by 16 inches in which to lie between decks often less than 4 feet apart; that they were often manacled on their sides so that more could be packed tighter; that 10% died of suffocation, apart from deaths due to a hundred types of disease and infection; that their food consisted of yams and beans twice a day, with one pint of stinking water; that they were imprisoned between decks for 16 hours out of 24 and that the famous dancing "consisted of jumping in their irons for exercise and that they were whipped when they refused to do it."[37]

There were also others who did not make it to the shore as, when the slavers saw a British anti-naval patrol on the horizon, they would get rid of the "evidence," being the people, who were thrown alive into the sea. This was almost the case for the progenitor of the Kindo family of Simon's Town and Ocean View who was thrown overboard a "slave" ship. Oral history has it that he was a young child thought to be about twelve years old when he was rescued and brought to the shores of Simon's Town. Reverend Barnabas Shaw is said to have given Kibo Kindo refuge at the Methodist Church, where he worked and lived during his young life.

In 1850 Kibo Kindo married Aletta Davidse. The couple were childless and sadly Aletta died in April 1866. Some months after the loss of Aletta, Kibo married his second wife, Johanna Sebastian, who also hailed from Simon's Town. The couple had thirteen children and though he was never

---

[37] Lloyd, *The Navy and the Slave Trade*, 8.

given access to formal education and worked as a labourer, Kibo Kindo supported his family and provided them with a home in Cardiff Road, Simon's Town. Were Kibo to have a lens to the future, he would have been proud of all his descendants and particularly so of (the late) Christopher Kindo, who became a world famous dancer. He would have also been happy to know that though his entire family had been forcibly removed from Simon's Town during apartheid, another of his descendants, namely Christopher's brother Percy along with his wife Mary, would return to Cardiff Road in the post-apartheid era, rebuilding the family home and in this way the legacy of the Kindo family of Simon's Town.[38]

Fig. 5-2. Mary and Percy Kindo outside the family home in Simon's Town
Source: Mary Kindo

Certainly, with the abolition of the "slave-trade," "slave-holders" were incentivised to improve the treatment of the enslaved people on their "slave-

---

[38]It appears the young boy worked for Barnabas Shaw and later for the mayor of Simon's Town, William Runciman, from whom the young Kindo is said to have bought a piece of ground in Cardiff Road in Simon's Town.

holdings." For purely economic reasons, "slave-holders" started improving the living and working conditions of enslaved people, the mindset being that these enslaved people were irreplaceable assets from whom they could derive a profit, provided they were healthy. On the other hand, with the tap of supply being shut, the womb of the enslaved woman became the supplier of the "slave-trade," which rendered enslaved women even more vulnerable to sexual exploitation by "slave-holders." However, for many enslaved people, the abolition of the "slave-trade" created a psychological turning point, making it possible for them to imagine their lives differently. People were hungry for freedom and the abolition of the "slave-trade" strengthened their resolve to overcome enslavement.

It is therefore no accident that this was also the year of the first revolt of enslaved people when, on 27 October 1808, more than 300 enslaved people and "servants" from the Zwartland, Koeberg and Tygerberg districts staged an armed uprising.[39] Though this was far from the very remote district of Simon's Town, this was a time when enslaved people generally were becoming restless for their freedom. To this end, by 23 June 1809 the numbers of people who had escaped from slavery were so great that "runaway slaves" were offered "a general pardon" provided they were not guilty of "capital crimes."[40] That such an edict was issued is indicative of the successful network available to enslaved people amongst the "Free Black Malay" community in Simon's Town and elsewhere.[41]

Fishing had become a traditional lifestyle for many in the "Free Black Malay" community in Simon's Town who were managing to carve out livelihoods from the sea. By 1808, Mey of Batavia was earning enough to invest in a second boat.[42] It is possible that he was one of the many "Free Black Malay" fishermen from Simon's Town who assisted enslaved people who had

---

[39] Nicole Ulrich, "Abolition from Below: The 1808 Revolt in the Cape Colony" in *"Humanitarian Intervention" and Changing Labour Relations: Long-Term Consequences of the British Act on the Abolition of the Slave Trade, 1807*; edited by Marcel van der Linden. (Leiden: Brill, 2011), 193.

[40] WCARS, SO 17/1, "Notes collected from the Colonial Placcards" (23 June 1809).

[41] For an insight into the Hanglip maroons see Donna Corns, "Offended Shadows: Marronage in the Cape Hanglip 1720s-1730s" Thesis, (BA Hons), University of Cape Town, 2011.

[42] WCARS, Memorials Colonial Office, CO 3873, Ref. 401 (23 July 1809).

escaped, many of whom had formed the maroon community at Hanglip.⁴³ Another avenue of assistance for enslaved people was through friendships with sailors, which made it possible for enslaved people to escape by ship.

On 8 September 1808 it was reported to the Simon's Town magistrate that an enslaved female named Clara had run away from the household of "Mr Misteer" and was on board the ship *Phoenix* where she was thought "to have a connection with one of the ship's people."⁴⁴

It was also during this year that Johan Willem Hurter died and his forty-two year old wife, born Martha Maria Munnik, carried on running their boarding house, which from then on became known as "The Widow Hurter's Lodging House."⁴⁵

"Prize Negroes"—The Royal Navy versus Private Indentureships

Whereas the Navy had certain codes of treatment considered to be humane, the plight of people described as "prize negroes" who were indentured to private individuals prompted Sir Jahleel Brenton to express his opinion on the matter in official correspondence when he wrote:

> The tender mercies of the original Dutch Boor in this colony are but too well known, and the unfortunate black, not called a slave but an apprentice, lost all the benefit which he would have derived from being a slave, when being a marketable commodity, his health was taken care of, and like other animals belonging to the farm he was well fed, and kept in good condition that he might fetch the better price if it seemed expedient to sell him. But the Boor having only a life interest, (for such indeed it became in many instances when the negro did not outlive his apprenticeship) tasked him to the utmost; and as he had been in the habit of acting towards the unhappy Hottentot, the more the man's

---

⁴³Corns, "Offended Shadows."

⁴⁴WCARS, Records of the Magistrate of Simon's Town (1/SMT 2/5), Letters received (1808) Simonstown 1/SMT 10/2, Ref. 122 (8 September 1808).

⁴⁵Boet Dommisse, *Admiralty House, Simon's Town* (Cape Town: CTP Book Printers, 2005), 13.

health was impaired, made the greater efforts to get work out of him, before he died.[46]

Certainly, the treatment of people referred to as "prize-negroes" who were indentured to the Navy contrasted significantly compared to the treatment of so-called "prize-negroes" in private homes, where levels of trauma were particularly great and violence commonplace. Unlike private individuals, the Royal Navy had a mandate to ensure that people indentured to the navy were not "oppressed or ill treated with impunity."[47] These sentiments notwithstanding, the males referred to as "prize negroes" were still assigned the worst and most trying forms of labour within the Navy and the Army where they were required to perform "those duties of fatigues and labour which would be injurious to a European constitution."[48] Yet compared to so-called "prize negroes" indentured to private individuals, when abusive behaviour of private individuals spilled over onto people indentured by the Navy, there were repercussions.

Such was the case in 1813 when G Rossouw of Simon's Town assaulted Dic Hamaloos, a man indentured to the Navy. In correspondence from Alfred Johnson, superintendent of "His Majesty's Victualling Establishment" to Johannes Hendricus Brand as "His Majesty's Attorney General for the District" he requested that he "put this business in legal train, and collect such evidence as may be conducive to attain the ends of impartial justice."[49]

The "Negroes Employed in the Dock-Yard"

From 1810 Commissioner Shield ensured that "the negroes employed in the dock-yard should be put on the same footing as landsmen on board His

---

[46]Jahleel Brenton, *Memoir of the Life and Services of Vice-Admiral Sir Jahleel Brenton...*; edited by the Rev. Henry Raikes (London: Hatchard and Son, 1846), 437.
[47]WCARS, Records of the Magistrate of Simon's Town (1/SMT 2/5) 10/, Letters received (1813) Simonstown 1/SMT 10/2, Ref. 108 and Ref. 110 (23 October 1813).
[48]Letter from W Merry to Henry Goulburn, War Office (16 July 1821), Theal, *Records of the Cape Colony*, volume 14: 53, 79.
[49]WCARS, Records of the Magistrate of Simon's Town (1/SMT 2/5), Letters received (1813) Simonstown 1/SMT 10/2, Ref. 108 and Ref. 110 (23 October 1813).

Majesty's ships."[50] They were paid the same salaries, which amounted to £14 per annum. He arranged that after deductions for the clothes the balance was to be kept in credit for these indentured workers so that they would have some savings after their indentureships had been completed. However, after his departure the payments stopped.

After Sir Jahleel Brenton had taken over he petitioned the Navy Board to reinstate this arrangement from 31 May 1814. The Navy Board agreed to his request, but refused to back pay the wages that were in arrears.[51]

People indentured under the "prize negro" system and absorbed into the services of the Navy, formed a primary labour pool for a number of building developments during this period.[52] These included a jetty in the dockyard, "a spacious mast house erected, with a working sail loft over it, and a very ornamental range of houses for the officers of the yard constructed upon a terrace overlooking the bay."[53] These buildings were enclosed with a wall to resemble a compound, which Brenton described as "forming a remarkably neat and compact arsenal."[54] Another development was the construction of a cattle yard in the Bay.[55]

Certainly the British authorities considered themselves to hold the higher moral ground when it came to the people referred to as "prize negroes." Random checks on private households were ordered by the colonial officer. The modus operandi was that he would send a list of names to the local magistrate, who was asked to call on these households to appraise the treatment of people described on the census as "prize negroes," and to report back to the colonial office.

On 1 March 1811 the list included the following people:[56]

---

[50] Brenton, *Memoir*, 438.
[51] Brenton, *Memoir*, 438-441.
[52] Brenton, *Memoir*, 431.
[53] Brenton, *Memoir*, 432-433.
[54] Brenton, *Memoir*, 433.
[55] Brenton, *Memoir*, 434.
[56] WCARS, Records of the Magistrate of Simon's Town (1/SMT 2/5), Letters received by Resident Magistrate (1811), Simonstown 1/SMT 10/4, Ref. 26 and 26A (1 March 1811).

Table 5:-1: "Prize negroes" (1 March 1811)

NAME	GENDER	INDENTURED TO
Tenetihanks	Female	J G Aspeling
Sangorkalik	Male	W H I Benezer
Bettie	Male	John Osmond
Obios	Male	John Osmond
Sarika	Female	John Osmond
Boongah	Female	F Rossouw
Chumoonie	Female	Mrs Chater
Sakina	Female	Widow Rossouw

It is revealing that just ten days after this survey was conducted it was reported that a group of Mozambican people listed as "prize negroes" had escaped. The group comprised two men, two women and one child aged about one year of age.[57] A further attempted escape occurred on 25 May 1811 when "Louis of Mauritius" was found on board the *Cartel Willesley*.[58]

The predicament of people taken off "slave" ships who were indentured to private individuals was in many cases inhumane and for the people so indentured, there was little recourse.

When four "apprentices" of the former "slave-trader" Alexander Tennant petitioned against Tennant's ill-treatment and their illegal detention as "slaves," the Fiscal, in rejecting their plea, spoke of their entertaining "ideas of such uncurbed liberty and freedom as no Hottentot or Free person of colour ever enjoyed in this Colony."[59] This statement is illuminating of the trauma experienced by vulnerable people in the colony.

A complaint of ill-treatment by a woman described as "Catharina a Prize Negress belonging to Lieut. Steele" was treated with similar disdain by

---

[57] WCARS, Records of the Magistrate of Simon's Town (1/SMT 2/5), Letters received by Resident Magistrate (1811) Simonstown 1/SMT 10/4, Ref. 31 (11 March 1811).

[58] WCARS, Records of the Magistrate of Simon's Town (1/SMT 2/5), Letters received by Resident Magistrate (1811) Simonstown 1/SMT 10/4, Ref. 55, (25 May 1811).

[59] Saunders, "Liberated Africans in Cape Colony," 228.

Charles Blair in his correspondence to Johannes Hendricus Brand in the Simon's Town Magistrates office saying: "May I beg you will have the kindness to enquire if she has any just cause of complaint if not she ought to be punished which you can order from this letter."[60] This led to Catharina being jailed at the Simon's Town prison for three months before Lieutenant Steele himself requested her release.[61] In a case such as this where a socially vulnerable person complained to a socially powerful person about ill-treatment by another socially powerful person, the odds were always stacked against the former. There were also people described as "prize negroes" who were never made aware of the fourteen year indentureship limit and through this ignorance were exploited by "slave-owners" well beyond the levels that were legally allowed, keeping them in a state of permanent bondage that long outlasted slavery.[62]

Family Separations

The trauma of family separations overshadowed the lives of many families described as "prize negroes" at the Cape, as the law held that "prize negro" children could be indentured for fourteen years from the age of five. This law compelled mothers either to stay on in the indentured households while their young children were still indentured or face the trauma of being separated from their children.

The worst case scenario, of course, was the separation of mother and child when children were indentured separately to their mothers from the age of five. On 14 August 1810 a "prize negro" mother named Selva escaped to Simon's Town with her daughter, hoping to find safety there. However, without social or material capital, this escape was doomed. They managed to evade the authorities for two weeks before their presence in Simon's Town was reported and a warrant issued for their arrest.[63]

---

[60]WCARS, Records of the Magistrate of Simon's Town 1/SMT 2/5 (Letters received by Resident Magistrate (1818) Simonstown) 1/SMT 10/10, Ref. 98 (24 May 1818).

[61]WCARS, Records of the Magistrate of Simon's Town: 1/SMT 2/5 (Letters received, 1793-1932), 1/SMT 10/10, Ref. 137 (12 August 1818).

[62]WCARS, SO 2/12, (21 March 1831), pages 120, 163 and 169.

Fig. 5-3. Fishermen in Simon's Bay, circa 1860
Source: Watercolour by John Haverfield, Library of Parliament, 28864

The Growth of Islam among "Prize Negroes" in Simon's Town

A powerful psychological form of escape for enslaved people and for the newly-arrived people referred to as "prize negroes" during this period was through the practise of Islam, which created a psychological bridge out of slavery and also offered a vital support system for many enslaved people, particularly through their access to the Muslim Free Black fishing community

---

[63]WCARS, Records of the Magistrate of Simon's Town (1/SMT 2/5), Letters received by Resident Magistrate (1810), Simonstown 1/SMT 10/3, Ref. 80 (28 August 1810).

of Simon's Town. Unsurprisingly, the majority of people described as "prize negroes" who arrived at the Cape from 1808 onwards, converted to Islam.

Certainly the colonial authorities were not pleased with the growth of Islam and on 19 October 1812 the law concerning the sale of Christian "slaves" was altered to incentivise "slave-holders" to promote Christianity in their "slave-holdings." Their reasoning for this was that the law up until that time was based on the decree of the Council at Batavia dated 10 April 1770, wherein it was stated that enslaved people who had "professed the Christian faith" were not to be sold. From the perspective of the British colonial authorities this gave "slave-holders" no incentive for themselves to encourage Christianity amongst enslaved people when they stood to lose economically by not being allowed to re-sell the said enslaved persons.[64]

A strong proponent of Islam in Simon's Town at this time was Sheikh Musdin. He was a member of the "Free Black" community who assisted enslaved people and offered them a sense of dignity through the adoption of Islam. Through Islamic religious ceremonies enslaved people in Simon's Town experienced a sense of agency. For Sheikh Musden and his contemporaries, organising such activities was no small feat as permission needed to be received from Johannes Hendricus Brand, the Simon's Town magistrate. In one such letter to Brand dated 13 October 1813, Sheikh Musdin used flattery as his entry point.

In his correspondence he wrote:

> Sir
>
> Your Excellent disposition will I trust pardon the freedom of my laying before you this Humble Address in the hopes that some attention will be given towards it.
>
> As we intended a play for tonight which according to our Religion being an Atonement to the Almighty for our transgressions as well as to implore his Divine Assistance for the Restoration of our Health from sickness which some of us are at present afflicted with—we were given to understand that you prohibited the same for the Present night—as this being a particular night (in our Religion) for the Per-

---

[64]WCARS, SO 17/1 "Notes collected from the Colonial Placcards," (23 January 1813).

formance of such works. We do therefore earnestly entreat you will under the Circumstances above mentioned permit us to perform it for tonight for two hours only; after which we will finish entirely.

We humbly beg you will take our case into Consideration & grant us that which will be of very great benefit to us.

I am, Sir

With the greatest respect

Your most Obedt & very Humble Servt

Shaik Musden, For Himself and the Rest[65]

An eloquent and intelligent man, his letter shows how he had to engage in just the right balance between dignity and restraint in this "uncomfortable" society.

The Social Value of a Fair Complexion

The value of a fair complexion and European appearance was entrenched early into the psyches of all people at the Cape colony. This is not surprising given that people with European appearances held positions of power. Overwhelmingly the majority of "slave-holders" and landowners were, or were considered to be, European. Legislation passed during the VOC period was repeated by the British, which stated that "slaves who wilfully jostle or push against a European, even of the lowest class, or otherwise insult him is [sic] to be punished with flogging."[66] The message was clear: European ancestry carried currency and access to social power.

Because of the sexual abuse of enslaved women in the households of "slave-holders" and also at the Slave Lodge, a sizable number of enslaved people at the Cape carried European ancestry and thus appeared European. It is then not surprising, given the conditions of their enslavement, that fair-skinned enslaved people would seek to use their appearances as a key to freedom.

---

[65] WCARS, Records of the Magistrate of Simon's Town (1/SMT 2/5), Letters received by Resident Magistrate (1810) Simonstown 1/SMT 10/3, Ref. 119 (13 December 1810).

[66] WCARS, SO 17/1 "Notes collected from the Colonial Placcards," (3/5 September 1754). See also Letter from Fiscal Denyssen to Sir John Cradock (16 March 1813) in Theal, *Records of the Cape Colony* volume 9, page 143 (point 39).

While not always successful, this seems to have been the case with a young enslaved man named Abraham, described as "the Slave boy Abraham formerly belonging to Mr Roselt" who ran away to Simon's Town. In a letter to the Simon's Town Magistrate regarding Abraham's escape, it was mentioned that "his appearance resembling so much that of a soldier's child (being so very fair) that he may escape the notice of your *Dienders* [officers]."[67]

The case of a young fair-skinned enslaved boy named Hendrik who escaped from the Munnik family in Simon's Town is another case in point, although Hendrik's escape was infinitely more dramatic.

The Story of Hendrik

On 13 July 1811 a poster was erected in Simon's Town by Gerhardus Munnik, which read simply

> Strayed. On 23 June last from Gerhardus Munnik in Simons Town, about 13 years of age, white complexion and nearly 4 feet high. Whoever will deliver him at the prison shall be rewarded.[68]

When thirteen year old Hendrik decided to escape his enslavement from the Munnik residence on 23 June 1811, he had no money and no social connections that he could tap into. However, young as he was, he understood the power of "whiteness" in Cape colonial society. This was the only resource he had at his disposal and he tapped into this very innovatively. Hendrik had decided to stowaway on a ship bound for England and he knew that by his appearance, he would blend into the country he had chosen to escape to. Understanding the currency of his "whiteness" and having first-hand knowledge that Gerhardus Munnik was owed three rix dollars by a Javanese resident in Simon's Town, Hendrik duly knocked on his door and demanded the money on behalf of Munnik. With the cash in his pocket Hendrik clandestinely hid away on the frigate *The Crusoe*, which was bound for England. Little is known about how he survived the journey. It is likely that he was put to work as a deckhand and given food as compensation. It was on his arrival

---

[67]WCARS, Records of the Magistrate of Simon's Town (1/SMT 2/5), Letters received (1813) Simonstown 1/SMT 10/2, Ref. 64 (2 July 1813).

[68]Simon's Town Museum, Slavery file, ST Museum, (13 July 1811).

in England that his problems started. Having no foreign currency, no family and no benefactor, Hendrik found himself in the ranks of England's poor urchins, a homeless street child begging and otherwise foraging for survival on the streets of England. However, Hendrik was at a distinct disadvantage. He was a foreigner with no networks in the social underbelly of nineteenth-century England, so his chances of survival were even bleaker than that of the English poor.

Literally starving to death "on the Public Streets in England, in the most deplorable state,"[69] fortune smiled on Hendrik when the Captain of a packet ship happened to take a stroll down the road where Hendrik was begging.[70] Recognising the naval uniform, Hendrik sprang into action, telling him that he was from Simon's Town and begging the Captain to offer him work so that he could return home. The Captain took pity on him and offered him a job on the packet ship, where Hendrik spent the bulk of his teenage years as a sailor, returning to Simon's Town five years later at the age of eighteen. On his return he lived as a free person, much to the ire of Gerhardus Munnik who came across Hendrik on the streets of Simon's Town. Munnik applied to the Fiscal to have Hendrik punished in the town prison and returned to him. However, although Hendrik was arrested he was released without charge or punishment, the Fiscal stating that he was not able to grant this request. Incensed, Munnik took the matter to the courts who upheld the ruling of the Fiscal. Munnik finally petitioned Lord Charles Somerset to ensure that Hendrik was returned to him as a "slave."[71] In his petition he stated:

> That Memorialist, being in the uncertainty of the result, and fearful of entering into havy [sic] and expensive Law-suits, as also the danger of the Boy running away; has moved him to Pray your Lordship most humbly that said slave Boy Hendrik, Memorialist's own Lawfull [sic] property may be ordered home, and by that means prevent a

---

[69] WCARS, Colonial Office Memorials, CO 3906, Ref. 337 (9 October 1816).

[70] Originally, a "packet ship" was a ship used to carry post office mail packets carrying to the furthest outposts. In addition, a packet service is a regular, scheduled service, carrying freight and passengers. [online resource] https://en.wikipedia.org/wiki/Packet_trade (accessed 20 July 2023).

[71] WCARS, Colonial Office Memorials, CO 3906, folio 337 (9 October 1816).

severe loss to a Man who is obliged to maintain a wife and six children by a daily hard labor.[72]

Ironically on 2 July 1811 Dadalus of Bengal was granted his freedom by Lord Caledon, for which 50 Rixdollars was paid to the church as was prescribed by law at the time.[73]

In that same month, on 6 July 1811, a memorial was addressed to "the Earl of Caledon," requesting a remission of punishment for a young enslaved woman named Rosina. The letter stated the following:

> To His Excellency The Earl of Caledon Governor and Commander in Chief
>
> The Memorial of the Widow Munnik Humbly Sheweth
>
> That a female Slave named Rosina (given by her to her son Mr F Munnik) has for some time since been confined on account of having been charged with being an accomplice in the burglary committed at the store occupied by Mr McDonald. That the investigation before the worshipful the Court of Justice having now been terminated she has been condemned to be scourged in the prison. Memorialist upon recollection of the faithful services of the said female slave and of the very good character she has otherwise always borne, has thought it only a reciprocal duty on her part to entreat your Lordship gracious to remit or at least to mitigate the punishment awarded on her as Your Excellency in wisdom may deem meet.
>
> Signed: de weduwe Munnik

Such was the complexity of the experience of slavery in Simon's Town.

It was not an experience that was static and the experience of each enslaved person depended on a number of variables such as the personality of the "slave-holder," the disposition of a "slave-holder" towards a particular

---

[72] WCARS, Colonial Office Memorials, CO 3906, folio 337 (9 October 1816).
[73] WCARS, Records of the Magistrate of Simon's Town (1/SMT 2/5), Letters received by Resident Magistrate (1811) Simonstown 1/SMT 10/4, Ref. 74 (2 July, 1811).

enslaved person and sometimes even the shade of the enslaved person's skin. However, a singular feature of slavery was the absolute power of the "slave-holder" to manipulate and control the lives of those they enslaved. Of interest with respect to the case of Rosina and others, is the following statement in Slave Office correspondence:

> It is a well known fact, [74]that many Slaves are frequently committing thefts, for the express purpose of collecting money, wherewith to purchase their freedom.[75]

Hendrik, of whom we learnt earlier, was not the only enslaved person to have escaped by sea and conversely, a number of British sailors also deserted in Simon's Town.[76] This opened networks between enslaved and indigenous people with deserting sailors, which facilitated escapes. A twenty-five year old woman named Sanna van der Kaap is one such example. Described as "masculine-looking" and being of "white yellowish in colour" she escaped on the *Prince Regent,* dressed up in sailor's clothes.[77]

By 1813 the Cape Colony was nearing the end of the period of transition, which began in 1795. The state of slavery in the Cape Colony at this time is encapsulated in a document signed by Fiscal Denyssen titled *Statement of the Laws of the Colony of the Cape of Good Hope regarding Slavery.* The document included the following:

> Point 10: The Masters being Christians are obliged to bring up their slaves in the Christian faith, to catechize and have them baptised provided they can be brought thereto without making use of absolute means of constraint.
>
> Point 21: Children begotten by a master with any of his slaves may never be sold, whether the estate be solvent or

---

[74]WCARS, Colonial Office CO 3883, Ref. 245 (6 July 1811).

[75]WCARS, SO 7/35, Notes on "Proclamation by Lord Charles Somerset," (18 March 1823).

[76]WCARS, Records of the Magistrate of Simon's Town 1793-1985: 1/SMT 2/5 (Letters received by Resident Magistrate (1818) Simonstown) 1/SMT (10 October 1818).

[77]WCARS, Records of the Magistrate of Simon's Town 1793-1985: 1/SMT 2/5 (Letters received, 1793-1932), 1/SMT 10/10, Ref. 184 (10 October 1818).

insolvent, but must be emancipated after the death of the master.

Point 25: Slavery has this consequence that slaves have not any of those rights and privileges which distinguish the state of the free in civil society; they cannot marry, they do not possess the right of disposing of their children, even if they be minors, they cannot possess any money, or goods in property, they cannot enter into any engagements with other persons, so that they can compel them to the fulfilment of such engagements, they cannot make a will, and they are therefore considered in the civil law as not existing.

Point 27: One of the consequences of this principle is, that although slaves cannot marry, still however they can cohabit together as man and wife, which is approved of by law; such cohabitation cannot be allowed between persons who by the Civil Law are forbidden to marry on account of consanguinity, affinity, or decency. The breaking of the faith of such cohabitation among slaves is not punished as adultery, because no marriage can subsist among them.

Point 30: However when death is the consequence of extravagance of the master in punishing his slave without a premeditated intention to kill him the master is not considered a wilful murderer, nor is he subject to the punishment prescribed for wilful murder which has been also adopted in the modern laws, it being specifically prescribed in the Statutes of India, that if any person should beat his slave to death or otherwise deprive him of his life … he shall be corporally or otherwise punished …

Point 31: Among the consequences of this principle can also be brought, that slaves being ill-treated by their master or representatives, or not being properly provided with the necessities of life, have a right to complain to the fiscal, deputy fiscal, or landdrosts under whose jurisdiction their masters reside, who are then obliged to investigate the complaint, and finding it to be true to bring the same to the cognizance of the Court of Justice ...

Point 36: Crimes committed by slaves are amenable the same as those committed by free persons, to the judgment of the Court of Justice, and are punished with the same punishments.

Point 37: Crimes against the life or safety of the master's person are however more severely punished than those against others, whence it comes that slaves, in case they proceed so far as to assail their master, although without weapons, they must suffer death without mercy, agreeably to the express commands of the law.

Point 39: Such is the law enacting that a constable seeing a slave wilfully jostle or push against a European, even of the lowest class, ... or otherwise insult him is obliged, in the absence of the master, immediately to apprehend such slave and have him punished with flogging by order of the magistrate.

Point 44: On Sundays and holidays slaves are forbid [sic] to come into the church or porch at the end of Divine Service or as the congregation are going out, or from making any noise or committing any wantonness during church time, on pain of, if caught in the fact, being severely flogged.

Point 46: No slaves unless accompanied by their master, or sent for the purpose of taking care of their children, may enter the government garden on pain of being beaten.

Point 48: No slave may walk in the street with a lighted pipe on pain of being flogged.

Point 58: No slave may rent a house or room, neither beside or lodge out of the house of his master, on pain of corporal punishment, besides the penalties of the owner and the landlord of the house or room who may transgress this order.[78]

Simon's Town after the Dutch Cession of the Cape to Britain

In 1814 the Dutch formally ceded the Cape to Britain. This set the tone for a sense of Britishness in Simon's Bay where the Dutch-looking thatch roofs gave way to Victorian balustrades, giving the town a distinctly British appearance. This sense of Britishness was reinforced with the establishment of the Royal Navy in Simon's Town in that same year, being the only naval establishment at the Cape. Although the Dutch wagons continued to be in use, a more sophisticated mode of transport was the British-inspired coaches.

One of the British recipients of land grants in 1814 was Captain Thomas Talbot Harington [sometimes spelt Harrington]—after whom Harrington Street in Simon's Town is likely named—who penned a letter to Lieutenant Colonel William Wilberforce Bird, Colonial Secretary at the Cape, wherein he mentioned his intention to use the labour of artisans from England working aboard the *Scaleby Castle* to build his home in Simon's Town, stating:

> I have further to request that I may be permitted to leave behind from the *Scaleby Castle*, here and at Cape Town, three English Masons, as many English Carpenters and thirty Chineese [sic] of different descriptions who are necessary to the execution of my House and outhouse, and to bring into cultivation the land which His Majesty's Government has been pleased to grant me in this neighbourhood.[79]

By this time there were already Chinese people living in Simon's Town at the home of "the Chinese Azam," one of whom was "the Chinese Lako who had been living there for some time."[80] At this time too, enslaved wagoners

---

[78] Letter from Fiscal Denyssen to Sir John Cradock (16 March 1813) enclosing a "Statement of the Laws of the Colony of the Cape of Good Hope regarding Slavery," in Theal, *Records of the Cape Colony* … volume 9: 143-161, particularly points 27 on pages 150-151, and point 58 on pages 155-156.

[79] WCARS, Records of the Magistrate of Simon's Town (1/SMT 2/5), Letters received by Resident Magistrate (1814) Simonstown 1/SMT 10/6, Ref. 59A (10 June 1814). Harington captained the British East India Company ship, *Scaleby Castle,* from 1811-1815.

[80] WCARS, Records of the Magistrate of Simon's Town (1/SMT 2/5), Letters received by Resident Magistrate (1814) Simonstown 1/SMT 10/6, Ref. 85 (23 July 1814).

like thirty-six year old Manes of the Cape (owned by John Osmond) and twenty-five year old Abraham of the Cape, travelled the dusty main road in Simon's Town alongside enslaved coachmen like forty-seven year old Michiel of the Cape, owned by Pieter Daniel Rossouw and Jonas of the Cape listed initially as owned by Carel Jeremias Auret, but resold to I Bam of Cape Town.

The First Church in Simon's Town, 1814

There was growing concern by the colonial authorities that there was no Christian church in the town, and even though there were those who felt that "a Church capable of containing five to six hundred persons could not be completed in a place so isolated as Simon's Town,"[81] this matter was corrected in 1814 when a storeroom in the town was converted into a makeshift church. The first minister to lead the Christian flock of Simon's Town was Reverend George Hough.[82] However, in terms of slavery, the one who left an uncomfortable scar on the lives of many enslaved people was Reverend George Sturt, of whom we will learn later in this text.

Clandestine "Slave-Trading"

During this period people taken off "slave" ships were also at the mercy of being re-sold into slavery by unscrupulous people to whom they were indentured, and who carried on clandestine "slave-trading" operations after the abolition of the "slave-trade." On the death of Alexander Tennant at the age of forty-two in 1814, his wife made a request to the Fiscal to re-indenture Tennant's ninety-nine "prize negroes" for a further seven years.

---

[81] Letter from Mr Schutte to the Colonial Office dated 10 December 1812, Theal, *Records of the Cape Colony*, volume 9: pages 29, 178, 180, 249, 357, 362, 463, 498 especially 180.

[82] Reverend George Hough (1787-1867), born in Gloucester, England, sailed to the Cape Colony in 1813 where he was appointed Colonial Chaplain of Simon's Town. In 1817, he was relocated to Cape Town where he served as Colonial Chaplain until leaving the Colony in 1846 [online resource] University of Newcastle (Australia), School of Humanities and Social Science. *The Wellington Valley Project* https://downloads.newcastle.edu.au/library/cultural%20collections/the-wellington-valley-project/wellpro/h/hough.html (accessed 18 July 2023).

When the Fiscal requested that the said "negroes" be brought before him, it became apparent that a number of these people had been resold into slavery. An investigation into tracing the missing so-called "prize negroes" proved futile and the secrets of how Tennant disposed of these unfortunate people for his own monetary gain, went with him to the grave.[83] When Tennant's estate was wound up it was discovered that he was in fact insolvent.[84] However, this would have offered little comfort to all the people whose lives were traumatised by Tennant's actions during his lifetime.

On 13 May 1818 the Portuguese brig *Flor da Bahia* rolled ominously into the Bay, carrying within it a cargo of death. Lord Charles Somerset was faced with a dilemma as, due to the close of the Napoleonic war, it was no longer permissible for "slave" ships to be impounded in Simon's Bay. As a result he could not "save" these people through the indentureship process. However, on his instruction the sick were landed and treated by the medical officer. In a letter to Earl Bathurst dated 13 May 1818, Lord Charles Somerset described the situation as follows:

> Upon the arrival of the vessel in Simon's Bay the crowded state of the Negroes on board had caused so much mortality and disease was making such rapid progress that the common dictates of humanity urged a speedy interference and in consequence of the reports, copies of which are herewith transmitted, I directed the sick to be landed, succoured and treated by the medical officer at Simon's Town during the stay of the vessel in that harbour … The Negroes, having been dying at the rate of four a day previous to my having afforded them relief.[85]

Having saved their lives, the *Flor da Bahia* went on her way, taking along with her this cargo of vulnerable people, into an unknown future.

---

[83]Theal, *Records of the Cape Colony*, Volume 12: 75.
[84]Philip, "The Vicissitudes of the Early British Settlers at the Cape," 164.
[85]Letter from Lord Charles Somerset to Earl Bathurst, Theal, *Records of the Cape Colony*, Volume 12: 3-4.

The Establishment of Black Town

Black Town came into being largely at the instigation of Sir Jahleel Brenton,[86] who took a philanthropic interest in a group of "recaptured slaves" who had been indentured to the British Navy for nine years, but had five years left to serve.

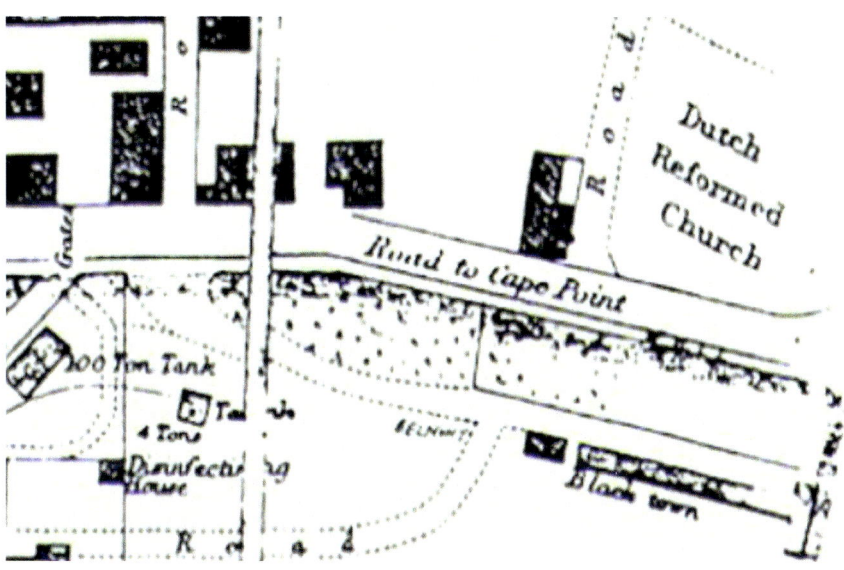

Fig. 5-4. A street plan showing Black Town in Simon's Town
Source: Shell, From Diaspora to Diorama page 1798; original in Simon's Town Museum

In correspondence he described being very impressed by the quality of their work and felt that they had been a great asset to the British Navy. In 1817 Sir Jahleel Brenton asked that a piece of ground "a part lying behind the Commissioner's garden, and part beyond the Naval Hospital" [the site of the present Simon's Town Library] be given to the indentured workers described as "prize negroes," saying that "Upon each lot a small house should be built by the black artificers themselves, to whom two days in the week

---
[86] Audrey Read, "Black Town in Simon's Town" *Simon's Town Historical Society* 20, 4 (July 1999): 139-142.

should be given up for that purpose." This took some negotiation after which the Navy Board agreed provided that

> such an indulgence to the black people, will not afford any just ground of dissatisfaction and complaint to the European artificers; and provided an absolute power is reserved to the Commissioner to deprive the people of their houses and grounds in case of misbehaviour, or if required for the public convenience.

A further condition was as follows:

> No man to have more than a life interest in the property; but as deaths occur, you will in giving the houses to others, make it a condition that the family of the deceased shall have some small sum paid by the new occupant.[87]

Black Town was eventually established in 1819 when the Commissioner "selected four of the most meritorious blacks" who were given one day off their labour at the Dockyard to prepare the foundations for their cottages and lay out their gardens.[88]

The earliest residents of Black Town were households registered under the fathers who, in colonial records, were recorded under the following names: Monday and Joseph, George and Ceroffe, Adam and Morrison, Charlie and Adam, Layeff and Simpson, Friday 2nd and Friday 3rd, Chuff and Chengur and William and Figami.[89] The separate housing arrangements for the "prize negroes" indentured to the British Navy were a feature of British colonial rule that saw people segregated.

There were Madagascan people settled into tin houses in Black Town, a separate settlement of Mozambican people housed in mud huts in the town and a further settlement of Javanese people, also referred to as "prize negroes," in Noordhoek. People described as "prize negroes" were also housed in the Naval Yard.[90]

---

[87] Jahleel Brenton, *Memoir of the Life and Services of Vice-Admiral Sir Jahleel Brenton*; edited by the Rev. Henry Raikes (London: Hatchard, 1846), 445-448.

[88] Brenton, *Memoir*, 448.

[89] Audrey Read, "Black Town in Simon's Town" Simon's Town Historical Society, 20, 4 (July 1999): 139.

Reverend George Sturt

In the same year that Black Town was established, the Simon's Town church welcomed the arrival of George William Milner Sturt. Described as a "wild character"[91] George Sturt arrived in Simon's Bay on 13 October 1819, where he was ordained as colonial chaplain.[92] His application for a piece of land in Simon's Bay measuring one acre was dealt with swiftly by Colonel Bird of the Colonial Office who, on 19 November 1819, urged Johannes H Brand "to have the land measured and reduced to diagram, that Mr Sturt may receive the grant thereof without delay."[93]

The Colonial Office's eagerness to please Reverend Sturt was no doubt due to their desire to firmly establish Christianity in Simon's Bay, where the first church had been established in an old storehouse just five years earlier. The need for a church in Simon's Bay was strongly felt, not least by Lady Anne Barnard's butler Samuel Hudson, who viewed Simon's Bay as a place of "wickedness."[94] There was also concern at the growing momentum of Islam amongst the enslaved. Clearly Sturt was unhappy with the makeshift church in a storeroom as on 6 December 1819 the Colonial Office corresponded with Johannes Hendricus Brand, Simon's Town magistrate, about the "insecure state of the church in Simon's Town." To this end he was urged to provide "temporary accommodation" to the congregation under the charge of Sturt.[95]

This saw the birth of St Francis Church and from 1819 to 1830 George Sturt was on the list of clergy serving St Francis Church in Simon's Town.[96]

---

[90] WCARS, Records of the Magistrate of Simon's Town (1/SMT 2/5), Letters received by Resident Magistrate (1811) Simonstown 1/SMT 10/4, Ref. 87 (11 August 1811).

[91] Reginald Robert Langham-Carter," George Sturt, Colonial Chaplain" *Simon's Town Historical Society Bulletin* 10, 1 (January 1978): 12-17.

[92] "Some Facts in the History of the Parish of St Frances [sic] Simon's Town" (Claremont: *Peninsula Herald*, 1903), 28.

[93] WCARS, Records of the Magistrate of Simon's Town 1793- 1985: 1/SMT 2/5 (Letters 1819), 1/SMT 10/11, Ref. 179 (18 November 1819).

[94] WCARS, A 602/9, Samuel Eusebius Hudson, Essay on "Improvements" [1807 to 1814].

[95] WCARS, Records of the Magistrate of Simon's Town 1793 – 1985: 1/SMT 2/5 (Letters 1819), 1/SMT 10/11, Ref. 201.

[96] "Some Facts in the History of the Parish of St Frances," 28.

However, it was as a "slave-holder" that Sturt showed himself to be devoid of the principles of true Christianity. This is ironic. As a man of the cloth he would have been expected to practise charity and compassion. We will return to Sturt later.

John Osmond and Hegemonic Masculinity

The carpenter John Osmond was typical of many European men of his time, in that while their behaviour towards all women was that of establishing control, their behaviour towards non-hegemonic males was destructive and cruel.

Fig. 5-5. Untitled portrait
Source: Sketch by Lionel Davis

A study on social dominance conducted by the psychologists Jim Sidanius and Felicia Pratto explores this phenomenon. They assert that the primary motives driving discrimination against men from socially vulnerable groups by men from socially dominant groups, is a desire to harm.

They go on to say that discrimination against out-group males appear to have a distinctly aggressive and debilitative character.[97] This was particularly evident in the treatment of men referred to as "prize negroes."

One morning in May 1821, Osmond used a sjambok to assault a man named Obiah, whose name suggests that he was West African. The assault with a *sjambok* caused lacerations to Obiah's skin that were striking enough to enable a medical doctor to count "twenty marks of blows given he says by a *sambuc* [sic]."[98] Osmond incurred no penalty for his behaviour.

Another person, also referred to as a "prize negro" who experienced brutish treatment from Osmond was a man named Francois. Francois was a carpenter[99] by trade and he had been indentured to John Osmond in 1811 under the "prize negro" indentureship practice. When he attempted to complain about Osmond's ill-treatment, which included being prevented from visiting the woman he loved, Osmond used his power as Justice of the Peace to have Francois lodged in prison.

Some twenty years later it was brought to the attention of George Jackman Rogers, the "Protector of Slaves," that Francois had not been released after his fourteen year "indentureship" had expired and had been held in perpetual slavery by Osmond.[100]

In these and possibly many other cases that went unreported, one has to consider not only the physical pain and suffering, but the trauma of humiliation for these men at their experiences of emasculation. Osmond's attempts at emasculating dark-skinned males were not restricted to the enslaved or indentured. Sheikh Musden, whose written communication suggests a higher education and certainly more refinement than Osmond, was at the receiving end of an attempt by Osmond to humiliate him. This incident he expressed eloquently in a letter to the local magistrate, as follows:

---

[97] Jim Sidanius and Felicia Pratto, *Social Dominance* (Cambridge: Cambridge University Press, 2001), 295.
[98] A *sjambok* or whip. WCARS, Records of the Magistrat of Simon's Town 1793-1985: 1/SMT 2/5 (Inkomende briewe 1821), 1/SMT 10/13. Ref. 37 (14 May 1821).
[99] Database of enslaved people in Simon's Town compiled by Joline Young.
[100] WCARS, Slave Office SO 2/12 (21 March 1831): 120.

Worthy Sir,

Your Benevolent & human disposition will I trust pardon the freedom of my laying before you this Humble Address—for the reason of my not being able personally to relate the Circumstances undermentioned:

The day before yesterday I called at the [?Plainting] shop to get a pound of pepper by order of Mr Osmond, which he delivered but very much less than the pound by weight of this colony which I immediately remarked to him offering at the same time to bring the Pound weight of three or Four Tradesmen of this Town which he refused with making of abuses to me in the most Indecent & mean languages & in which he was joined with by his wife. The words that they made use of towards me are too vulgar to be stated in writing. I had therefore given him to understand I would not take the Pepper till he gave me proper & honest weight upon which I understand he has lodged a Complaint against me before your Worship—I therefore trust Worthy Sir you will take the Circumstances into Consideration & in your Judicial Capacity exercise the necessary measures for which we shall ever pray.

I am Sir with the greatest respect your most obedient and very humble Servt

Shaik Musden Servt,

For himself & Conns—Findall, Gobbmoo Tindall, Norah Laicass[101]

---

[101]WCARS, Records of the Magistrate of Simon's Town (1/SMT 2/5), Letters received by Resident Magistrate (1810) Simonstown 1/SMT 10/3, Ref. 120 (15 December 1810).

PART 6

AMELIORATION 1816-1834

The false reports of general emancipation by Government, and opposition against effecting it by their Masters, have found but too ready beliefs and have already caused the blood of the innocent to flow.[1]

—Cape of Good Hope, "Slave Office" Correspondence

In August 1817 the colonial authorities received a request from Lieutenant James William Crutwell[2] of the 83rd (County of Dublin) Regiment of Foot who sought permission for Catherine, "a Hottentot Servant Girl," to accompany him when his Regiment was transferred to Ceylon on 1 October 1817 "in case of sickness, bad-health or being dismissed in Service with or without good reason." For this privilege he offered the security of a bond for £100 sterling.[3] Of interest is that this request was made during the period of amelioration at the Cape.

With the rise of the abolition movement in England, a strong anti-slavery sentiment was developing, with abolitionists lobbying for an end slavery. This included calls "for acts of Legislation for the Distant Slave Colonies."[4] However, their rallying cries were met with fierce resistance by "slave-hold-

---

[1] WCARS, Slave Office, SO 7/35: Notes on Proclamation of 18 March 1823. For text of the Lord Charles Somerset's Proclamation (18 March 1823), see George McCall Theal, *Records of the Cape Colony* (London: William Clowes for the Government of the Cape Colony, 1903), volume 15: 336-342.
[2] Peter Philip, *British Residents at the Cape, 1795-1819* (Cape Town: David Philip, 1981, 83.
[3] WCARS, Records of the Magistrate of Simon's Town 1793-1985: 1/SMT 2/5 (Letters received, 1793-1932), 1/SMT 10/9, Ref. 134 (14 August 1817).
[4] WCARS, Slave Office, Confidential reports, Protector of the Slaves 1829-1834, SO 3/20A, signed by Major George Jackman Rogers, Protector of Slaves, (June-December 1830). See also John Edwin Mason, "The Slaves and Their Protectors: Reforming Resistance in a Slave Society, the Cape Colony, 1826-1834" *Journal of Southern African Studies* 17, 1 (March 1991): 103-128.

ers" at the Cape. Their resistance was supported by the Cape Colonial "Slave Office" who argued that "with respect to this Colony, Slaves are of considerable higher pecuniary value than perhaps anywhere else and constitute the greatest property of the Inhabitants." This statement rings true when one considers the large numbers of highly skilled people who were enslaved at the Cape. In addition to labourers, housemaids and nursery maids, there were masons, cabinet makers, carpenters, tailors, seamstresses, shoemakers, coopers, wagoners, coachmen, fishermen, cooks, boatmen, bakers, gardeners, bricklayers, tanners, blacksmiths, knitters, butchers and husbandmen.[5] Through their labour, great wealth was generated for "slave-holders."

Enslaved people were also used as collateral to raise mortgages. In 1830 the bonded debt of "slave" mortgages registered at the Cape Colony by 1,424 "proprietors of slaves," some of this jointly with landed property, amounted to "Seven Million Five Hundred and Twenty One Thousand dollars or about Five Hundred and Sixty Thousand Pounds Sterling."[6] For those benefiting from this system, there was a lot of money at stake. In "Slave Office" correspondence it was stated that "Slave Holders in the Country Districts are, by the Promulgation of this last Order in Council, in a state almost of insurrection." In order to appease "slave-holders," enslaved people and abolitionists until it was possible to end slavery by financially compensating "slave-holders," the colonial authorities sought to ameliorate the conditions of enslaved people. This they asserted was necessary so "that the Slave will be satisfied with his improved condition, and the Master with the remaining share of authority, thereby allotted to him over his Slave."[7]

This set in motion ameliorative conditions for enslaved people, which included the appointment of a "Protector of Slaves" in 1816 to oversee the treatment of enslaved people. For the first time a "Slave Register" was instituted, which obliged "slave-holders" to register all enslaved people in their "slave-holdings" and report pertinent matters such as births and deaths

---

[5]Simon's Town slavery database compiled by Joline Young.
[6]WCARS, Slave Office, Confidential reports, Protector of the Slaves 1829-1834, SO 3/20A, signed by Major George Jackman Rogers, Protector of Slaves (June-December 1830).
[7]WCARS, Slave Office Confidential reports Protector of Slaves 1829-1834, SO 3/20A (June-December 1830).George Jackman Rogers, Protector of Slaves (June-December 1830).

affecting enslaved people. By 4 July 1817 the wardmaster, Johan Friedrich Kirsten wrote to the magistrate, Johannes Hendricus Brand, informing him that "all the slaves in this ward" had been reported.[8]

Sunday labour was abolished and many enslaved people used this day to work for their own accounts. Corporal punishment for enslaved women was also abolished. In the words of the Earl of Bathurst, this was to "raise this unfortunate class above their present degraded level, and to restore to the female slaves that sense of shame, which is at once the ornament and the protection of their sex."[9]

As part of the ameliorative conditions, "slave-holders" were no longer allowed to use a whip or other instruments as a stimulus to labour. All punishments were to be "accurately recorded" and witnesses needed to be present during the punishment of an enslaved person. "Slave-holders" were also no longer allowed to delay punishments for delayed times after an "offence" which no doubt created added psychological torture for enslaved people in this predicament. Unlawful punishments by "slave-holders" could be prosecuted if this was proven and a "slave-holder" "twice convicted of inflicting cruel and unlawful punishment to be declared incapable to be the owner or manager of slaves and every slave of such person to be forfeited to His Majesty."[10]

Punishments of enslaved people and people described as "prize negroes" continued to take place in the Simon's Town court. This is evident in a letter from the Naval Hospital in Simon's Town signed by J Chenowith on 3 May 1817, when he complained that the "Negro Apprentice Jack" is "idle and disobedient" and requested that he "be punished agreeable to the Customs of the Colony."[11]

---

[8]WCARS, Records of the Magistrate of Simon's Town 1793-1985: 1/SMT 2/5 (Letters received, 1793-1932), 1/SMT 10/9, Ref. 109.

[9]WCARS, Slave Office, SO 7/35: Notes on Proclamation of 18 March 1823. For text of the Lord Charles Somerset's Proclamation (18 March 1823), see Theal, Records of the Cape Colony, volume 15: 336-342.

[10]WCARS, Slave Office SO 7/35 Notes on Proclamation of 18th March 1823 on Slaves (18 March 1823).

[11]WCARS, Records of the Magistrate of Simon's Town 1793-1985: 1/SMT 2/5 (Letters received, 1793-1932), 1/SMT 10/9, Ref. 60.

As part of the ameliorative laws the Court of Justice was ordered to grant an enslaved person "who has any apparent right to sue" an Advocate to attend their interest in a court case. Furthermore, the Fiscal was bound to "attend to the complaint of every slave and if public inquiry appears necessary, to report the case to the Court of Justice."[12]

However, in practice it was not easy for enslaved people to attain any form of meaningful justice within this hierarchy. Enslaved people were up against a social network from which they were excluded, making it difficult though not impossible to lay charges against someone who had social connections. Furthermore, if an enslaved person laid a charge against a "slave-holder" and the "slave-holder" was found to be not guilty, which was very likely in this unfair society, the enslaved person would be punished. The modus operandi when an enslaved person laid a charge against the "slave-holder" was that the enslaved person would be incarcerated pending the outcome of the case.[13] In this way laying a charge would have created a lot of fear and anxiety for the complainant.

In his book, *Children of Bondage*, Robert Shell acknowledged that the "slave-holding" class included "the usual complement of psychopaths among them."[14] However, this acknowledgement held little comfort for enslaved people at the receiving end of the behaviour of psychopathic people who legally held power over them. The resultant trauma to themselves and subsequent generations has yet to be explored or acknowledged.

For people born into a state of slavery, it would have been very difficult to perceive their lives differently. Yet within this psychologically confusing and traumatic environment enslaved people were by this time experiencing a semblance of family life that had previously been denied them. Certainly, even though the power balances continued to be stacked against them, changes were afoot in the landscape of slavery. In a strong drive towards encouraging Christianity among enslaved people, religious instruction in the Christian faith was encouraged.

---

[12]WCARS, Slave Office SO 7/35 Notes on Proclamation of 18th March 1823 on Slaves (18 March 1823.)

[13]WCARS, Slave Office SO 7/35 Notes on Proclamation of 18th March 1823 on Slaves, (18 March 1823).

[14]Shell, *Children of Bondage*, 227.

On 9 January 1824 Charles Henry Somerset sent a letter from his Newlands home to the Chief Justice and Members of the Court of Justice saying that the House of Commons had "unanimously agreed" to certain resolutions. He emphasized that he was asked to give his "particular attention to the amelioration of the state of slavery."[15] He went on to say:

> Fortunately the steps I took by my Proclamation of the 18th March last have anticipated the views of His Majesty's Government in most of the points which have attracted its attention—some other regulations will be gradually introduced but there is one to which I am to call your earliest notice it is that of abolishing flogging in all cases of female prisoners whether Slaves, Hottentots or others.[16]

This he claimed had the unintended effect of "lowering the value of property in them," with an official asking "What is to become of public Justice, if a female is not to be subject to corporal punishment?"

After the appointment of Christiaan Michiel Lind[17] as the functionary in Simon's Town in 1824, there was a noticeable increase in the listings of enslaved people in the "Simon's Town Slave Register."

Certainly with the implementation of key ameliorative laws, all the elements of family life that were denied to enslaved people at the Cape prior to 1824 were now made accessible. For the first time, "slave-holders" were no longer allowed to sell young children separately from their mothers. A savings bank was instituted for enslaved people and enslaved people were able to own property if they had the means. Enslaved men who had acquired sufficient property were granted the right to purchase the freedom of their spouses and children. From 1824 enslaved people were no longer compelled

---

[15]WCARS, Records of the Magistrate of Simon's Town 1793-1985: 1/SMT 2/5 SMT 10/16 (Inkomende briewe 1824) Simon's Town, Ref. 4 (9 January 1824).

[16]WCARS, Records of the Magistrate of Simon's Town 1793-1985: 1/SMT 2/5 SMT 10/16 (Inkomende briewe 1824) Simon's Town, Ref. 4 (9 January 1824). Text of Proclamation by Lord Charles Somerset, Theal, *Records of the Cape Colony*, volume 15: 336-342.

[17]George McCall Theal, *History of South Africa since September 1795* (London: Swan Sonnenschein, 1908) volume 1: 433. See also *Family Search* [online resource] https://www.familysearch.org tree/ person/about/2CBT-1DZ (accessed 27 July 2023).

to work on Sundays. By this time highly skilled artisans were able to benefit from the hiring out system, whereby they were able to hire out their labour privately and pay an agreed amount to the "slave-holder." There were also those who resorted to desperate measures. As mentioned previously, in "Slave Office" correspondence it was stated to be "a well known fact, that many slaves are frequently committing thefts, for the express purpose of collecting money, wherewith to purchase their freedom."[18]

The Free School

The primary aim of the Free School system was a "drive towards instructing the slave class in Christianity." "Slave-holders" were obliged to send "slave" children aged three to ten years to free schools at least three days a week "where free schools are or are to be established."[19]

Whereas before this time, and during the Dutch period in particular, "slave-holders" were more interested in gaining the benefits of strong male labour rather than either the procurement of enslaved females or the survival of children and the old and infirm; the Amelioration Law of 1823 sought to address this. To this end the law stipulated that "slave-holders" were responsible for "securing the subsistence of superannuated slaves and children under six years of age."[20]

The Free School in Simon's Town unfortunately had its own challenges. In correspondence dated 17 September 1825 it was noted that George Clarke, the schoolmaster at the free school in Simon's Town "was not qualified for the situation of schoolmaster" and that "there was no visible improvement" in the education of the children.[21] This matter was obviously under discussion in the wider community as, in a letter addressed to The Residents and

---

[18]WCARS, Slave Office SO 7/35 Notes on Proclamation of 18th March 1823 on Slaves (18 March 1823).

[19]WCARS, Slave Office SO 7/35 Notes on Proclamation of 18th March 1823 on Slaves (18 March 1823).

[20]WCARS, Slave Office SO 7/35 Notes on Proclamation of 18th March 1823 on Slaves.

[21]WCARS, Records of the Magistrate of Simon's Town 1793-1985: 1/SMT 2/5, SMT 10/18 (Letters Received from 22nd April 1825 to 29th December 1825) Ref. 82 (17 September 1825).

Members of the School Committee, Simon's Town on 7 October 1825, a hopeful J Coleman wrote:

> Understanding that the situation of Master to the Free School at this place is likely to become vacant, I beg leave to offer my services in that capacity and have not the least doubt that by Assiduity and attention, I shall be able to give satisfaction.[22]

George Clarke had an ally in Reverend Sturt to whom he wrote, seeking his protection. In his correspondence to Sturt he stated:

> from your knowledge of my conduct and regularity in attending the School, [you] will have sufficient weight with His Excellency the Governor, not to deprive me of a situation without cause or reason.[23]

In response to Clarke's request, Sturt saw fit to write to the Governor in Clarke's favour.[24] Nevertheless, on 26 October 1825 the Colonial Office intervened in the matter and George Clarke was removed "from his situations of Schoolmaster, Church Clerk, Sexton & Bellringer at Simon's Town."[25] Sturt tried to calm these waters by writing to Blake in his capacity as Resident of Simon's Town, stating that George Clarke was "truly penitent for having so far forgotten himself towards the Residents," adding that he was normally "orderly, submissive and respectful."[26] Nevertheless, by November Reverend Sturt had to concede defeat when John Coleman

---

[22] WCARS, Records of the Magistrate of Simon's Town 1793-1985: 1/SMT 2/5, SMT 10/18 (Letters Received from 22nd April 1825 to 29th December 1825) Ref. 107 (7 October 1825).

[23] WCARS, Records of the Magistrate of Simon's Town 1793-1985: 1/SMT 2/5, SMT 10/18 (Letters Received from 22nd April 1825 to 29th December 1825) Ref. 109 and Ref. 121 (12 October 1825).

[24] WCARS, Records of the Magistrate of Simon's Town 1793-1985: 1/SMT 2/5. SMT 10/18 (Letters Received from 22nd April 1825 to 29th December 1825) Ref. 109 and Ref. 121 (12 October 1825).

[25] WCARS, Records of the Magistrate of Simon's Town 1793-1985: 1/SMT 2/5 SMT 10/18 (Letters Received from 22nd April 1825 to 29th December 1825) Ref. 118 (26 October 1825).

[26] WCARS, Records of the Magistrate of Simon's Town 1793-1985: 1/SMT 2/5 SMT 10/18 (Letters Received from 22nd April 1825 to 29th December 1825) Ref. 132 (9 November 1825).

replaced George Clarke as Church Clerk[27] and teacher of the Free School in Simon's Town.[28]

On 31 December 1824 Major George Jackman Rogers, Protector of Slaves, noted in his register that there were forty enslaved children in Simon's Town aged eight and under, notably thirty males and ten females.[29] These children formed part of the 190 enslaved people listed in Simon's Town of whom 143 were males and 47 were females.[30]

A View from the "Slave Register"

The decision by the British colonial government to institute a "slave register" has provided researchers with a window into this historical era. Through the documents compiled by the "Protector of Slaves" we are able to view the inventories of "slave-holders."

One such example is the inventory of Gerhardus Hurter of Simon's Town, the son of Johan Wilhelm Hurter and Martha Maria Munnik, whose home was what we know as Admiralty House in Simon's Town. The recording of Gerhardus Hurter's household inventory commenced on 7 November 1816. The inventory hints at how the experience of slavery at the Cape was characterised by ethnic diversity, differential treatment, the trauma of separation and fragile and impermanent existences.

Apollos was a wagoner who, at the age of thirty-eight, was sold to G[erhardus] Munnik, a relative of Hurter's. The meals in the Hurter household were cooked by two Mauritian men—Pierre aged thirty and Toon aged fifty—while two Mozambican men (David aged forty and Asai aged fifty) baked the bread, pastries and cakes. Fish was carried into the kitchen after being caught on the shores of Simon's Bay by a forty year old Batavian fisherman named Baartjoe. The hard labour and gritty work was done by a forty year

---

[27]WCARS, Records of the Magistrate of Simon's Town 1793-1985: 1/SMT 2/5 SMT 10/18 (Letters Received from 22nd April 1825 to 29th December 1825) Ref. 137 (16 November 1825).

[28]WCARS, Records of the Magistrate of Simon's Town 1793-1985: 1/SMT 2/5 SMT 10/18 (Letters Received from 22nd April 1825 to 29th December 1825) Ref. 138 (17 November 1825).

[29]WCARS, Slave Office, SO 7/36 (31 December 1834 entry) Slave Registry Office, Cape Town (7 October 1825).

[30]WCARS, CA 7/36, Slave Returns 1816-1834 (31 December 1834).

old Mozambican man named Mars. There were two herdsmen serving this household, namely forty year old Thomas from Mozambique and thirty-eight year old January from Malabar. The expansive gardens were tended by a fifty year old Batavian man also named Baartjoe aged fifty. In the parlour of this household sat the seamstresses: twenty-four year old Rosina of the Cape and twenty-five year old Bitja of Bengal. It is probably at the nearby waterfall that twenty-five year old Pegie from Mozambique scrubbed and rinsed the household's washing.

Two enslaved children were listed as having been sold, without any further explanation being given. They were Abdol aged just two years and a four year old girl child named April. It is likely that the sale of these children was to clear a debt by Hurter to A[lexander] Oxholm on 18 May 1816. Oxholm refers to such a sale in a letter to the local magistrate, where he states

> Mr Hurter, the bearer of this, waits upon you in order to give up the names of two of his slaves to be sold to pay the amount of the sentences of the Court of Justice against me, in case he cannot find the means of clearing the amounts.[31]

Births and deaths of enslaved people attached to the Hurter household included Louis, the son of Pegie of Mozambique, who was born on 22 December 1817 and died aged three years in August 1820. The exact date was not recorded. Pegie's twin sons, George and William, who were born on 9 March 1820 are also recorded as having died in August 1820. No further details were given or requested. Pegie had two more children: Justinus, born on 5 October 1821 and Fortuin, born on 4 June 1823.

Other enslaved children listed in this "slave-holding" whose mothers are not mentioned include the "houseboy" Cupido aged fourteen, Pieter aged six, Albert aged two, Charlotte aged ten and Carolina aged four. Only a few are identified with their mothers, such as Robert, the son of Rosina, born on 7 January 1818 and Jupiter, the son of sixteen year old Charlotte, born on 26 June 1821. Two years later on 24 January 1823, Charlotte bore another son named Charles.[32]

---

[31] WCARS, Records of the Magistrate of Simon's Town 1793-1985: 1/SMT 2/5 (Letters received, 1793-1932), SMT 10/8, Number 111 (18 May 1816).
[32] Simon's Town Museum, Register of Slaves, Simon's Town, page 79-80.

Essentially these were children without childhoods. Their fathers, unless this was the "slave-holder" himself, would have had no power to protect them from exploitation or cruelty. Their mothers were "slaves" and by extension so were they. They could be bought and sold at any time. There was no guarantee that they would remain in the "slave-holdings" where they were born and if sold, that they would ever see their mothers again.

The records for Simon's Town are replete with stories of traumatised enslaved children desperately trying to be re-united with their parents from whom they had been separated. Cases of children of enslaved mothers and "Free Black" fathers in Simon's Town were particularly painful, as the law overrode the ability of their fathers to protect them.

All in all, the British ameliorative laws were met with great resentment by the "Dutch" burghers who formerly had *carte blanche* in the way they treated enslaved people and who felt that the British were meddling in their personal affairs. Notwithstanding the pressure to end slavery outright, the British colonial government faced the dilemma of not being able to end slavery without paying compensation to the "slave-holders." However, a wind of change was blowing through the town as it was through the entire colony.

Escaping to and from Simon's Town

During this period many enslaved people and people described as "prize negroes" were "deserting" and seeking shelter with sympathetic members of the "Free Black" community in Simon's Town.[33] Being a port village, the list of incoming deserters also included seamen or passengers who jumped ship in Simon's Town and became absorbed into the "Free Black" community.[34] Also absorbed into the "Free Black" community in Simon's Town at this time were two Chinamen named Arsurie and Campoo.[35]

---

[33] WCARS, Records of the Magistrate of Simon's Town 1793-1985: 1/SMT 2/5 (Letters received, 1793-1932), SMT 10/8, Ref. 168 (2 August 1816); WCARS, Records of the Magistrate of Simon's Town 1793-1985: 1/SMT 2/5 (Letters received, 1793-1932), SMT 10/8, Ref. 203 (20 Sept 1816); WCARS, Records of the Magistrate of Simon's Town 1793-1985: 1/SMT 2/5 (Letters received, 1793-1932), 1/SMT 10/9, Ref. 38 (27 March 1817).

[34] WCARS, Records of the Magistrate of Simon's Town 1793-1985: 1/SMT 2/5 (Letters received, 1793-1932), 1/SMT 10/9, Ref. 98.

Still others were trying to escape from Simon's Town. A woman from Madagascar whose "slave" name was Sarah, managed to get as far as Muizenberg before she was unfortunately captured.[36]

Research on Simon's Town has revealed that the term "prize negro" was more related to the mode of enslaved people being taken off "slave" ships by the British anti-slavery squadron than about the people being exclusively African. A group of a hundred Javanese people located in Noordhoek were also referred to as "prize apprentices" as was a little girl named Finna from Batavia. However, overwhelmingly the term described people from Africa.

A Little Girl named Finna

The story of a little Batavian girl named Finna came as rather a surprise in that at face value it appears that her treatment deviated from the norm. At the age of eight she was indentured as a "prize negro" to Gerrit Buyskes and his wife who claimed to have formed such an attachment to her that they petitioned to return Finna to her family in Batavia for a period of two years.[37] The full letter is printed below:

> To His Excellency Major General Sir Rufane Shaw Donkin K.B. Acting Governor and Commander of the Cape of Good Hope
>
> 28 March 1820
>
> The Memorial of G[errit] Buyskes LLD humbly Sheweth
>
> That a Prize Negro girl named Finna born at Batavia was apprenticed to Memorialist at the age of about eight years & further educated by his wife to whom she consequently is most attached, & who she would leave most reluctantly.

---

[35] WCARS, Records of the Magistrate of Simon's Town 1793-1985: 1/SMT 2/5 (Letters received, 1793-1932), 1/SMT 10/9, Ref. 98.

[36] WCARS, Records of the Magistrate of Simon's Town 1793-1985: 1/SMT 2/5 (Letters received, 1793-1932), 1/SMT 10/9, Ref. 64 (13 May 1817).

[37] Advocate Gerrit Buyskes (1765-1832) emigrated from the Netherlands and arrived at the Cape of Good Hope in 1802 where he served as Secretary of the Court of Justice at the Cape. He was admitted to the Cape bar in 1806 and practised as an advocate thereafter. In Batavia he became Vice-President of the Supreme Court.

And whereas the object of the Abolition of the Slave Trade (a trade so contrary to the Laws of Nature) is to contribute to the Happiness of Those unfortunate creatures, who have been importuned contrary to these benevolent views, Memorialist supposed that this would be promoted if she was restored to her Native country (Batavia) her family & Friends by Memorialist.

And whereas the Dutch Government at Batavia has framed Laws, prohibiting the importation of Slaves especially stipulating that a Slave imported shall be Free it will guarantee Government here (should it doubt Memorialist's veracity) that he could not mislead.

And Memorialist always flattered himself, that on these grounds he would obtain liberty to take this Girl on for the assistance of his wife now 56 years old, & therefore made no other arrangements.

Memorialist therefore humbly requests that Your Excellency may be graciously pleased to allow him to take this girl on to Batavia he being willing to provide for her, and to give security that she will return either with his daughter, the widow of the late Lieut von Butlar or otherwise, within the term of two years,

And Memorialist as in duty bound

Shall ever pray[38]

Francis Dashwood

An interesting person to emerge as having influenced the course of history in the lives of at least some enslaved people in Simon's Town is Francis Dashwood.[39] A powerful man who served as the president of the Lombard Bank[40] from 1808 to 1814, he was also a member of the liquor licensing and auctioning committees between 1807 and 1815. On 29 April 1808 he was

---

[38] WCARS, Colonial Office Memorials (1820), CO 3917, Ref. 156 (28 March 1820).

also appointed to a committee enquiring into the clandestine importation of "slaves."

After resigning as president of the Lombard Bank in 1814, Dashwood took up farming for a while before being appointed Collector of Customs in Simon's Town on 9 April 1819 where he eventually bought a house on 10 September 1819.

Dashwood is notable for facilitating the largest number of manumissions of enslaved people in Simon's Town. Initial manumissions arranged by Dashwood were for the nineteen year old housemaid "Aida 1" of the Cape on 17 March 1819, the twenty-four year old tailor, "Africa of the Cape" and forty-four year old tailor "August 1" of the Cape on 13 April 1820 and the forty-three year old nursemaid "Clara of the Cape" on 17 March 1819. In addition, August and Yima of the Cape were manumitted on 13 April 1820.

When Dashwood returned to England on 15 February 1825 he freed the remaining enslaved people in his "slave-holding" and also procured property for them in Simon's Town.[41] They would have then joined the "Free Black" community in Simon's Town. This date is significant as it was in 1825 that Sir Richard Plaskett[42] requested from the Governor Resident in Simon's Town that the population statistics be altered so that people described as

---

[39]Francis Dashwood (1772-1828) married Lady Ann Maitland, sister to the Earl of Lauderdale on 1 July 1793. Dashwood was known for his royal family connections and particularly his colourful relative, his namesake Sir Francis Dashwood (1708-1781) who was linked to the notorious "Hellfire Club." The "Hellfire Club" referred to a group of exclusive—and notorious—clubs established for aristocratic libertines in Britain and Ireland.

[40]Lombard Bank (also known as the Bank van Leening) was the first commercial bank at the Cape of Good Hope, founded on 15 March 1793. "Lombard banks" originated in Lombardy in France and the street on which most banks in London were situated was Lombard Street. They typically provided credit at 5% per annum against "qualifying collateral" e.g. property or gold, and the Lombard Bank at the Cape followed suit. Roy Havemann and Johan Fourie, "The Cape of Perfect Storms: Colonial Africa's First Financial Crash, 1788-1793" *Economic Research Southern Africa (ERSA) Working Paper* 511 (March 2015), 12.

[41]WCARS Confidential reports, Protector of Slaves 1829-1834, Slave Office, SO 3/20A "Observations of the Protector of slaves from 24th December 1830 up to the 25th June 1831," signed by George Jackman Rogers, Protector of Slaves, 1831.

[42]Richard Plaskett was appointed Colonial Secretary of the Cape of Good Hope in 1824.

"Free Black" would thenceforth be identified as "Coloured."[43] This curious term would later become a blanket identity imposed on people formerly disparagingly described as "Bushmen," "Hottentot," "Bastard Hottentot," "Bastard," "Prize Negroes" and "slaves."

The Court Case of Figaro

The court case of Figaro is interesting in what it reveals about the society that existed during this time. In December 1818 Figaro was described as being an apprentice in the Dockyard aged around forty years and born in Mauritius. He was accused of breaking into the hut of Solomon Harmslier on "a certain Saturday in the month of September last" by cutting the thong that fastened his door. The items Figaro was accused of stealing from Solomon Harmslier were listed as follows:

1 Blue Great Coat
1 Blue Jacket
3 White Jackets
2 Jackets
1 Petticoat of Patchwork
2 shifts
1 red cloth Pocket book containing pins & needles
1 pair of scissors
1 Brass thimble
1 case containing two Razors with horn hands
1 Bag with 4 lb of sugar
1 plate with a piece of salt-meat &
2 English loaves of Bread

Figaro's movements were noticed by William Auret, the son of Jeremias Auret who, at the time, was accompanied by "a maid of his named Rebecca on their way to the place of said Auret" when they saw Figaro carrying goods out of the said hut. At the time he was carrying a blue Handkerchief under his arm, containing a Little Bag with Sugar, a plate with some meat & three English loaves of bread. On asking his name and Figaro replying that it was

---

[43]WCARS, Records of the Magistrate of Simon's Town 1793-1985: 1/SMT 2/5, Volume number SMT 10/18, folio 86 (21 September 1825).

Siegar, this seemed to satisfy William and Rebecca "not to entertain any bad suspicion against him." However, two days later it came to Rebecca's attention that Harmslier was missing all these items from his hut, at which stage she informed Harmslier of the encounter with Figaro.

Fig. 6-1. From the Hills above Simon's Bay, 1838
Source: Watercolour by Christopher Webb Smith. Library of Parliament, 19349 (ii)

It seems that Figaro's motive was to abandon his apprenticeship at the Simon's Town Dockyard, as he was eventually found "on the road to Rondebosch … having in his possession a pair of Scissors, an old blue great Coat, a can of Razors, and a red pocket book" all belonging to Solomon Harmslier. In court Figaro admitted to going into Solomon Harmslier's hut from time to time and forcing open the lock of the chest, which apparently was not very secure. He described taking the razors and the pocket book from the chest, a pair of scissors from the table and the great coat from the bed.

133

His sentence was extremely severe, justified by the judge as necessary "to deter others from doing the like." Figaro was ordered to be taken to the Place of Execution and to be

> delivered over to the Executioner to be tied to a stake & severely scourged with Rods on the bare back & thereupon to be confined to labor in irons without wages on the public Works at Robben Island, or elsewhere, for the term of the next insuing [sic] two years.[44]

Fig. 6-2. Osmond's home "The Palace" (double storey house on the right)
Source: The Author

"King John"

While people like Solomon Harmslier lived in simple abodes such as huts on the False Bay mountains, in December 1818 a visitor to Simon's Town

---

[44]WCARS, Court of Justice, CJ 812, Ref. 302-310 (10 December 1818).

commented on John Osmond's considerable landownership and growing power in Simon's Town in the following excerpt:

> He is now well known by the name of King John, on account of his extensive possessions in dwelling-houses and lands which, combined with his situation as magistrate, give him great power and influence in that town and neighbourhood.[45]

Another researcher describes Osmond as "a particularly shrewd operator" who, with the benefit of his wife's family's wealth, bought up insolvent estates at bargain prices, which resulted in him "owning most of Simon's Town." Of course Osmond also benefited from many land grants given to him by the British colonial government.[46] We will return to Osmond later in this text.

Locating People Referred to as "Prize Negroes" in Simon's Town

By 1822 the first of the people who were "liberated" from "slave" ships by the anti-slavery squadron back in 1808 would have reached the end of their fourteen year mandatory indentureships. They were then brought before the magistrate where they were informed that they were to provide for themselves a "Master" and to notify the Local Authorities of this engagement within a month of their emancipation,[47] and the Laws of the Colony in respect of vagrancy were made clear to them.[48]

Although the Cape authorities recorded the branding marks of indentured "prize negroes" in an official ledger in order to identify them once their indentureship periods had expired, this system cannot have been totally reliable as the onus was placed on the recipients of the indentured "prize negroes" to supply the authorities with the correct information regarding these indentureships. This becomes evident in a letter from Secretary Chris-

---

[45] James Holman, *A Voyage Round the World, Including Travels in Africa, Asia, Australasia* ... (London: Smith, Elder, 1834), volume 2: 107.

[46] Philip, "The Vicissitudes of the Early British Settlers at the Cape," 163-164.

[47] *Cape Town Gazette* (26 April 1823), page 1, column 2. WCARS, CCP, 08/1/18.

[48] *Cape Town Gazette* (26 April 1823), page 1, column 2. WCARS, CCP, 08/1/18.

topher Bird of the Colonial Office[49] to Captain Somerset dated 11 July 1823, asking him "to request from people in the area who had prize negroes indentured to them speedy returns of this information."[50]

Pierre Rocher of Imhoff's Farm reported three people—namely a "male negro" named Nakatinka who was indentured on 25 March 1815 and who was renamed "Present"; a person named Danatorcana who was indentured on 21 December 1816 who was renamed "Joseph;" and a man named "John" who was indentured in 1816.[51]

Another Simon's Town resident named Ed Miller reported on 7 July 1823 that a "female Negro" named Mameea was indentured to him on 15 March 1815 and that she had borne a daughter named Flora just sixteen months previously.

At the end of her indentureship period in 1824, this mother would then have been faced with the dilemma of either leaving her daughter behind or staying on in this household until her child completed the mandatory fourteen year indentureship after reaching her fifth birthday.

The fragmentation of families and the trauma of these childhood indentures is evident in the words of a man named Samboo, a "prize negro" indentured to Charles Blair, the Collector of Customs. Samboo was interviewed by the British Royal Commissioner John Thomas Bigge, one of the Commissioners of Enquiry sent to the Cape in 1823, with a particular view to investigating "the disposition and possible emancipation of government slaves and apprenticed Africans."[52] In answering Bigge's questions as to

---

[49]Lieutenant-Colonel Christopher Chapman Bird (1769-1861), Colonial Secretary at the Cape, 1818-1824.

[50]WCARS, Records of the Magistrate of Simon's Town 1793-1985: 1/SMT 2/5, SMT 10/15 (Inkomende briewe 1823) Simon's Town, Ref. 66 (11 July 1823).

[51]WCARS, Records of the Magistrate of Simon's Town 1793 – 1985: 1/SMT 2/5, SMT 10/15 (Inkomende briewe 1823) Simon's Town, Ref. 67) 21 July, 1823.

[52]John Thomas Bigge (1780-1843) and Major William Colebrooke were both Commissioners of Eastern Inquiry, the commission established by Great Britain to investigate all aspects of governance (including slavery) in various colonies and the laws and administration of justice of others (1823-1831). See Zoe Laidlaw, "Investigating Empire: Humanitarians, Reform and the Commission of Eastern Inquiry" *Journal of Imperial and Commonwealth History* 40, 5 (December 2012): 749-768 and *Australian Dictionary of Biography* [online resource] https://adb.anu.edu.au/biography/bigge-john-thomas-1779/text1999.

whether he was happy with his treatment, one should be aware that Samboo was at a distinct disadvantage in expressing his true feelings, lest there were repercussions. He responded by saying that he "had no complaints," before expressing his sadness about being separated from his children, saying "my children are all apprenticed out and I wish the one which is with Mr Moore, a baker at Wynberg, should be returned to his mother; it is only six years old."[53] This seemingly simple request may have taken great courage for Samboo to make, given the context of the time in which it was made and the fact that his questioners might have taken umbrage at his statement. Whether there were ramifications for Samboo we will never know, but at the time, the most common punishment for "prize negroes" was "thirty nine lashes with a rattan on the bare posterior."[54]

Another heartbreaking case is that of a five year old boy named Robert, born in Kalk Bay during 1817 to Mozambican parents named Jaccote and Mina. At some point he was separated from his mother Mina, who was indentured to Stephen Twycross, a merchant residing at 59 Long Street, Cape Town.[55] Mina then took ill and the severity of her illness must have been significant for a decision to have been made to take five year old Robert, described by Twycross as "a hearty robust healthy boy" to Cape Town to visit his "sick mother" on 13 November 1822.

It transpired that while Robert was standing in the doorway of the Twycross home, four men from Swellendam were unloading their wagons close-by at Messrs Cooke & Thompson. Before they departed, little Robert was "clandestinely taken away."[56] In a missive to all the magisterial districts concerning this case, the Fiscal D Denyssen wrote:

> You will oblige me by directing the field cornets in your respective Districts accurately to enquire whether any such child is detained within their field cornetcies and if it may

---

[53]Christopher Saunders, "The Case of Samboo" in "'Liberated Africans' and Labour at the Cape of Good Hope in the First Half of the 19th Century' (Centre for African Studies, UCT, 30.03.1983), 23-24.
[54]Saunders, "The Case of Samboo," 23.
[55]Philip, *British Residents at the Cape*, 433.
[56]WCARS, Records of the Magistrate of Simon's Town 1793-1985: 1/SMT 2/5, SMT 10/14 (Inkomende briewe 1822), Simon's Town, Ref. 122 (15 November 1822).

be found by taking proper measures for restoring the child to W Twycross and also making those who have kept the child under their custody answerable for such conduct.[57]

Though a search of all districts was ordered by Denyssen, there is no record of whether Robert was ever found. It is open to conjecture whether he ended up being absorbed into the farmworker system in Swellendam or not.

People in Simon's Town who benefited from free labour through the so-called prize negro indentureship system included Gerrit Hurter, John Osmond Senior, Francis Dashwood, David Oddy, Richard Howell, James Stone, John Clarence, John Goodwin, Christiaan Michiel Lind, James Richardson, Mariana Savory, I F van der Schyff and Thomas White. Within the Noordhoek area those who benefited from the labour of people taken off "slave" ships were Robert Cowdrey of Wildeschutsbrand, Field Cornet James Bailey of Oliphantsbosch, George Sturt of Rocklands Farm, Pierre Rocher of Imhoff's Gift and Johannes Frans Sebastiaan Kirsten of Krom Rivier.[58]

On 16 September 1823 an ill Reverend Sturt penned a letter in very shaky handwriting to John Goodwin (the Government Secretary for the Simon's Town district) requesting that he dispatch one of his constables to "take a prize boy to the Tronk" for speaking rudely to his wife. He ends the letter saying "I think a little corporal punishment will be of use, and I should feel obliged by his having it. Excuse this hasty letter but weakness [pleads] my excuse."[59] When it transpired on 18 September 1823 that Goodwin had not ordered the requested punishment, Sturt responded in correspondence saying "if it is not in your power to order the punishment, liberate the prisoner," claiming that being without his servant was a "great inconvenience."[60] It seems that Goodwin was less than eager to liberate the prisoner as, on 20

---

[57]WCARS, Records of the Magistrate of Simon's Town 1793-1985: 1/SMT 2/5, SMT 10/14 (Inkomende briewe 1822) Simon's Town, Ref. 122 (15 November 1822).

[58]WCARS, Opgaafrolle J181, 1826.

[59]WCARS, Records of the Magistrate of Simon's Town 1793-1985: 1/SMT 2/5, SMT 10/15 (Inkomende briewe 1823) Simon's Town, Ref. 66 (16 September 1823).

[60]WCARS, Records of the Magistrate of Simon's Town 1793-1985: 1/SMT 2/5 SMT 10/15 (Inkomende briewe 1823) Simon's Town, Ref. 93 (18 September 1823).

September 1823, Sturt penned a further letter to Henry Somerset requesting him to "liberate his boy."[61]

John Campbell

Sometimes people became absorbed into the "prize negro" indentureship system even when they did not fit the British colonial criterion of being found on "slave" ships. John Campbell is one such example. He is described in British colonial correspondence as a Sierra Leonean national who was "a Soldier in a Native Corps or Company at Banie Island."[62] On its disbandment he was "bound as an apprentice" to Major U Henry of the late Royal African Corps at Sierre Leone. When Major Henry travelled to the Cape Colony he took John Campbell along with him.

On the occasion of his death, Major Henry's widow arranged for Campbell to be indentured to Mr Moore, the baker. With the completion of the indentureship John Campbell worked as a paid servant for Mr le Brand, a resident of Simon's Town.

However, Campbell was in a vulnerable position as he had no official papers and Moore had refused to supply him with the necessary assistance to legalise his release from the indentureship. At this stage John Campbell himself petitioned the British colonial governor for a colonial passport, which led to an enquiry into the matter.[63]

The Story of Jean Ellé

The Collector of Customs, Charles Blair was unscrupulous in his dealings with people described as "prize negroes," and he would virtually trade these people off to cover his debts. As mentioned previously, the *modus operandi* was that once a human cargo of people described as "prize negroes" was

---

[61]WCARS, Records of the Magistrate of Simon's Town 1793-1985: 1/SMT 2/5 SMT 10/15 (Inkomende briewe 1823) Simon's Town, Ref. 95, Ref 96, Ref. 97, Ref. 98 (20 September 1823).
[62]WCARS, Records of the Magistrate of Simon's Town 1793-1985: 1/SMT 2/5, SMT 10/16 (Inkomende briewe 1824) Simon's Town, Ref. 95 (25 June 1824).
[63]WCARS, Records of the Magistrate of Simon's Town 1793-1985: 1/SMT 2/5, SMT 10/16 (Inkomende briewe 1824) Simon's Town, Ref. 95 (25 June 1824), page 145.

landed, Blair was to be notified. He would then make the journey to Simon's Bay or Table Bay, to view and allocate the "prize negroes" as he saw fit. The fittest were expected to be procured for the Navy and the Army and the rest were spread thinly throughout the colony, some of whom would remain with individuals in Simon's Town.[64] However, all of these placements were entirely at the whim of Blair who was given *carte blanche* over these individuals. This saw the inception of a trail of corruption in which people were bartered as a currency by Blair, who profited generously from these transactions.[65] However, one such "prize negro" was to be the catalyst for Blair's corrupt activities being exposed to the authorities. His name was Jean Ellé.

The exceptional story of Jean Ellé emerges from the court trial records in a case of alleged libel brought by Charles Blair against Lancelot Cooke, William Edwards and Jan Bernard Hoffman by His Majesty's Fiscal in 1824. Jean Ellé, formerly a "free citizen" of the Island of Bourbon (now Reunion), was a sailor cook on the French packet, *Le Victor* when it was captured by the British brig *Race Horse* in 1810, during the Napoleonic wars. Thus it was that the course of his life became irrevocably altered. Delivered into the hands of the Collector of Customs, namely Charles Blair, Jean Ellé was forced into servitude with a number of Blair's creditors, the first being Iver Phillipus Jacobus Tyrholm where he was placed for a number of years and the last being Samuel Murray.[66]

Murray hired Jean Ellé out as a cook to a wealthy Cape merchant, Lancelot Cooke, who in turn paid Murray a sum of 35 Rixdollars per month for Jean Ellé's service.

At the death of Samuel Murray, which occurred after Jean Ellé had been with Cooke for six years, Blair ordered the return of Jean Ellé, whom he had

---

[64]Christopher Saunders, "'Liberated Africans' and Labour at the Cape of Good Hope in the First Half of the Nineteenth Century," in Centre for African Studies, University of Cape Town: *Africa Seminar* (March 1983), 5: 226-227.

[65]"Memorial to the Lords of the Treasury, accusing Mr C Blair, Collector of His Majesty's Customs, of having committed divers malpractices in the distribution of Prize Negroes and of having, in many instances, made donations of these people to satisfy the claims of several of his creditors," Theal, *Records of the Cape Colony,* Volume 17: 178.

[66]Theal, *Records of the Cape Colony,* Volume 17: 189.

promised to a Mr Pegou, the son-in-law of his assistant, William Wilberforce Bird. Jean Ellé was reluctant to go and Cooke was reluctant to part with him.

He was now six months short of completing a fourteen year period of enforced indenture, which he had always claimed had been wrongly forced upon him and which was later blamed on the language barrier, i.e. Jean Ellé was French speaking.

In addition, with the death of Murray, Cooke had been paying the 35 Rix-dollars to Jean Ellé himself. Cooke, who spoke of the "good opinion he entertained of the man, acquired during his long and faithful service"[67] offered to pay the costs of another cook for Pegou in place of Jean Ellé. However, Blair refused and after a verbal altercation between the two, Cooke decided to take action against Blair. Thus with the assistance of Edwards and Hoffman, Cooke instituted the drawing up of a petition on behalf of a number of people named "prize negroes" citing Blair's ill-treatment and underhanded dealings in relation to them. The petition, which was addressed to the Lords of the Treasury, was intercepted and Lancelot Cooke, William Edwards and Jan Bernard Hoffman were accused of instigating it and sued by Blair for libel.[68] In retrospect, Blair might have re-considered his libel action, as the court case created a platform for Cooke to expose Blair's corrupt activities.

Giving evidence in the libel court case Cooke stated:

> If Mr Blair had been influenced by the benevolent spirit of the Abolition Act (and Jean Ellé had been a slave in reality), when he found him a man near thirty years of age, so good a cook and so well able to earn the bread of honest industry, he would have satisfied the law, by placing him in some family for a few months, instead of 14 years; but this would not satisfy the necessities or the wishes of Mr Blair, who acquired consequence and credit by disposing of so many Slaves of the most unfortunate order; and if your Lordships would afford your protection against the future oppressions of the Officers of Customs, several cases should appear

---

[67]Theal, *Records of the Cape Colony*, Volume 17: 189.
[68]Theal, *Records of the Cape Colony*, Volume 17: 24.

before you of Mr Blair's privity to such contracts that offered to Mr Pegou, at which he expresses such indignation; to contracts, even more corrupt, some wherein when persons have pressed him for payment of his debts, he has promised them greater advantages, which have ended in the donations of miserable Creatures, thus abandoned to those whom he dare not to assail, sacrifices to his necessities, victims of his oppressive partialities.[69]

When the libel case against Cooke et al was finally dismissed, after lengthy hearings, Blair was investigated for corruption with regard to his illicit practices, which included the disappearance of a number of "prize negroes" who disappeared after being indentured by Blair.[70]

After an investigation headed by British Royal Commissioner John Thomas Bigge and Colonial Administrator William Colebrooke, Blair was found guilty of corruption in 1825, but suffered no punishment for his actions.[71]

Forgotten Identities

By this time in Simon's Town a variety of distinct communities had formed, who were identified in the Cape colonial census in a variety of identity constructions. As mentioned previously, these categories of constructed identities were "Bushmen," "Hottentot," "Bastard Hottentot," "Bastards," "Prize Negroes," "whites," "Slaves" and "Free Blacks"—the latter group sometimes mimicked people described as "Bastards" or "Bastard Hottentots" who were more enfranchised than their peers.

Although the majority of enslaved people at the Cape were described as being of the "Mohamedan faith"[72] the parish Births and Deaths register

---

[69] Theal, *Records of the Cape Colony*, Volume 17: 191-192.
[70] WCARS: CO 414/6 12285, Correspondence to Lord Charles Somerset from P Brink et al, (27 August 1818), 501.
[71] Reidy, The Admission of Slaves and "Prize Slaves" into the Cape Colony, 1797-1818, Thesis (MA), University of Cape Town, 1997, 82.
[72] WCARS: Slave Office, Confidential reports, Protector of Slaves 1829-1834 SO 3/20A, George Jackman Rogers, Protector of Slaves (June-December 1830).

recorded by Reverend Sturt reveals a diverse congregation, with births and deaths for the period 1812 to 1823 listed as follows:

IDENTITY CONSTRUCTION	BIRTHS	DEATHS
Whites	85	30
Persons of Colour	44	6
"Bastard Hottentots"	9	0
Prize Apprentices	22	9

By 1824 the population of Simon's Town was listed as 1,275 people, who were divided into five categories. There were 514 people described as "white," 118 people described as "Hottentot," 311 people described as "Free Blacks," 190 people described as "slaves" and 72 people described as "Prize Negroes." This makes it safe to assume that the "Persons of Colour," recorded by Sturt, were people recorded as "Free Blacks" in the census, suggesting that enslaved people were not church-going at this time.

Among the people described as "Free Blacks" a material class structure was forming as some were becoming entrepreneurs and property owners, while others fell into the category of the working class and lived in rented homes. The "Free Black" community formed a distinct social class who intermarried with other people who were also listed in the census as "Free Blacks."

A search of marriage and death records has revealed further people described as "Free Blacks" in Simon's Town and/or their descendants. They are mentioned here—not in chronological order—as follows:

- Abdol Karriem Mondar born in 1811, was a fisherman who rented a cottage in Simon's Town belonging to H Brown. However, he owned a plot of ground in South End in Port Elizabeth, which at the time of his death on 24 June 1866 was worth thirty pounds. A daughter named Nasera was born from his marriage to Simara Mondar née David, who at his death signed his death certificate with an X.

- Another Simon's Town fisherman was Abdol Soeker alias Jongie Elias who was described as "Malay from the Cape Colony."

These records prove that within the category of people described as "Free Blacks," land ownership, literacy and skills were the preserve of some, but not of others.

- There were also many people like James Williams, who was born in 1814, who worked as a general labourer all his life and died of "pneumonia exhaustion" at the age of eighty-five. Property ownership and literacy were not something that he could pass on to his son, Daniel Williams, who signed his father's death certificate with an X in 1899.

- The widow Rackia Raven was born into the "Free Black" society in Simon's Town in 1837. In official documents she was described as a "mixed colonial." When she died an adult relative named Jatiem Raven signed her death certificate with an X.

Fig. 6-3. Simon's Town circa 1866
Source: Lithograph by Thomas Bowler. Library of Parliament, Bowler_6546, Plate10

- Saida Jardine was born in Simon's Town in 1842 to Majiet and Seba Jardine. Although she owned no property, she left her children the proceeds of a policy taken out with African Homes Trust when she died. Her daughter Laka Solomon signed her mother's death notice with an X.

- Marthinus Mentor, who was born in Simon's Town in 1820, worked as a farm labourer in Elsjes River, Simon's Town, where he died on 17 April 1896, having never married.

Oranje Arie Kleyn[73]

Arie Kleyn—of partial Khoe ancestry—was born in Wemmershoek in 1793 to Oranje Kleyn and Janitsche Brand. The 1826 opgaafsrolle shows that as an adult he owned two properties in the Simon's Town district, namely Klaas Jagers Rivier measuring thirty six morgen and Klipfontein, which measured ten morgen. He also owned grazing land in Wildeschutsbrand, which offered ample sustenance for his twenty oxen and seven breeding cattle. In addition to farming he was a wagoner and for years operated a delivery service in the Simon's Town. Much of the labour required for his enterprises would have fallen on his sons Joseph, Adrian Martinus and Tromp Arie Junior. He also had four daughters, namely Christina, Maria, Griet and Johanna. Compared to his peers he could be described as being comfortably off.

Arie Kleyn, who was also sometimes referred to as Oranje Kleyn, lived to the age of ninety-two when he died at his house on Klipfontein farm in 1885, having outlived his wife, Jacoba. Although Arie Kleyn had left two farms in the Simon's Town District to his children, namely Klaas Jagers Rivier and Klipfontein, it appears that for years he had been burdened with extremely high property taxes placed upon his property by the Cape Colonial government, as the following memorial by his children after his death suggests:

> Memorial by the children of Oranje Kleyn saying that they want to take transfer of the property left to them by their father namely Klaas Jagers Rivier in extent thirty six morgan and Klip Fontein in extent ten morgan, but that the

---

[73]Oranje Arie Kleyn's surname was sometimes spelt "Klein."

quitrent placed on it was so high and with the accumulated arrears coming to more than the value of the property.[74]

This Memorial raises questions about whether this property taxation was purposely inflated in order to dispossess Arie Kleyn and/or his descendants of their land.

Elias Davidse

It is possible that Elias Davidse, owner of the farm Wolfkloof in Noordhoek was the grandson of Elias van de Caab. The latter was an enslaved person owned by Christina Diemer of Imhoff's Farm in Noordhoek and listed in her will in 1765. His maternal lineage was indigenous Khoe. Elias Davidse first emerges in the records in 1816 in correspondence concerning his application for a licence to shoot game.[75] The 1826 *opgaafrolle* shows that Elias Davidse owned Wolfkloof in Noordhoek. Also resident on this farm were unnamed people of indigenous Khoe ancestry described in colonial records as "Hottentots" comprising an adult male and female and three male children.[76] On 14 December, 1862 the boatman and Khoe descendant Elias Davidse, who was likely his grandson, formalised his marriage to Elizabeth van Baale at the Dutch Reformed Church in Simon's Town. The couple signed their marriage certificate with an X.

Cornelius September

Cornelius September came as a huge surprise to me as I was not expecting to find my great-great-great grandfather in the Simon's Town district. For years I have felt an affinity with Simon's Town and became immersed in its history, without realising that I had a personal connection to this history. Imagine my surprise when researching my genealogy in 2020 that I discovered my maternal great, great, great grandparents Cornelius and Sara September (née Willemse) were from Noordhoek. At the time of their marriage in the Dutch Reformed Church in Wynberg on 10 February 1840, their res-

---

[74] WCARS, Colonial Office, CO 4021, Ref. 131 (April 1844).
[75] WCARS, Records of the Magistrate of Simon's Town 1793-1985: 1/SMT 2/5 (Letters received, 1793-1932), SMT 10/8, Ref. 273 (23 December 1816).
[76] WCARS, Opgaafrolle, J181, 1826.

idence was Zilvermyn Farm in Noordhoek. They were both illiterate and Cornelius worked as a labourer.[77]

My research suggests that Cornelius and Sara September had seven children, namely September September, Petrus Gabriel September, Willem September, Cornelius September, Jan Stephanus September, Sara Elisabeth September and Eva Jacoba September.[78] Their son Cornelis Pieter September (who was born in Noordhoek on 9 April 1835), was my great, great grandfather who married Lydia Aletta Overmeyer in the Dutch Reformed Church in Simon's Town on 10 October 1858. Though Aletta was not literate, Cornelius was literate and a mason by trade.[79]

Their marriage at the Dutch Reformed Church is interesting. During this historical period the Dutch school in Simon's Town was established for the offspring of people described as "emancipated slaves, negroes and other liberated Africans (formerly employed by HM Navy) together with the Dutch children living in the wards of Klaver Valley and Brand Wachet."[80] One wonders too whether Cornelius was one of the masons who worked on the church building completed in 1856. It may well be that his skilled labour is reflected in other heritage buildings in the town.

Cornelius and Lydia Aletta must have moved to Graaff Reinet, no doubt for better work prospects or a job contract as five of their children were born and baptised there between 1860 and 1866.

1. Johanna Margaretha September was born on 21 July 1860.[81]

---

[77] Cornelis September and Sara Willemse, married on 4 February 1840 in the Dutch Reformed Church, Wynberg. *Family Search* [online resource] https://www.familysearch.org/ark:/61903/1:1:6ZHB-XSBZ.

[78] Cornelis September personal family record. *Family Search* [online resource] https://www.familysearch.org/tree/person/details/KZSY-SYR.

[79] Cornelis Pieter and Lydia Aletta September, married on 10 October 1858 in the Dutch Reformed Church, Simon's Town. *Family Search* [online resource] https://www.familysearch.org/ark:/61903/3:1:S3HY-65S3-ZJK?i=91&cc=1392488

[80] Michael Whisson, "Group Areas: The Case of Simon's Town." Unpublished paper, 29-30.

[81] Johanna Margaretha September, baptised in the Dutch Reformed Church, Graaff Reinet on 9 September 1860. *Family Search* [online resource] https://www.familysearch.org/ark:/61903/1:1:6CBW-YFK9.

2. Sara Jakoba Elizabeth September was born on 23 October 1862.[82]

3. Cornelius Pieter September was born on 28 October 1863.[83]

4. Lydia Aletta Magdalena September was born on 10 November 1864.[84]

5. Margaretha Susanna Carolina September was born on 24 November 1865.[85]

A further three children were born after the September family returned to Noordhoek:

6. Eva Jacoba Elisabeth Septembers [sic] was born on 23 September 1867.[86]

7. Jan Stefanus September was born on 26 June 1870.[87]

8. Samuel Willemenus [sic; also recorded as Willimorus] September (my great grandfather) was born in Noordhoek on 16 December 1871 and was baptised at the Dutch Reformed Church in Simon's Town on 31 January 1872.[88]

---

[82]Sara Jakoba Elizabeth September, baptised in the Dutch Reformed Church, Graaff Reinet on 14 December 1862. *Family Search* [online resource] https://www.familysearch.org/ark:/61903/1:1:623L-Z91Q.

[83]Cornelius Pieter September, baptised in the Dutch Reformed Church, Graaff Reinet on 11 December 1863. *Family Search* [online resource] https://www.familysearch.org/ark:/61903/1:1:623L-LR3Y.

[84]Lydia Aletta Magdalena September, baptised in the Dutch Reformed Church, Graaff Reinet on 9 December 1864. *Family Search* [online resource] https://www.familysearch.org/ark:/61903/1:1:623R-MCXL.

[85]Margaretha Susanna Carolina September, baptised in the Dutch Reformed Church, Graaff Reinet on 12 February 1866. *Family Search* [online resource] https://www.familysearch.org/ark:/61903/1:1:623Y-DBFJ.

[86]Eva Jacoba Elisabeth Septembers [sic], baptised in the Dutch Reformed Church, Simon's Town on 8 December 1867. *Family Search* [online resource] https://www.familysearch.org/ark:/61903/3:1:3Q9M-CSV8-69C4-L?cc=1478678.

[87]Jan Stefanus September, baptised in the Dutch Reformed Church, Simon's Town on 27 July 1870. *Family Search* [online resource] https://www.familysearch.org/ark:/61903/1:1:6KN5-4VS6.

At some stage Cornelius September moved his family from Noordhoek to Wynberg where Aletta died on 5 May 1899. Cornelius then married his second wife Caroline September, born Paulsen, with whom he had no children. Cornelius died at his home in Ottery Road, Wynberg on 30 July 1903. At the time he was also recorded as owning three other properties, however, the details of these properties are not listed.

Evidently the extended September family remained in Noordhoek, as the anthropologist, Michael Whisson, cites a visitor to Noordhoek in 1902 mentioning the September family in particular, saying:

> Lower down, and close to the beach, is a family of coloured people—the "Septembers," who are hardworking gardeners and also keep cattle. There are lots of very well to do coloured small farmers upon 10-20 twenty acres of land—hardworking and very well-disposed towards a stranger. I have never seen in all my travels a prettier place than Noordhoek.[89]

My great grandfather Samuel September was a wood merchant, however, at the time of his marriage he was recorded as a labourer. He married my great grandmother Johanna Elizabeth Sassman on 9 February 1892 and they lived on a smallholding in First Avenue, Grassy Park, where Samuel died on 22 February 1944.[90]

The couple had eight children namely Cornelius Pieter September (born on 20 March 1892);[91] Abraham John September (1894-1976); Johanna Elizabeth September (1900-1952); Anne Elizabeth September (born circa

---

[88] Samuel Willemenus September, baptised in the Dutch Reformed Church, Simon's Town on 31 January 1872. Samuel's second name changed in some records to "Willowmore" (and variants) in subsequent years. *Family Search* [online resource] https://www.familysearch.org/ark:/61903/1:1:6KJC-X4QC.

[89] Extract from an article in the *Wynberg Times* (3 May 1902) cited by Michael Whisson in *The Fairest Cape: An Account of the Coloured People in the District of Simonstown* (Johannesburg: South African Institute of Race Relations, 1972), 10.

[90] Samuel September, Death Notice, 22 February 1944. *Family Search* [online resource] https://www.familysearch.org/ark:/61903/1:1:WYBQ-X23Z.

[91] Cornelius Pieter September served in the British armed forces during World War 1 and died in Paris on 31 July 1918 while on active service. *Family Search* "United Kingdom, World War I Service Records, 1914-1920" [online resource] https://www.familysearch.org/ark:/61903/1:1:QVBG-PR2S.

1909); Daniel George September; Johannes Peter September; Lydia Aletta September and Samuel Peter September.[92]

Their daughter Johanna Elizabeth September was my grandmother and she married James Watson Coffen/Coffin on 3 November 1919 in St John's Anglican Church in Wynberg.[93] Their daughter, Barbara Ellen Coffen, born on 6 November 1927, was my mother.[94]

Fig. 6-4. Zilvermyn Farm
Source: André Pretorius Collection, Manuscripts Section (MS 408), Stellenbosch University

---

[92]Records for these family members may be located on *Family Search* [online resource] https://www.familysearch.org/search/.

[93]Record of the marriage between Johanna Elizabeth September and James Watson Coffin/Coffen, in St John's Church, Wynberg on 3 November 1919. Family Search [online resource] https://www.familysearch.org/ark:/61903/1:1:6ZH5-D6FQ.

[94]Barbara Ellen Coffen, baptised 4 December 1927 in the Parish of Wynberg.

Today the descendants of Cornelius September live throughout the Western Cape, other parts of the country and also span several continents and I honour them all. However, for the purposes of this book I have personalised the connection.

A complicated society was forming where people's life experiences were advantaged or disadvantaged by racial identity constructions and also by enslaved or "free" status. This was a society where, peculiarly, people were separated into socially constructed groups; and where 'free" fathers had no legal right to care for or protect their enslaved children. Essentially this was a world where the socially disadvantaged used whatever resources there were at their disposal to survive within these structures and where people were beginning to form groups along the lines of their particular ethnic mix. Though they were up against colonial hierarchies, in 1825 the surnames Leeuwendal, Klein and Pietersen were among those in memorials petitioning for land in Noordhoek and Simon's Town, reinforcing the view that within the Khoe descendant and "Free Black" communities there was a class hierarchy.[95] However, the vast majority of indigenous people were disenfranchised. They were made to carry a pass and in 1825 archival correspondence reflects this through the case of the Khoe man disparagingly described as the "Hottentot named Adriaan Kaffer" who was said to be "in the service of Mr J N Joone" of Poespaskraal farm in Noordhoek. Adriaan was imprisoned in the Simon's Town prison (today's Simon's Town Museum) for "wandering about without a pass."[96]

Cases tried at the Simon's Town Prison

Most of the cases tried at the Simon's Town prison were for the theft of basic foodstuffs, giving an insight into levels of desperation.

The "apprentice Thom" also referred to as "Mr Hurley's slave," was sentenced to be punished for stealing some coffee.[97] The Reverend Sturt sent the "negro" Jan to prison for stealing rice to give to a family living nearby.[98]

---

[95]WCARS, Records of the Magistrate of Simon's Town 1793-1985: 1/SMT 2/5, SMT 10/17 (Letters Received August 1824 to March 1825) Ref. 239.
[96]WCARS, Records of the Magistrate of Simon's Town 1793-1985: 1/SMT 2/5, SMT 10/18 (Letters Received from 22nd April 1825 to 29th December 1825) Ref. 10 (29 April 1825).

Sturt also sent for a constable to take the "Prize Apprentice, Philip" to prison for stealing potatoes.[99] Although Phillip ran away to Cape Town to avoid arrest, he was found and arrested. However, by 3 April 1823 Sturt was eager for the said Phillip to be returned to him, stating in a letter to Somerset "it is by no means my desire to forfeit every benefit of his services."[100]

Hunger was a common theme of life, particularly for people indentured to private individuals like Sturt, so it is not surprising that they were reduced to stealing food to assuage their hunger or to help family and friends who were faced with starvation. Sturt's mean-spiritedness and lack of Christian charity is glaringly apparent.

There were also many cases of "desertion." "Patientie, Apprentice, in the service of Pierre Rocher and Afrika Hottentot in the service of I Jones" were among a number of people who were either enslaved, indigenous or described as "apprentices, who were jailed for desertion" before being returned to the households that they so desperately wished to escape from.[101]

Punishments were also meted out at the whim of "slave-holders" and Reverend Sturt was one of the Simon's Town residents who cruelly—and often—took advantage of this system. Sentences were set by the magistrate and punishments carried out by the "Black constable Absolom."[102]

---

[97] WCARS, Records of the Magistrate of Simon's Town 1793-1985: 1/SMT 2/5, SMT 10/14 (Inkomende briewe 1822) Simon's Town, Ref. 132 (6 December 1822).

[98] WCARS, Records of the Magistrate of Simon's Town 1793-1985: 1/SMT 2/5, SMT 10/15 (Inkomende briewe 1823) Simon's Town, Ref. 3 (2 January 1823).

[99] WCARS, Records of the Magistrate of Simon's Town 1793-1985: 1/SMT 2/5, SMT 10/15 (Inkomende briewe 1823) Simon's Town, Ref. 12 (12 February 1823).

[100] WCARS, Records of the Magistrate of Simon's Town 1793-1985: 1/SMT 2/5, SMT 10/15 (Inkomende briewe 1823) Simon's Town, Ref. 12 (12 February 1823).

[101] WCARS, Records of the Magistrate of Simon's Town 1793-1985: 1/SMT 2/5, SMT 10/14 (Inkomende briewe 1822) Simon's Town, Ref. 23 (22 April 1822).

[102] WCARS, Records of the Magistrate of Simon's Town 1793-1985: 1/SMT 2/5, SMT 10/21 (Letters Received from December 1827 to December 1830) Ref. 197 (27 July 1830).

The Koue Bokkeveld uprising led by Galant and its impact in Simon's Town

On 12 January 1825 a letter arrived at the Simon's Town Magistrates office penned by Daniel Denyssen, respecting "the murder committed on Koue Bokke Field."[103] A further letter from the Landdrost's Office in Worcester dated 8 February 1825 read as follows:

> I have the painful duty to report for the information of His Excellency The Governor, that a conspiracy has been formed among the Slaves & Hottentots of Barend and Willem van der Merwe in the Veldcornetcy of W F du Toit voorste omtrek van Koude Bokkeveld which had for its object the destruction of the white population and before the plot was discovered the Conspirators succeeded in murdering Willem N[icolaas] van der Merwe, Johannes H T van Rensburg & Johannes [Martinus] Verlee all at the place of the above ...[104]

On 22 February 1825 Sir Richard Plaskett sent further correspondence to Simon's Town on the matter, speaking of the "most lamentable atrocity which has been committed in the Bokkeveld."[105] The Koue Bokkeveld uprising and murders sent a wave of fear amongst the colonial authorities and inhabitants. Sir Richard Plaskett was keen to avoid panic and in a letter to the Government Resident in Simon's Town stated that he had

> not the slightest cause to believe that there is any disaffection generally amongst the Slaves of the Colony, and that He considers the expressing such apprehension might lead to serious evil.

---

[103] WCARS, Records of the Magistrate of Simon's Town 1793-1985: 1/SMT 2/5, SMT 10/17 (Letters Received August 1824 to March 1825) Ref. 23 (12 January 1825).

[104] WCARS, Records of the Magistrate of Simon's Town 1793-1985: 1/SMT 2/5, SMT 10/17 (Letters Received August 1824 to March 1825) Ref. 235 (14 February 1825).

[105] WCARS, Records of the Magistrate of Simon's Town 1793-1985: 1/SMT 2/5, SMT 10/17 (Letters Received August 1824 to March 1825) Ref. 243 (22 February 1825).

Certainly he was concerned about vigilante action. However, he went on to say that he considered

> it advisable to call upon you to be extremely vigilant of the Black Population in your Residency, avoiding however, most carefully the creating the slightest alarm or distrust.[106]

Certainly the Koue Bokkeveld set the tone for introspection by the colonial authorities to ask themselves the pertinent question: "How are we treating these people? Do we have reason to be afraid?" This set in motion an initiative by the colonial authorities to communicate with enslaved people themselves, albeit indirectly. On 25 April 1825 P Wikboom and I P de Wet were tasked with going from house to house to explain the Proclamation of 18 March 1823 to enslaved people, "in front of two credible witnesses."[107]

The following day Peter Jacob Arendze Raven, wardmaster to John F Goodwin, Secretary to the Residency Simon's Town, confirmed that he had also duly explained the Proclamation of 18 March 1823 to the "slave" population.[108] On 4 May 1825 James Bailey Field Cornet, District Wildschutsbrand to Major J B Blake, Olaphantsbosch [sic] sent a similar message of confirmation.[109]

The blasé attitude by "slave-holders" to the deaths of enslaved people is also hinted at in correspondence from Sir Richard Plaskett who ordered the Government Resident of Simon's Town to inform "slave-holders" that remission of fines for non-disclosure of "slave" deaths would no longer be entertained. The Government Resident was ordered to ensure

---

[106] WCARS, Records of the Magistrate of Simon's Town 1793-1985: 1/SMT 2/5, SMT 10/17 (Letters Received August 1824 to March 1825) Ref. 243 (22 February 1825).

[107] WCARS, Records of the Magistrate of Simon's Town 1793-1985: 1/SMT 2/5, SMT 10/18 (Letters Received from 22nd April 1825 to 29th December 1825) Ref. 3 (27 April 1825).

[108] WCARS, Records of the Magistrate of Simon's Town 1793-1985: 1/SMT 2/5, SMT 10/18 (Letters Received from 22nd April 1825 to 29th December 1825) Ref. 4 (28 April 1825).

[109] WCARS, Records of the Magistrate of Simon's Town 1793-1985: 1/SMT 2/5, SMT 10/18 (Letters Received from 22nd April 1825 to 29th December 1825) Ref. 5 (4 May 1825).

that instructions be given to all the Field Cornets to explain to the proprietors of Slaves in their Fieldcornetcies the nature of the Proclamation 30 January 1818 and at the same time to inform them that after the date of such Explanation being made to them, His Excellency will not allow the remission of any such fine in case of future neglect.[110]

The colonial authorities also felt it pertinent to ensure that enslaved people were aware of their rights within this system of law and, on 1 October 1825, P Hugo wrote to Lieutenant Colonel Blake, the Government Resident in Simon's Town, stating

I beg leave to inform you that I have distinctly explained to the slave population in my district the nature of His Excellency the Governor's Proclamation dated the 30th January 1818, as directed by your letter dated 27th September 1825.[111]

The Government Resident of Simon's Town was requested to institute an annual census report of all births and deaths in Simon's Town from 1824, distinguishing the white and the *Free Black* as *"coloured"*[112] from the "slave" population and also the sexes.[113]

On 14 October 1825, under order of his superiors, the Governor Resident of Simon's Town began a series of visits to interview enslaved people who fell within his area of control. The purpose was to enquire as to their treatment by their "slave-holders." The farms visited were Silvermine [Zilvermyn], Noordhoek, Slangkop and Poespaskraal.[114] Certainly it was wishful thinking to presume that socially vulnerable people would risk the obvious backlash of "slave-holders" by complaining. In any event the concerns of the

---

[110]WCARS, Records of the Magistrate of Simon's Town 1793-1985: 1/SMT 2/5, SMT 10/18 (Letters Received from 22nd April 1825 to 29th December 1825) Ref. 85 (20 September 1825).
[111]WCARS, Records of the Magistrate of Simon's Town 1793-1985: 1/SMT 2/5, SMT 10/18 (Letters Received from 22nd April 1825 to 29th December 1825) Ref. 99 (1 October 1825).
[112]Author's emphasis.
[113]WCARS, Records of the Magistrate of Simon's Town 1793-1985: 1/SMT 2/5, SMT 10/18 (Letters Received from 22nd April 1825 to 29th December 1825) Ref. 86 (21 September 1825).

colonial authorities were rudimentary, questioning whether they had clothes to wear and food to eat. Unsurprisingly, few complained. However, at Noordhoek where the Governor Resident interviewed a huge contingent of Javanese people, there were three children without clothes.[115] At Slangkop (owned by Pierre Rocher), an unnamed person described as a "Freeblack" complained of ill-treatment and having been flogged. He was nevertheless left in a precarious position when his peers failed—were too afraid?—to corroborate his story.[116]

Archival records reveal another complaint of ill-treatment levelled against Pierre Rocher in 1835, by the "apprentice" named Jack.[117] At Poespaskraal where people described as "4 hired men slaves—a female Hottentot"[118] were interviewed, they were said to have no complaints.

Ordinance 19 of 1926

On 19 June 1826, Ordinance 19 came into effect. Through this ordinance the "Inspector of the Registry was appointed Registrar and Guardian of Slaves." Central to this law was the "propagation of Christianity, and the general diffusion of religious instruction amongst slaves." Ordinance 19 made lavish provision for the amelioration of the condition of enslaved peo-

---

[114]It is rumoured that J N Joone (probably Johan Nicolaas Josephus Joone) was murdered by an enslaved man at Poespaskraal, with the aforementioned enslaved person then hanging himself in the kitchen of this homestead. Personal communication with the current owner of Poespaskraal (April 2016).

[115]WCARS, Records of the Magistrate of Simon's Town 1793-1985: 1/SMT 2/5, SMT 10/18 (Letters Received from 22nd April 1825 to 29th December 1825), Loose page with other pages of data concerning Report of the Government Resident's visit to post of the Field Cornetcy of Noordhoek (14 October 1825).

[116]WCARS, Records of the Magistrate of Simon's Town 1793-1985: 1/SMT 2/5, SMT 10/18 (Letters Received from 22nd April 1825 to 29th December 1825), Loose page with other pages of data concerning Report of the Government Resident's visit to post of the Field Cornetcy of Noordhoek (14 October 1825).

[117]WCARS, Records of the Magistrate of Simon's Town 1793-1985: 1/SMT 2/5, SMT 10/23 (1835) Ref. 10.

[118]WCARS, Records of the Magistrate of Simon's Town 1793-1985: 1/SMT 2/5, SMT 10/18 (Letters Received from 22nd April 1825 to 29th December 1825), Loose page with other pages of data concerning Report of the Government Resident's visit to post of the Field Cornetcy of Noordhoek (14 October 1825).

ple and the registrars in the various districts were now styled "Assistant Registrars and Guardians of Slaves."[119]

In line with the thinking *"how are we treating these people and do we have reason to be afraid?"* Sir Richard Plaskett requested the Government Resident of Simon's Town to supply him with information on "the nature and description of the several instruments used in the prison of your district, for flogging in prison, or for public scourging."[120]

Fig. 6-5. Cottage and mosque in Simon's Town, circa 1902
Source: Pastel by George Salisbury Smithard, Library of Parliament, 285

---

[119]WCARS, Records of the Magistrate of Simon's Town 1793-1985: 1/SMT 2/5, SMT 10/17 (Letters Received August 1824 to March 1825) Ref. 191 (17 December 1824).
[120]WCARS, Inventory, Slave Office, SO 1/21, page 3 (19 June 1826).

As part of the new Amelioration laws in 1826 compulsory manumissions were instituted, which allowed enslaved people to buy their freedom without the consent of the "slave-holder." Opportunities for compulsory manumission benefited mostly Asian males who had skills that were sought after within the British colonial society at the Cape.

Two Men from Mozambique

Evidence of clandestine "slave-trading" comes through in the case of two men from Mozambique. In 1826, Major George Jackman Rogers, the "Registrar of Slaves," wrote to the "Assistant Registrar of Slaves" about a case that was linked to Alexander Tennant, which was brought about by two "slaves" who asserted their right to freedom as "prize negroes."

A man named Present was initially recorded in the British Colonial "Slave Register" on 12 November 1816, as a "slave" of Pieter Francis Hugo, with his occupation listed as labourer. Lendor was registered on 26 February 1825 as the jointly-owned "slave" of Pieter Francis Hugo and Pieter Wikboom. Lendor was listed as a baker.[121]

Present's Claim

On Saturday 4 November 1826, the man named Present, described as a "boy" in colonial records, presented himself to the Landdrost of Stellenbosch claiming his freedom on the grounds of being a "prize negro." In his statement he said that he arrived at the colony as a child and that his birth name was Sima. Although he could not remember the name of the ship that he was landed on, he clearly recalled that the ship's captain was Captain Mosinti.

He related how he was sent to Tennant, from whose hands he was passed on to "old Mr Rossouw of Simon's Town." On the death of Rossouw he was sold as a "slave" by Rossouw's son Frans, to Pieter Hugo (also of Simon's Town) where he laboured for a further ten years before being re-purchased by Frans Rossouw (by then living in Banhoek) in 1823. Significantly, he mentioned the names of two other "prize negroes" who were brought on the

---

[121] WCARS, CAD, SO 6/78, folio number 4, 12 November 1816 and folio number 5 (26 February 1825).

same ship with him, these being "the slave Lendor belonging to Hugo Wikboom of Simon's Town" and "the boy James who was in the service of Mr Moore, a baker at Wynberg," the latter having obtained his freedom some five years previously.[122]

Lendor's Claim

Lendor's claim was lodged with the "Registrar of Slaves" in Cape Town on 13 November 1826. He claimed that he was "formerly a prize slave of Tennant" and claimed his freedom on the basis of being "illegally detained as a slave." Lendor identified a number of people who were on the same vessel as himself and who were free, such as "the boys Africa, Camiella and Apollos, living he believes in Cape Town" as well as "James of Mr Moore and April of Mr Dury, both of Simon's Town."[123]

Whatever hopes Present and Lendor had of an imminent release from bondage were dashed as the wheels of justice ground slowly for them. In an inversion of justice, they were kept in the prison cells while the matter was being investigated. On 26 December 1826, Christiaan Michiel Lind, the "Registrar of Slaves" in Simon's Town, seemed to be at a loss as to how to proceed with the matter, when he wrote to Major Rogers, the "Registrar of Slaves" in Cape Town, stating: "Having perused the 25 Ordinance, I find nothing by which I might be guided [by] in such cases."[124] Rogers in response wrote back saying that until the matter was resolved the men should be returned to the service of their respective owners, adding further:

> I cannot possibly state the period at which I may have it in my favour to bring the case forward and you will therefore endeavour to *impress upon the minds of the slaves*[125] the necessity of their conducting themselves obediently with propriety until such period, and to assure them that

---

[122]WCARS, Slave Office, SO 1/23 Slave Registry Department, Extract from the Day Book of the Landdrost of Stellenbosch (Saturday, 4 November 1826).

[123]WCARS, Slave Office, SO 1/23, Slave Registry Department, Extract from the Day Book of the Guardian of Slaves (13 November 1826); signed by George Jackman Rogers.

[124]WCARS, Slave Office, SO 1/23, Slave Registry Department, Correspondence, Lind to Rogers (26 December 1826).

[125]Author's emphasis.

everything will be done which their case may be found to merit.[126]

These statements held little comfort to these two men who had to return to the homes of the people they were seeking to be liberated from.

Maintaining Marriages During Indentureships

Even though the law held that there should be no impediment to marriage for people indentured as "prize negroes,"[127] for those who were indentured to private individuals, maintaining marriages was fraught with difficulty and dependant on the goodwill of those to whom they were indentured.

Any concessions given could be withdrawn at any time, as was the case with Rosana who was indentured to Henry Dray of Castle Street in Cape Town, whose wife had given Rosana "permission" to live with her husband in Simon's Town "until her services should again be required." With four years of her indentureship still outstanding, Henry Dray requested her return. When Rosana refused to leave her husband and home in Simon's Town, Dray contacted the police to have her removed from her husband and returned to the Dray household.

In another case John Williams of Simon's Town petitioned the colonial government as he was apparently prevented by a Mr Miller of Simon's Town from having any communication with his wife, described as a "negro" in the service of Miller.[128]

The woman Saartje described as a "Prize Negro"

Whether Saartje arrived in Simon's Town with her husband or whether they met and married in Simon's Town is unknown, although the latter is likely as by the time the pregnant Saartje was indentured to Frans Becker

---

[126]WCARS, SO 2/16 Letters Despatched by Slave Registry Office Simonstown 1822-1826 (26 December 1826).

[127]WCARS, Records of the Magistrate of Simon's Town 1793-1985: 1/SMT 2/5, SMT 10/17 (Letters Received August 1824 to March 1825) Ref. 191 (17 December 1824).

[128]WCARS, Records of the Magistrate of Simon's Town 1793-1985: 1/SMT 2/5, SMT 10/17 (Letters Received August 1824 to March 1825) Ref. 191 (17 December 1824).

and his wife in Wittebome, Saartje's husband was no longer indentured and was described as "an inhabitant of Simon's Town."[129]

By Becker's own admission, Saartje had run away from the Becker household after his wife had slapped Saartje across the face. This he said was necessary to "keep her at home in future."[130]

A glimpse into Saartje's trauma emerges through three letters penned by Frans Becker and addressed to J F Goodwin Esq, Secretary to The Residency of Simon's Town. The first was dated 10 February 1825, a week after Saartje ran away. In this letter Becker stated:

> I beg leave to inform you that a prize negress of mine named Saartje absconded on the 3rd of this month, & I suppose is with her husband Joseph Brown in Simon's Town. If this should prove to be the case as Mrs Becker is much in want of the Girl for a nurse, I beg you will be good enough to send her to me by the bearer accompanied by a constable & oblige.[131]

From a second letter dated 15 February 1825 it emerges that Saartje had given birth prematurely. Deflecting any blame that her stressful unpaid work environment may have been responsible for her premature delivery, Becker asserted: "I believe the Prize Negress who is the subject of this correspondence to be highly capable of practising such an imposition." To back his statement he accused Saartje of being a "troublesome character" who conducted herself with "insolence and violence."

Certainly Becker should have asked himself whether the staff at the magistrate's office would not have questioned why he would want such a "troublesome character" to nurse his wife. However, this seemed lost on Becker

---

[129]WCARS, Records of the Magistrate of Simon's Town 1793-1985: 1/SMT 2/5 SMT 10/17 (Letters Received August 1824 to March 1825) Ref. 242 (18 February 1825).

[130]WCARS, Records of the Magistrate of Simon's Town 1793 – 1985: 1/SMT 2/5, SMT 10/17 (Letters Received August 1824 to March 1825) Ref. 237 (15 February 1825).

[131]WCARS, Records of the Magistrate of Simon's Town 1793-1985: 1/SMT 2/5, SMT 10/17 (Letters Received August 1824 to March 1825) Ref. 232 (10 February 1825).

whose sole concern was to have a postnatal Saartje return from Simon's Town to Wittebome by foot, saying "I hope she may be by this time so far recovered to be able to follow the Boy I have sent for her."[132]

On 18 February 1825, the same day that a request for the arrest of Joseph Mashoshy (who may well have been Joseph Brown) was refused, a final letter arrived at the Simon's Town Magistrate's Office from Frans Becker. In this letter he refuted his earlier claim that Joseph Brown was Saartje's husband, stating instead that Saartje was being "illegally detained by a person of the name of Joseph Brown an inhabitant of Simon's Town."[133] Through this correspondence he requests that Saartje be "forwarded to the Landdrost of the Cape District," adding arrogantly:

> I do not understand how any cognizance can be taken at the Residency of Simon's Town of a crime said to have been committed by me in the Cape District: the worshipful Court of Justice as the Board of Landdrost & Heemraden being my competent judges.[134]

With this final letter Saartje disappears from the records, a life captured through three letters, which leaves so many questions unanswered. Experiences such as these are very likely to have induced separation anxiety, a form of trauma known to impact on mental well-being.

Abdol Gaviel: a Religious Leader—an Enslaved Man

Abdol Gaviel was a notable resident of Simon's Town and his presence and status was twofold. To the colonial residents it was his talent as a highly skilled carpenter whose practised eye and craftsmanship created masterpieces out of pieces of wood. However, to the residents of the "Malay Quarter" and enslaved people in and around Simon's Town, he was first and foremost their

---

[132]There is evidence in the literature of premature births among "slave" women in consequence of the brutality of enslavement, for example, see *The Anti-Slavery Reporter and Aborigines' Friend* 2, 20 (2 August 1847): 119.

[133]WCARS, Records of the Magistrate of Simon's Town 1793-1985: 1/SMT 2/5, SMT 10/17 (Letters Received August 1824 to March 1825) Ref. 237 (15 February 1825).

[134]WCARS, Records of the Magistrate of Simon's Town 1793-1985: 1/SMT 2/5 SMT 10/17 (Letters Received August 1824 to March 1825) Ref. 242 (18 February 1825).

Imam. Abdol Gaviel's role in his community encompassed that of teacher, spiritual leader and carer.

Through his teaching this familiar figure, who resided up the cobbled lanes of the Alfred Lane area of Simon's Town, was engraving the presence of Islam on the landscape at this time. Despite his standing in the community, he was also an enslaved person. However, as already mentioned, there was a "hiring out" system that benefited mostly skilled Asian enslaved men who were allowed to live separately and hire out their services on the condition that the "slave-owner" received the lion's share of their income, and Abdol Gaviel was a beneficiary of this system.

Abdol Gaviel's life was entirely enmeshed in the powerful Rossouw family, and, although the relationship was that of "slave-holder" and "slave," it appears that he received preferential treatment. By 1822 he had rented a cottage in the "Malay Quarter" in Simon's Bay from Susanna de Necker (the widow of Gideon Rossouw, mother of Margaretha Johanna Rossouw who was the wife of John Osmond).[135]

His neighbours in the Malay Quarter area included Oude Betje, Manual, Marie, Wary, Sam Evans, Gert, Thomas and Maniesa from Batavia, Manuel Joseph & January, Carolus, Marie, Rejap van de Kaap and Lendor from Bengal[136] who occupied cottages in Thomas Street, Hospital Lane and Wikboom Lane.[137]

In 1823 Abdol Gaviel led a memorial that was sent to the British Colonial authorities by a delegation of Muslim people.

The memorial formally requested that a piece of land that had long been used for the interment of members of their faith be officially recognised as the Muslim burial ground. The cosmopolitan nature of the Muslim community in Simon's Town is evident by the origins listed in the memorial signed as follows:

---

[135] Cape Transcripts, MOOC 8/45, 92, Will of Johanna Susanna de Necker (9 May 1828).

[136] Cape Transcripts, MOOC8/45, 92, Will of Johanna Susanna de Necker (9 May 1828).

[137] Merle Muller, Aspects of Social Composition of Twelve Malay Households in Simonstown. Thesis (Social Anthropology Hons), University of Cape Town, September 1969, 1.

Abdol Gaviel (Priest/Slave), Thomas and Maniesa from Batavia; Manuel Joseph & January, Carolus, Marie, Rejap van de Kaap & Lendor from Bengal, the first a slave and the latter a free black.[138]

Fig. 6-6. The Malay Quarter, Simon's Town
Source: Pastel by George Salisbury Smithard, Library of Parliament, 6940, 4, vi

The Callous Clergyman

On 4 May 1822 the Reverend George Sturt wrote to John Goodwin at the Magistrates Office in Simon's Town, requesting punishments for two people. His letter reads as follows:

> Upon consulting Mrs Sturt; she really thinks as it is not the first time that the boy were in the prison has been guilty of

---
[138]WCARS, Records of the Magistrate of Simon's Town 1793-1985: 1/SMT 2/5, SMT 10/14 (Inkomende briewe 1822) Simon's Town, Ref. 129 (4 December 1822).

quitting my home at night; he deserves a small punishment. I shall therefore have to ask you to order him one dozen, as a taster; it may prove most beneficial.

The girl as an old offender; and I believe was pardoned and about 2 dozen or 30 stripes will do her some good. After the punishment you will have the kindness to confine them on Prison allowance till the following morning, when they may be sent home.[139]

In addition to benefiting from the free labour of vulnerable people in this way, Sturt also derived an income through an informal arrangement with a fisherman named Manuel from the "Malay Quarter," who used Sturt's boat for an undisclosed fee.[140] However, after some time Manuel obtained his own boat, which prompted Sturt to inform the local authorities of Simon's Town in 1822 that he had "nothing further to do with "Manuel the Malay."[141]

Sturt also took into his service two impoverished young British women named Fanny and Mary Bray who had arrived at the Cape on the *Brilliant* on 9 May 1820. In a similar vein to the way he treated the people whose labour he benefited from through the "prize negro" indenture system, Sturt complained to the Acting Government Resident of Simon's Town on 6 April 1822 about Fanny Bray. In his letter he complained about her "insolence and carelessness," requesting that she be "summonsed to appear before the Government Resident."[142]

---

[139]WCARS, Records of the Magistrate of Simon's Town 1793-1985: 1/SMT 2/5, SMT 10/14 (Inkomende briewe 1822) Simon's Town, Ref. 28 (4 May 1822).

[140]WCARS, Records of the Magistrate of Simon's Town 1793-1985: 1/SMT 2/5 (14 November 1822). SMT 10/14 (Inkomende briewe 1822) Simon's Town, Ref. 121.

[141]WCARS, Records of the Magistrate of Simon's Town 1793-1985: 1/SMT 2/5 (1 March 1824); SMT 10/16 (Inkomende briewe 1824) Simon's Town, Ref. 40 (1 March 1824).

[142]WCARS, Records of the Magistrate of Simon's Town 1793-1985: 1/SMT 2/5, SMT 10/14 (Inkomende briewe 1822) Simon's Town. These details are recorded at the back of this file, but with no reference number. The details are also not listed in the index.

For all the free labour that Sturt benefited from through the system of colonial rule, he was not a good manager of money and his life was constantly plagued by debt. He tried to offset these circumstances in ways that were particularly mean.

George Watson of Simon's Town complained that although Sturt was too ill to perform a full church ceremony for Watson's marriage to Mary Bray on 22 July 1823, he nonetheless retained the full fee of twenty Rix dollars for a church wedding. Watson was particularly put out that after his complaint, Sturt had only refunded him five Rix dollars even though he had to go to Sturt's home for the marriage to be performed. He was further vexed that Sturt refused to issue a marriage certificate without a further payment of four Rix dollars![143]

Hendryn

After having benefited from the indentureship system from the time of his arrival at the Cape in 1824, Reverend Sturt made his first and only purchase of an enslaved person. Her name was Hendryn. The transfer of Hendryn, a young woman aged twenty-nine, from Major Matthew George Blake to Sturt, shows how she was used as a pawn in so many ways. On 30 October 1824 Hendryn, described as a housemaid, was sold for an undisclosed amount by Major Blake to George Sturt. Both men lacked astuteness in financial management, hence the fact that Hendryn was registered in the name of Maria Carolina Blake, Minor Daughter of Major Blake. In this way she could not be attached in the event that Blake became sequestrated. In a similar vein Hendryn as a "slave" was transferred to "Mary Elisa Sturt, the minor daughter under the Guardianship of her Father the Rev. George William Sturt." In a fantastic manoeuvre, which raises questions about inside connections, on the same day that Hendryn was transferred to Mary Elisa Sturt, she was mortgaged "by Bond of 30th October 1824 before the Directors of the Government Discount Bank for seven thousand two hundred guilders 7200 in favour of said Bank for which a certificate was granted on the 2nd instant."[144]

---

[143]WCARS, Records of the Magistrate of Simon's Town 1793-1985: 1/SMT 2/5, SMT 10/17 (Letters Received August 1824 to March 1825) Ref. 117 (17 August 1824).

Clearly, as a man of the cloth, Sturt had a certain degree of clout which he used unashamedly. When Christiaan Michiel Lind, the "Registrar of Slaves" in Simon's Town, was admonished in a letter from the "Slave Registry Department" for omitting details of Sturt's transaction in terms of Hendryn,[145] Lind apologised for having "erred in supposing that I was to wait for Mr Sturt's communication."[146] The transfer of Hendryn seems to have caused some discomfort with Smith of the "Slave Registry Department" as he further admonished Lind in a letter dated 10 December 1824, for not having reported "the transfer of Hendryn to Miss Sturt." There were also questions about certificates issued, with Smith asking Lind to "state the authority under which such entry was made in his books."[147]

Juxtaposed between the enslaved people and the people described as "prize negroes" were those people who were either completely or partly descended from the indigenous hunter-gatherer and herder societies. The 1826 *Opgaafrolle* (census) for people residing in the area records 135 indigenous Khoe people working on farms in Noordhoek and a total of 118 indigenous Khoe people in Simon's Town.

In understanding the challenges imposed on the lives of indigenous people during the time of British colonial rule, we need to consider how their freedom of movement was severely curtailed through the Caledon Code of 1 November 1809, the brainchild of the Earl of Caledon, as indigenous people were required to have a fixed place of abode or be charged with vagrancy. It is through this legislation that we have to understand the following correspondence to the Simon's Town magistrate, which stated:

> The Hottentot woman Elsje Jeptha, who hired herself by legal contract to Mr W [?U] Dempers on the 26th of March last for one year, absented herself from her Masters service some time ago and as she is now in the employ of

---

[144]WCARS, Slave Office, SO 2/6, Slave Registry Dept Correspondence (5 November 1824).

[145]WCARS, CAD SO 2/16 Slave Registry Dept Correspondence (3 December 1824).

[146]WCARS, CAD SO 2/16 Slave Registry Office Correspondence (6 December 1824).

[147]WCARS, CAD SO 2/16 Slave Registry Dept Correspondence (10 December 1824).

Mr J Hurter, I request that she may be apprehended and sent to the prison at the Three Cups.[148]

In accordance with the Caledon Code, Elsje Jeptha was bound to her employment contract with Dempers for a year. Whether Elsje was literate, whether she understood the contract and whether she was ill-treated in this household, are all open to conjecture. However, the freedom to choose to move from one employment situation to another was taken away from her through a complicated set of legislation that she may or may not have not understood. Her very decision to change jobs rendered her a criminal.

The Caledon Code of 1809, followed by the Apprenticeship Law of 1812, created a system through which children of indigenous hunter-gatherer and herding societies, referred to by the colonial authorities as "Bushmen" and "Hottentots," were drawn into a net of enforced labour on the farms for ten years, commencing at the age of eight.[149]

The Vulnerability of Indigenous "San" and Khoe Children

The ramifications of these colonial systems reverberated through the indigenous community of Simon's Town in a multitude of ways. When the boy child named "Hottentot Gerrit" ran away after being taken to work for the farmer Dirk van Renen Jacob Zoon, his mother was not able to protect him as according to the authorities "the consent of his mother was not necessary."[150] In another incident an eleven year old Khoe boy child named Valentyn was forcibly removed at the behest of Major Blake, the Colonial Resident of Simon's Town, from the home of his Aunt Caatjie, "under whose protection he had been left." In the memorial of "Caatjie Hottentot woman" it transpires that Major Blake requested her permission to retain the service of eleven year old Valentyn for a period of three years, a request she refused. Using his position of power, Major Blake then sent a police constable to her home to fetch her nephew, stating that Valentyn was compelled to enter his

---

[148]WCARS, Records of the Magistrate of Simon's Town 1793-1985: 1/SMT 2/5, SMT 10/17 (Letters Received August 1824 to March 1825) Ref. 197 (22 December 1824).

[149]Wayne Dooling, "The Origins and Aftermath of the Cape Colony's 'Hottentot Code of 1809'" *Kronos* 31 (November 2005): 50.

[150]WCARS, Records of the Magistrate of Simon's Town 1793-1985: 1/SMT 2/5 (Letters received, 1793-1932), 1/SMT 10/9, Ref. 221 (16 December 1817).

service. However, the little boy (who was described as having "a strong repugnance in the first instance to enter Major Blake's service") ran back to his aunt's home. Though not literate, Caatjie petitioned the office of Sir Richard Plaskett, colonial secretary of the Cape about the illegal arrest of her nephew in a bid to protect him. Her memorial is signed with an X followed by the words "Cross of Caatje, Hottentot Woman."[151]

When Plaskett contacted Blake his tone was placatory. In his initial contact he stated:

> you would have acted more wisely had you not authorised the Undersheriff & Constable to interfere in the business & without raising any question as to the propriety of the Woman's conduct or her right to complain or to apprentice her Nephew it is in the Governor's opinion most advisable that a public officer of your rank should not avail yourself of such a Contract, if the Parents desire it should be annulled.[152]

Blake was nevertheless not put under any direct pressure to release Valentyn to his family. In the last correspondence on the matter dated 15 February 1827, Plaskett stated "The Lieutenant Governor has no doubt you will agree with Him as to the propriety of His former recommendation to you of parting with the Boy."[153] The terminology used was asking Blake to do the right thing, but not compelling him to do so.

In that same year Plaskett addressed a further complaint to Blake, that of Jannetjie Brand complaining "that her son has been forced to live with other persons against her will and praying for redress."[154] In all these cases, these

---

[151]WCARS, Colonial Office, Memorials (1827), CO 3933, Ref. 6 (2 January 1827).

[152]WCARS, Records of the Magistrate of Simon's Town 1793-1985: 1/SMT 2/5, SMT 10/20 (Letters Received from 4 October 1826 to December 1827) Ref. 99 (8 February 1827).

[153]WCARS, Records of the Magistrate of Simon's Town 1793-1985: 1/SMT 2/5, SMT 10/20 (Letters Received from 4 October 1826 to December 1827) Ref. 112 (17 February 1827).

[154]WCARS, Records of the Magistrate of Simon's Town 1793-1985: 1/SMT 2/5, SMT 10/17 (Letters Received August 1824 to March 1825) Ref. 234 (12 January 1825).

strong "Ausi" women challenged the system in order to protect the children.[155] However, they were not always successful.

A photo of a Khoe girl child discovered during archival research tells a thousand stories of trauma. In the photo the little girl is made to pose wearing a long skirt, but no clothing from her waist upwards. The expression on the little girl's face suggests that she is awkward, confused and ashamed as she stares into the distance. She is made to pose both facing the camera and then posing to the side, as if in a mug-shot. The child is described as having being left by her parents with "Mr Huskisson of Noordhoek." The truth of this statement is debatable, as well as the truth of who decided on her name. She was disparagingly named "Nappy," which in South Africa is a diaper, something that holds a baby's excrement. Out of respect for this little girl, the photograph is not reproduced here.[156]

"Your Boy is in the Tronk!'"

Reverend Sturt increasingly showed himself to be malicious, particularly towards people who lacked social power. On 8 January 1825 he ordered that a man indentured to Colonel Scott as a "prize negro" be put in jail for chopping some wood apparently on the premises of the firm of Sinclair and Murdock. He proceeded to write to Scott informing him "your boy is in the tronk." Barely skipping a beat, in the same letter he goes on to say

> Mr de Wet appears to take no note of the fine you informed me was levied upon him. I beg to acquaint you that forty-eight sheep were trespassing yesterday and that you will immediately summon him to appear before the Government Resident.[157]

However, in the ensuing weeks Sturt may have had more serious matters to consider. While occupied with repairs to the parsonage,[158] Sturt received the

---

[155] June Bam offers wonderful insights into the indigenous "Ausi" women. They were the carers, the knowledge-holders. See June Bam, *Ausi Told Me: Why Cape Herstoriographies Matter* (Auckland Park: Jacana Media, 2021).

[156] WCARS, Elliot Collection, Ref. E.3271.

[157] WCARS, Records of the Magistrate of Simon's Town 1793-1985: 1/SMT 2/5, SMT 10/17 (Letters Received August 1824 to March 1825) Ref. 210 and Ref. 211 (8 January 1825).

news of the uprising of enslaved people led by Galant, which had started with the murder of farmers in the Koue Bokkeveld area.[159] This news was received via a circular reporting the "conspiracy against the whites."[160] A major concern for the Governor was calming the seas of further uprisings; a fear that the Bokkeveld Uprising brought to light in the most sensational way. To this end a survey was undertaken to examine the state of the black population."[161]

Included in the survey was Hendryn and the people identified as "prize negroes" indentured to Sturt. On 18 October 1825 they were assembled at Rocklands farm and listed as "one female slave and the prize slaves." While for the most part they were fearful of complaining, Phillip bravely spoke out about the fear induced by the constant threats of violence from Sturt.[162] Complaining about ill-treatment was courageous as the complainant ran the risk of being flogged. A major indicator of the threat of violence was when people ran away. It is therefore no coincidence that just two months after Phillip's complaint to the Heemraad, a man described by Sturt as "the prize boy Sunday," ran away from Rocklands Farm.[163]

Through the "prize negro indentureship system" Sturt benefited from the free labour of people who were each "apprenticed" to him for a period of

---

[158]WCARS, Records of the Magistrate of Simon's Town 1793-1985: 1/SMT 2/5 SMT 10/18 (Letters Received from 22nd April 1825 to 29th December 1825) Ref. 30 (1 July 1825).

[159]WCARS, Records of the Magistrate of Simon's Town 1793-1985: 1/SMT 2/5, SMT 10/17 (Letters Received August 1824 to March 1825) Ref. 23 (12 January 1825).

[160]WCARS, Records of the Magistrate of Simon's Town 1793-1985: 1/SMT 2/5, SMT 10/17 (Letters Received August 1824 to March 1825) Ref. 235 (14 February 1825).

[161]WCARS, Records of the Magistrate of Simon's Town 1793-1985: 1/SMT 2/5, SMT 10/18 (Letters Received from 22 April 1825 to 29 December 1825), Report of the Commission of Heemraad on the visit to the Field Cornetcy of Wildschutsbrand (18 October 1825) signed by J Hurter, Heemraad (18 October 1825).

[162]WCARS, Records of the Magistrate of Simon's Town 1793-1985: 1/SMT 2/5, SMT 10/18 (Letters Received from 22 April 1825 to 29 December 1825), Report of the Commission of Heemraad on the visit to the Field Cornetcy of Wildschutsbrand (18 October 1825) signed by J Hurter, Heemraad (18 October 1825).

[163]WCARS, Records of the Magistrate of Simon's Town 1793-1985: 1/SMT 2/5; SMT 10/19 (Letters Received from 3 January 1826 to 30 August 1826 & September) Ref. 8 (11 January 1826).

fourteen years without any financial compensation. By 1826 Sturt had control over six people described as "prize negroes"—five men and one woman.[164] They were housed in a small cluster of stone hovels on the Rocklands Farm estate. Sturt exacted control over them all using institutionalised violence in the form of the Simon's Town prison, where they were sent for beatings ordered by Sturt himself.

Some might call it karmic fate and others would say more simply that his bad debt was catching up with him, but by 1826 Sturt's position in the church no longer guaranteed him impunity from his actions. This started with the local baker refusing to supply the Sturt household with bread, telling Sturt's servant that he should go and get it elsewhere.[165] The Government Discount Bank too was also becoming less tolerant of Sturt's financial woes, refusing to honour a cheque drawn by Sturt, stating that his account was "already overdrawn."[166] Caught in a quagmire of debt, he was quick to take up the temporary position of Collector of Customs on the death of Kirsten.[167] Foremost in his mind must have been the exorbitant mortgage he had been allowed to take out on Hendryn. There were also other debts, such as the loan from the Lombard Bank registered in the name of his son, George William Sturt.

At the end of September 1827 Reverend Sturt's entire salary of sixty pounds sterling was paid into the Lombard Bank on account of proportion of Capital and interest due linked to a promissory note for £16.18.9¾.[168] However, by this time the Lombard Bank had already begun legal proceedings against Sturt's son, referred to in documents as "GW Sturt, jr."[169] In

---

[164]Reginald Robert Langham-Carter," George Sturt, Colonial Chaplain" *Simon's Town Historical Society Bulletin* 10, 1 (January 1978): 12-17.

[165]WCARS, Records of the Magistrate of Simon's Town 1793-1985: 1/SMT 2/5, SMT 10/19 (Letters Received from 3 January 1826 to 30 August 1826 & September,) Ref. 21 (26 January 1826).

[166]WCARS, Records of the Magistrate of Simon's Town 1793-1985: 1/SMT 2/5; SMT 10/19 (Letters Received from 3 January 1826 to 30 August 1826 & September) Ref. 121 (23 May 1826).

[167]WCARS, Records of the Magistrate of Simon's Town 1793-1985: 1/SMT 2/5, SMT 10/20 (Letters Received from 4 October 1826 to December 1827) Ref. 8 (11 October 1826).

[168]WCARS, Records of the Magistrate of Simon's Town 1793-1985: 1/SMT 2/5, SMT 10/20 (Letters Received from 4 October 1826 to December 1827) Ref. not numbered but in this file (August 1827).

addition to this, Sturt was having to deal with a lawsuit for money owed, cited in the case of Thomson versus Sturt.[170]

By this time Sturt was becoming more and more isolated from members of his community, with both Wikboom and Leibbrandt, "the privileged bakers of this town," refusing to supply bread for the Sturt family to Sturt's "servant" who, Sturt asserted, "tendered ready money."[171] However, he seemed to have a steady friend in M G Blake and on 28 September 1827, the Discount Bank wrote to Blake stating:

> You are hereby requested to use payment for your 2 acceptances drawn by the Revd Sturt on Mr Sturt Jr amounting to £76.18.9¾ on the 30st Instant on which day it becomes due.[172]

By October 1827 the Discount Bank were calling in two loans, one registered in the name of Reverend George Sturt and another in the name of his son. In correspondence from R Loedolff of the Discount Bank he stated: "Unless the two bills in question are paid forthwith they will be under the necessity of reporting the same to Government."[173]

Word was getting around about Sturt's financial problems, his serial indebtedness and his underhand dealings. On November 1827, he faced further accusations when John Osmond asserted that "Sturt seized 84 prints & caricatures, which were landed from the French ship *Le Fils de France*." He duly requested that these be delivered to their rightful owners.[174]

---

[169] WCARS, Records of the Magistrate of Simon's Town 1793-1985: 1/SMT 2/5, SMT 10/20 (Letters Received from 4 October 1826 to December 1827) Ref. 213 (22 August 1827).

[170] WCARS, Records of the Magistrate of Simon's Town 1793-1985: 1/SMT 2/5, SMT 10/20 (Letters Received from 4 October 1826 to December 1827) Ref. 215 (24 August 1827).

[171] WCARS, Records of the Magistrate of Simon's Town 1793-1985: 1/SMT 2/5, SMT 10/20 (Letters Received from 4 October 1826 to December 1827) Ref. 140 (21 April 1827).

[172] WCARS, Records of the Magistrate of Simon's Town 1793-1985: 1/SMT 2/5, SMT 10/20 (Letters Received from 4 October 1826 to December 1827) Ref. 228 (28 September 1827).

[173] WCARS, Records of the Magistrate of Simon's Town 1793-1985: 1/SMT 2/5, SMT 10/20 (Letters Received from 4 October 1826 to December 1827) Ref. 251 (30 October 1827).

Letitia Clarence

A British woman who deviated from the norm in Simon's Town society—and who was no doubt disliked by Reverend Sturt—was Leticia Clarence who, with her husband, owned the Clarence Hotel (later the British Hotel) in Simon's Town. Leticia was outspoken about the ill-treatment of enslaved people, particularly those indentured as "prize negroes." The close proximity of the mud huts housing Mozambican people taken off "slave" ships to the Clarence Hotel meant that Leticia would have noticed many of the daily events. Leticia Clarence also called out racism and classism in the church when her dark-skinned "maidservant" accompanied her to church, causing an uproar among the congregants. On 2 March 1827 she penned a letter to the minister of the church, which challenged the status quo. In her letter she wrote:

> Mr Clarence and myself both feel particularly obliged by your kind attention in appointing us a seat in the Church, a privilege we have never before had since we have been in this Colony: from circumstances which have transpired since we have occupied the Seat; I regret to observe it is deemed an encroachment, as such we shall decline the Seat in future, and if there is any other part of the Church where Mr Clarence, myself, and our Servant, can be accommodated without intruding ourselves; we shall feel further obliged by your appointing us the same.[175]

People of Khoe ancestry

In 1826, according to the Simon's Town district and Noordhoek census, Arie Kleyn Senior, Joseph Kleyn, Tromp Kleyn and Arie Kleyn Junior owned Wildschutsbrand, which was also grazing land for their twenty oxen and seven breeding cattle. Cornelius Pietersen lived in Klaver Valley where he owned nine oxen, Marthinus Pietersen lived in Modder Fontein and Jan Pie-

---

[174] WCARS, Records of the Magistrate of Simon's Town 1793-1985: 1/SMT 2/5, SMT 10/20 (Letters Received from 4 October 1826 to December 1827) Ref. 260 (19 November 1827).

[175] WCARS, Records of the Magistrate of Simon's Town 1793-1985: 1/SMT 2/5, SMT 10/20 (Letters received from 4 October 1826 to December 1827) Ref. 121 (2 March 1827).

tersen in Klaas Jager Rivier. Marthinus Pietersen and Aron Mozes each owned twelve oxen. Elias Davidze lived in Wolfkloof (Noordhoek) and Isaac Flip (who owned twelve oxen) lived in Buffelsfontein. In terms of the Caledon Code, these descendants of indigenous people would all have had to experience the indignity of carrying passes.

The Carpenter and the Tailor

The authorities themselves were often confused by the status of Abdol Gaviel and in 1826 he was noted as a "free black" on the *opgaafrolle*.[176] However, his enslaved status is confirmed on the "slave register." Abdol Gaviel was initially part of the "slave-holding" of Pieter Francois Rossouw, John Osmond's brother-in-law.

The transfer of the twenty-eight year old carpenter Abdol and the thirty-five year old tailor Solomon from the estate of the late Pieter Francois Rossouw to John Osmond was processed on 1 April 1826.[177] Their descendants would form the majority of the Muslim families who lived in the Malay Quarter right up until the time of the forced removals during the apartheid era.

Vaccinations in Simon's Town

Epidemics such as smallpox, which arrived aboard ships in March 1812, gave rise to the introduction of vaccinations at the Cape. Simon's Town had an Officer of Health and by this time the Simon's Town Hospital had become known as the "Naval Medical and Surgical Centre."[178] Vaccines sent to Simon's Town were administered to the children who were required by law to be vaccinated. Children named for vaccinations during this period included two children of "Mr John Osmond's house," two children of the "Boats Crew of L[ieutenant] Weatherley" and one child in the household of Thomas Bend.

---

[176]WCARS, Opgaafrolle, J181, 1826.
[177]WCARS, SO 2/16 Slave Registry Dept Correspondence (1 April 1826).
[178]Percy Ward Laidler, "Medical Establishments and Institutions at the Cape During the Opening Years of the Nineteenth Century" *History of Medicine* (10 July 1937): 484-485.

Also included, on 20 October 1827, was the female child of Morrison in Black Town.[179] However, it is notable that in the period 1816 to 1834 twenty-two child deaths are recorded for Simon's Town, fourteen males and eight females. At least half of these children died in the first year of their lives.[180]

From indigenous people to "vagrants"

In just over a hundred years after Anthonij Visser set up his homestead in this area in 1725, the majority of indigenous people of this area were experiencing the paradox of being "surplus people" on their ancestral land. In the society that had formed, their way of life was denounced as vagrancy and a crime. Colonel John Bell, Colonial Secretary to the Cape of Good Hope, responded to an enquiry from the Simon's Town Magistrate for advice on "how to act in regard to certain Hottentots" sent to the prison for vagrancy as follows:

> By the Law of Holland Vagrants are to be punished by being fed on bread & water and sent out to the country, the first part of this punishment may be awarded by the Resident Magistrates, but not the latter. I should recommend that in aggravated cases vagrants be put upon the treadmill.[181]

Although Ordinance 50 of 1828 repealed the Pass laws for indigenous people and their mixed-race descendants, they were considered vagrants unless employed.[182] People in the Simon's Town area who were arrested as vagrants during this period included "Kallas Bartman, Jacob Hugtes, Mietje Jephta & Gail Hugters."[183]

---

[179]WCARS, Records of the Magistrate of Simon's Town 1793-1985: 1/SMT 2/5, SMT 10/20 (Letters Received from 4 October 1826 to December 1827) Ref. 243.

[180]WCARS, CAD CA 06/78 (1816-1834).

[181]WCARS, Records of the Magistrate of Simon's Town 1793-1985: 1/SMT 2/5, SMT 10/21 (Letters Received from December 1827 to December 1830) Ref. 191, Ref. 192,193 and 194 (15 July 1830).

[182]Vertrees Candy Malherbe, "Colonial Justice and the Khoisan in the Immediate Aftermath of Ordinance 50 of 1828: Denouement at Uitenhage" *Kronos* 24 (November 1997): 77-90.

It was also at this time that Abdol Gaviel died in Simon's Town on 1 March 1829. He is buried in the Muslim burial ground in Runciman Drive, Simon's Town. Although his life was short, his contribution to his community was profound. His gravestone has survived nearly two centuries in this windy landscape.

In 1831, in his capacity as Justice of the Peace, John Osmond commented on certain "slave proprietors in the Residency who practice great cruelty on their slaves." Ironically although Osmond's treatment of enslaved men was certainly found wanting, on the surface of things he appeared to show a totally different approach towards enslaved women.

When the aged enslaved woman Rosetta sought Osmond's assistance after repeated sadistic beatings by Hendrina Carolina Woolls, wife of the Simon's Town harbourmaster Thomas Brownrigg Woolls, Osmond arranged for a wagon "at his own expense" to take her to the Protector of Slaves in Cape Town. At the time he remarked this was necessary to prevent a return of inflammation as she was beaten "with great severity on the instep of her right foot, which bore evident marks of very severe treatment."[184]

On 4 March 1830 Hendryn brought a charge against Sturt, claiming that she was being "illegally detained in Slavery by her pretended owner."[185] Her case was dismissed because of lack of evidence. Though the surviving documents do not mention the reasons for this decision or Sturt's comments on the matter, that same month Sturt wrote to Christiaan Michiel Lind, the Registrar of Slaves in Simon's Town, about supposed defamation of his character, though not referring to Hendryn specifically.[186] This is the last documented correspondence from George Sturt. It is likely that he took ill soon

---

[183] WCARS, Records of the Magistrate of Simon's Town 1793-1985: 1/SMT 2/ 5, SMT 10/21 (Letters Received from December 1827 to December 1830) Ref. 191, Ref. 192, 193 and 194 (15 July 1830).
[184] WCARS, CSC, 2/1/1/15. Reference 5, Part 1, Record of proceedings of illiquid case Hendrina Carolina Woolls, wife of Thomas Brownrigg Woolls versus Thomas King, Assistant of Slaves, ill-treatment of slave (1831).
[185] WCARS, CAD, SO 4/12 Book of Complaints, Guardian of Slaves 1826-1830 Folio number 140 (4 March 1830).
[186] WCARS, Records of the Magistrate of Simon's Town 1793-1985: 1/SMT 2/ 5, SMT 10/21 (Letters Received from December 1827 to December 1830) Ref. 171 and 173, 174 and 175 (15 March 1830).

after this as he died five months later on 24 August 1830, at the age of fifty-three years.[187]

Fig. 6-7. Watercolour of Rocklands Farm
Source: Attributed to Mary Brenton[188]

On 30 December 1830 Rocklands farm was ordered to be sold by the Supreme Court, in the matter of "The Lombard Bank and G W Sturt jnr, defendant."[189] As indicated in correspondence from the Masters Office to C

---

[187]"Some Facts in the History of the Parish of St Frances [sic], Simonstown" (Claremont: *Peninsula Herald*, 1903), 37.
[188]Mary Brenton was the sister of Sir Jahleel Brenton. Judy Rowe, *The History of Rocklands Farm: Simon's Town ... 1815-1910*, 9.
[189]WCARS, Records of the Magistrate of Simon's Town 1793-1985: 1/SMT 2/5; SMT 10/21 (Letters Received from December 1827 to December 1830) Ref. 227 (30 December 1830).

M Lind on 14 February 1831, the property was sold by public auction to John Osmond, the highest bidder.[190]

Hendryn remained under the ownership of George Sturt's daughter, Olisa, until 1832. Because Hendryn was registered in the name of Olisa Sturt, she would not have been incorporated into the sequestration sale. The whereabouts of the Sturt family after the sale of Rocklands will need to be traced. However, a year and nine months later, on 5 November 1832, Hendryn died. She had lived for thirty-seven years, all of them as an enslaved person. With her one desperate attempt at freedom thwarted two years earlier, it is possible that she took her own life.[191]

Rosetta of the Cape—A Case of "Great Cruelty'"

The case of Rosetta gives us an insight into the challenges and barriers that enslaved people encountered when trying to lodge a complaint against cruel slave-holders.

At the Brownrigg's residence in Elsje Mill, Simon's Bay on Saturday 16 October 1830, an old woman was beaten with a broomstick and the attack was so severe that she was left with an injured wrist. The woman was known as Rosetta of the Cape. Her torturer was also a woman, namely Hendrina Carolina Woolls.[192]

Desperate and in pain, Rosetta sought help from John Osmond in his capacity as Justice of the Peace.[193] Osmond's response was to have her "forwarded" to the Protector of Slaves in Cape Town, stating that "the Protector having desired me to do so in all cases of such a nature."[194]

---

[190]WCARS, Records of the Magistrate of Simon's Town 1793 – 1985: 1/SMT 2/5, SMT 10/22 (1831-1833) Ref. 21 (14 February 1831).

[191]See Joline Young, The Enslaved People of Simon's Town. Thesis (MA) University of Cape Town, 2013). Appendix II, Database (UCT: MA thesis, 2013).

[192]WCARS, Records of the Magistrate of Simon's Town 1793-1985: 1/SMT 2/5, SMT 10/20 (Letters Received from 4 October 1826 to December 1827) Ref. 179 (3 July 1827).

[193]WCARS, Records of Civil Cases in the Supreme Court, Cape Town, CSC 2/1/1/15 Ref. 5 (28 January 1831).

[194]WCARS, Records of Civil Cases in the Supreme Court, Cape Town, CSC 2/1/1/15 Ref. 5 (28 January 1831).

Although on paper the Ameliorative Laws were supposed to offer protection for enslaved people, most notably through the "Protector of Slaves," in reality there were many obstacles for enslaved people who sought protection or redress. Such attempts were rendered prohibitive through complicated legislation. For example, if an enslaved person complained of being "cruelly treated," but lost the case, the enslaved person would be "severely whipped & returned to their Owners." Furthermore, if an enslaved person was found guilty of "falsely" accusing a "slave-holder" "of anything shameful" they would "be Whipped & put in irons, or be otherwise punished according to circumstances."[195]

Traumatised enslaved people who tried to get help in cases of physical cruelty by "slave-holders" were also further traumatised by the legal process, as the *modus operandi* for enslaved people who complained of ill-treatment was that they would either be housed in the prison until their cases were investigated or returned to the households of their enslavement until their cases were brought to court.

It is against this background that we need to understand Rosetta's desperation in approaching Osmond for help. In laying this complaint, Rosetta had enormous power dynamics stacked against herself, given that her assailant's husband, the Simon's Town harbourmaster Thomas Brownrigg Thomas, had replaced Christiaan Michiel Lind as the "Registrar and Guardian of Slaves" on 3 July 1827.[196]

Following the lodging of the complaint, the "Protector of Slaves" had Rosetta returned to the Brownrigg household and on 24 December 1830 she once again sought the help of John Osmond after Hendrina Carolina Woolls had beaten her with a broomstick two days previously. On this occasion Osmond reported that Rosetta had been beaten "with great severity on the instep of her right foot" which he stated "bore evident marks of very severe treatment recently committed."[197]

---

[195]WCARS, Slave Ofice, Document titled "Relative to Slavery," SO 7/35, 1833.
[196]Cape Archives, Records of Civil Cases in the Supreme Court, Cape Town, CSC 2/1/1/15 Ref. 5, 28 January, 1831.
[197]WCARS, Records of Civil Cases in the Supreme Court, Cape Town, CSC 2/1/1/15 Ref. 5 (28 January 1831).

In response to Rosetta's complaint, Thomas Brownrigg Woolls called on Osmond and asserted that her claims were false. To corroborate his assertion, he sent two witnesses in the form of an enslaved woman named Mena and Thomas Crow, an "indentured servant" who hailed from India. They were meant to say that Rosetta was lying, however, Mena broke down in tears and told the truth. According to Osmond the "slave girl Mena cried very much to Sarah Brevis in my presence," saying that she "hoped that Rosetta might not be sent back, for it was heart-breaking to hear the cries of this poor Old Slave from the punishment she almost daily received from her Mistress." Thomas Crow concurred with these statements.

As before, Osmond once again responded by having Rosetta "forwarded" to the "Protector of Slaves" in Cape Town, this time personally paying the cost of a wagon to transport Rosetta so as to "prevent a return of the inflammation."[198] However, in the eight day delay between Rosetta having been taken to Cape Town and a medical doctor examining her, the swelling had subsided leading the doctor to assert that there was no swelling. As a result Rosetta was returned to the home of her tormentor "by a constable" on Saturday 8 January 1831, where she was left to face the wrath of Hendrina Carolina Brownrigg whose venom towards Rosetta knew no bounds. It was at this stage that she took to beating Rosetta with a horsewhip. By the time Rosetta managed to find her way to Osmond on Wednesday 12 January 1831, the wounds inflicted were of such severity and in such intimate parts of her body, that Osmond called on Sarah Brevis—whom he described as his "servant," but in court papers was referred to as an enslaved person—to examine Rosetta's injuries in his presence. It seems that even Osmond was confounded by this case. Where he had shown himself to be cruel, it had never been to this degree of severity. He had never been physically cruel to a woman and there is no evidence to suggest that he had ever previously, in his capacity of Justice of the Peace in Simon's Town, had to encounter a case where a woman had done this to another woman. The assault on Rosetta by Hendrina Carolina Woolls was of such a severity that the lash marks on her back were too numerous to count. The lashes also extended to her loins, shoulders and the sides of her breasts.[199]

---

[198]WCARS, Records of Civil Cases in the Supreme Court, Cape Town, CSC 2/1/1/15 Ref. 5 (28 January 1831).

As there was no District Surgeon available in the town at the time, Osmond arranged for two further witnesses whom he described as the "two late maid Masters of this maid" namely W Anderson and P J Arendze Raven, to witness and make a statement of Rosetta's injuries at his home on 15 January 1831. They concluded that "such cruel severity as appears to have been inflicted on this old Slave is wholly unauthorised by the existing Laws of the Colony—and to the truth of the above, we are prepared to make Solemn Oath whenever required."[200]

On the strength of their statement, formal charges were laid against Hendrina Carolina Woolls on 25 January 1831. This was followed by a Supreme court hearing, which took place on 28 January 1831 with her crime listed as follows:

> Contravening an Order in Council made and published at the Court at Windsor in England 2nd day of February 1830 and promulgated in this Colony 12th day of August following that the Defendant on or about the 12th January inst at her dwelling house did wrongfully and unlawfully maltreat Rosetta Female Slave of Said Thomas Brownrigg Woolls, by beating her with a Whip with many blows upon her back and other parts of her body, and other injuries to the said Rosetta then and there did.[201]

Although she appealed the charge, Hendrina Carolina Woolls was found guilty and sentenced to a fine of ten pounds sterling[202] which Thomas Brownrigg Woolls paid off in instalments.[203] This was a hollow victory for Rosetta as the fine did not benefit her in the least. Fines levied by Governments went into Government coffers. Furthermore, whereas every time

---

[199] WCARS, Records of Civil Cases in the Supreme Court, Cape Town, CSC 2/1/1/15 Ref. 5 (28 January 1831).
[200] WCARS, Records of Civil Cases in the Supreme Court, Cape Town, CSC 2/1/1/15 Ref. 5 (28 January 1831).
[201] WCARS, Records of Civil Cases in the Supreme Court, Cape Town, CSC 2/1/1/15 Ref. 5 (7 February 1831).
[202] WCARS, Records of Civil Cases in the Supreme Court, Cape Town, CSC 2/1/1/15 Ref. 5 (7 February 1831).
[203] WCARS, Records of the Magistrate of Simon's Town 1793-1985: 1/SMT 2/5, SMT 10/22 (1831-1833) Ref. 31 (31 March 1831).

Rosetta sought redress from the Hendrina Carolina Woolls's cruelty through the justice system, she was either housed in prison or returned to the household of her abuser. Hendrina Carolina Woolls on the other hand was never arrested or imprisoned. At worst she incurred financial—and possibly reputational—damage.

However, the cruellest way that the Justice system failed Rosetta was that she was returned to the Woolls household, where she was at the mercy of the full-blown wrath of Hendrina Carolina Woolls and her husband Thomas Brownrigg Woolls. Not long after her return, Rosetta was assaulted again, this time by Thomas Brownrigg Woolls.

Notwithstanding her extreme vulnerability, Rosetta reported the matter and, on 5 February 1831, George Jackman Rogers the "Protector of Slaves" laid a formal charge against Thomas Brownrigg Woolls "for beating his Slave Woman Rosetta." A hearing was set for the Simon's Town court on Friday 11 February 1831, to be attended by "Mr King, Assistant Protector of Slaves" from Cape Town and C M Lind was asked to "direct all the parties Summonsed."[204] However, in a follow up letter from Rogers to Lind on 7 February 1831, Rogers asserted that

> the offence with which Mr Woolls is now charged is not in the opinion of the Attorney General and myself of such a heinous nature as to render it necessary that it brought by indictment before the Supreme court.[205]

Rogers continued saying

> there is no proof whatever against Mr Woolls, but the solemn asseverations of Rosetta herself, and that as solemn protestations from Mr Woolls & his Sister in Law together with the testimony of the other persons are made on the other side, so that it will require some address to come at the truth.[206]

---

[204]WCARS, Records of the Magistrate of Simon's Town 1793-1985: 1/SMT 2/5, SMT 10/22 (1831-1833) Ref. 16 (5 February 1831).

[205]WCARS, Records of the Magistrate of Simon's Town 1793-1985: 1/SMT 2/5, SMT 10/22 (1831-1833) Ref. 18 (7 February 1831).

[206]WCARS, Records of the Magistrate of Simon's Town 1793-1985: 1/SMT 2/5, SMT 10/22 (1831-1833) Ref. 18 (7 February 1831).

After her charge against Thomas Brownrigg Woolls, Rosetta disappears from the archival record, thus we have no knowledge of what became of Rosetta. Yet it is only because of Rosetta's brave and relentless attempts to seek justice that we know of her at all and in this way Rosetta has rescued herself from historical oblivion.

However, an incident that occurred in April 1831 suggests that there were further ramifications for Woolls in what could be conjectured as a case of "slave" justice by persons offended at the way Rosetta was treated. Thus it was that on 29 April 1831 Thomas Brownrigg Woolls reported "a most daring, wanton and malicious outrage" having been committed during the night. From his account we learn that unseen hands cut his boat off its moorings and sent it adrift. The boat was found "near the residence of J D Thompson Esq," but two oars and a boat-hook marked "TBW" were missing. Woolls also reported that "a boat in the employ of the Port Captain" where he worked as harbourmaster, was similarly cut from her moorings and eventually found on the beach at the Dock Yard minus "Boat Hook, lose [sic] thwarts, and stores in several places." Furthermore, the fastenings of another boat belonging to Woolls, which had been "hawld [sic] on the beach for repairs" was cut to pieces.[207] Although Woolls offered a reward of "One Hundred Rix Dollars on conviction of the Offenders," no-one attempted to take up the reward and the persons responsible were never reported or found.[208]

If "Rosette" and "Rosetta" were one and the same person—which is highly likely given administrative spelling errors—then Rosetta initially ran away from the Woolls household some time previously as "Rosette" was apprehended as a "deserter" in Cape Town on 23 May 1829.[209] As this case has shown, Rosetta had good reason to want to get as far away from this household as possible.

---

[207] WCARS, Records of the Magistrate of Simon's Town 1793-1985: 1/SMT 2/5, SMT 10/22 (1831-1833) Ref. 35 (29 April 1831).

[208] WCARS, Records of the Magistrate of Simon's Town 1793-1985: 1/SMT 2/5, SMT 10/22 (1831-1833) Ref. 35 (29 April 1831).

[209] WCARS, Records of the Magistrate of Simon's Town 1793 – 1985: 1/SMT 2/5, SMT 10/21 (Letters Received from December 1827 to December 1830) Ref. 125, 6 June, 1829.

Manumissions in 1831

A number of the enslaved people who were ordered to be manumitted by Francis Dashwood in 1825 were only in fact freed from bondage on 24 February 1831. They were listed as follows:

- The housemaid Rosina of the Cape and her five children named August, Aviva, Clarinda, Japie and Pamela.
- August of the Cape (occupation not mentioned)
- The shepherds Phillis of the Cape and Sylvester of Mozambique
- The housemaids Rachima of the Cape, Selima of the Cape and Sima of the Cape
- The washerwoman Spasie of Mozambique.

Japie of the Cape, who was listed as owned by Johannes Henricus Brand, was also manumitted on this date. He was the youngest enslaved coachman in Simon's Town, being just fifteen years old at the time of registration in the "Slave Register" in 1816.

All the above people would have joined the ranks of the people who were socially constructed in the colonial census records as "Free Blacks." Some of the "Free Black" Javanese fishermen in Simon's Town formed romantic relationships with enslaved women, and fathered children with them. Unfortunately, they were unable to protect the women they loved, nor were they able to protect their offspring from the chains of enslavement.

Such was the case of William, who was described as a "stout male of a dark complexion" who ran away from the "slave-holding" of J Murray to his father, a Javanese fisherman described as a free Man of Colour named Daniel in Simon's Town.[210] Another son of a "Free Black" Javanese fisherman in Simon's Town was a young man also named Daniel, described as "short and slightly built" who ran away from the "slave-holding" of C Pohl.[211]

---

[210] WCARS, Records of the Magistrate of Simon's Town (1/SMT 2/5), Letters received by Resident Magistrate (1811) Simonstown 1/SMT 10/4, Ref. 58 (28 May 1811).

[211] WCARS, Records of the Magistrate of Simon's Town (1/SMT 2/5), Letters received by Resident Magistrate (1812) Simonstown 1/SMT 10/4, Ref. 184 (15 September 1812).

In some cases "Free Black" fathers were in a position to buy their children's freedom. This was a costly exercise and therefore an option only for those who had amassed enough savings to do so. One such person was a "Free Black" fisherman named Bakkaar Bull who manumitted and legally adopted his son Gamieldien Bull at a very young age. Unfortunately, he did not free Gamieldien's mother. Gamieldien was born in Simon's Town in 1826, however, in later years he described having had no knowledge of his mother "who was a slave."[212] His experience resonates with that of the Oromo child Gilo Kashe of whom Sandra Rowoldt Shell has written "whatever that trauma was, it left Gilo with no memory of his mother, not even her name.[213]

---

[212]Gamieldien Bull's five children from his first wife "Ricera" all took the surname Gamieldien, namely Hadjie Spaar Gamieldien, Samdan Gamieldien, Omar Gamieldien, Abduragman Gamieldien and Ada Gamieldien. After Ricera died, Gamieldien Bull married Martha Pietersen according to "Malay rites." Gamieldien Bull supported his family as a fisherman and on his death on 18 December 1898, he left a house and furniture at 24 Sea Street, Cape Town.

[213]See Sandra Rowoldt Shell, "Trauma and Slavery: Gilo and the Soft, Subtle Shackles of Lovedale" *Bulletin of the National Library of South Africa* 71, 2 (December 2017): 141-156 and her *Children of Hope: The Odyssey of the Oromo Slaves from Ethiopia to South Africa* (Ohio: Ohio University Press, 76-77, 225.

PART 7

Emancipation and the "Apprenticeship" Period: 1834-1838

> You will watch with an anxious eye and report to me for His Excellency's information the progress of feeling amongst both Proprietors and Slaves on this subject i.e. the approaching Settlement of the Slaves.
>
> —*Acting Secretary to Government, Colonial Office, Cape Town to the Magistrate of Simon's Town, 13 December 1833*[1]

On 16 January 1835, Christiaan Michiel Lind opened the seal of a letter from Colonel John Bell[2] which commenced:

> I have the honor to transmit to you herewith a commission under the Great Seal of this Settlement appointing you special Justice for the second Special district of the Colony as defined by the Proclamation of the 6th Instant for giving effect to the provisions of the Act of Parliament for the Abolition of Slavery.[3]

On 11 February 1835, Lind opened the seal of a second letter from Colonel John Bell, the contents of which read:

> In consequence of doubts having arisen as to the legal interpretation of certain clauses of the Ordinance No. 1 of 1835, the opinion of the Law Officer of the crown has been

---

[1] WCARS, Records of the Magistrate of Simon's Town 1793-1985: 1/SMT 2/5, SMT 10/22 (1831-1833) Ref. 225 (13 December 1833).

[2] Sir John Bell (1782-1876), British soldier and magistrate, was deputy quartermaster-general at the Cape of Good Hope in 1821 and Colonial Secretary from 1828 to 1841.

[3] WCARS, Records of the Magistrate of Simon's Town 1793-1985: 1/SMT 2/5, SMT 10/23 (1835) Ref. 4 (16 January 1835).

taken thereon, and I have deemed it fit to acquaint you therewith for your guidance in similar cases should any such occur within your jurisdiction.[4]

Whether the child of a female apprenticed labourer whose indenture is about to be sold, such child being under 6 years of age, must be indentured under prior to such sale; or whether the Indenture can be effected after the sale, in the name of the purchaser of the Mother's indenture?

It may be unnecessary to apprentice the child at all. It can only be apprenticed in terms of the 13th section of the abolition Act, provided "it shall appear to the satisfaction of the Special Justice that such child is unprovided with an adequate maintenance." The person disposing of the mother's services has nothing to do with such child.

Whether the Indenture of such child can be sold under the 10th clause of the Abolition Act?

No—neither in that nor any other manner.

Whether the services of the Mother and her indentured Children (whether above or under 6 years of age) must be sold in one lot or is it allowed to sell them separately.

The 10th clause of the Abolition Act provides that children may not be separated from their Parents or reported Parents.

In what form, and before who transfers of the services of apprenticed laborers are to be executed?

Such transfers are to be made before the Keepers of the late Slave Registers in the form & upon payment of the same fee and stamp duty as hitherto observed in effecting the change of property in Slaves.

As at 1 December 1834, a total of 193 people were still enslaved in the Simon's Town district comprising 119 males and 74 females. The largest

---

[4]This letter included the original questions with the responses, which are printed in italics.

"slave-holders" in the town were Pierre Rocher, John Osmond and William Rousseau Osmond.[5]

Although Emancipation was set for 1 December 1834, the period from 1834 to 1838 was referred to as the Apprenticeship period, but was effectively a guise to extend slavery for another four years. Essentially, this enabled those controlling the economy to make a smooth financial transition from enslaved labour to wage labour. Archival records show that during this period enslaved people were still changing hands as "slave-holders" were actively trading them for their unexpired terms.[6] Through the Apprentice Ordinance of 1835, their unexpired indentureships could be "disposed of by public sale."[7] As a result many enslaved people were again put through the trauma of being publicly exhibited at auctions, until the Government intervened as the latter practice was apparently in contravention of Ordinance No. 1 of 1835.[8] It was also possible for enslaved people to buy themselves out of their unexpired terms if they were able to raise the money to do so.[9]

A greater government focus was also placed on the age-old system that saw enslaved people being sent to the local prison by "slave-holders," who requested that they be punished. From 24 December 1835 the Special Magistrates were ordered to keep a record of all punishments of apprentices.[10]

This was also a time when enslaved families were filled with the hope of being reunited with their kin and following emancipation many formerly enslaved people walked from farm to farm, trying to find members of their families, particularly their children. It was a time when enslaved people were

---

[5]WCARS, Records of the Magistrate of Simon's Town 1793-1985: 1/SMT 2/5, SMT 10/23 (1836) Ref. 9 (27 January 1836).

[6]WCARS, Records of the Magistrate of Simon's Town 1793-1985: 1/SMT 2/5, SMT 10/23 (1836) Ref. 33 (2 September 1836).

[7]WCARS, Records of the Magistrate of Simon's Town 1793-1985: 1/SMT 2/5, SMT 10/23 (1835) Ref. 46 (30 September 1835).

[8]WCARS, Records of the Magistrate of Simon's Town 1793-1985: 1/SMT 2/5, SMT 10/23 (1835) Ref. 46 (30 September 1835).

[9]WCARS, Records of the Magistrate of Simon's Town 1793-1985: 1/SMT 2/5, SMT 10/23 (1835) Ref. 58 (27 November 1835).

[10]WCARS, Records of the Magistrate of Simon's Town 1793-1985: 1/SMT 2/5, SMT 10/23 (1835) Ref. 61 (24 December 1835).

starting to imagine their lives as "free" people. However, there were also huge challenges. The biggest challenges were financial.

Unlike the "slave-holders" who were paid compensation from Britain for their financial losses incurred through the freeing of people who formed their "slave-holdings," the majority of enslaved people were released into states of poverty. In the Simon's Town district the three people who stood to gain the highest compensation from Britain were Pierre Rocher, John Osmond and his son William Osmond. As previously mentioned, they had the largest "slave-holdings" in the town.[11]

For the enslaved, the biggest casualties during this period were the old and infirm and young children. The fear of family separations, one of the most traumatic aspects of slavery, became an exacerbated concern during this time for enslaved families with children aged six and younger. This was due to a loophole in the Abolition Act, whereby "slave-holders" were allowed to retain young children if they could show either that the mother did not have the means to take care of the child/children or that the mother was (conveniently accused of being) a woman of "loose morals." Ruthless and unscrupulous "slave-holders" used these laws to their benefit. This was a time when children were extremely vulnerable and child labour the norm.

Bernard Keane

Bernard Keane stands out as an anomaly in this society as he was an Irish boy who lived in Simon's Town with his mother Anna Keane.[12] At the age of eleven he was a "bound apprentice" to the shoemaker Robert Haywood, a boot and shoemaker in Simon's Town, for a period of seven years. Bernard's hours of work were "from six in the morning till eight or nine in the evening." Bernard described leaving work at 8pm one evening "leaving about an hour's work undone" due to extreme exhaustion and staying home the next day for fear that Haywood would beat him. This was not an unfounded fear, as Haywood had beaten him badly in the past.[13] On returning to work

---

[11] WCARS, Records of the Magistrate of Simon's Town 1793-1985: 1/SMT 2/5, SMT 10/23 (1836) Ref. 9 (27 January 1836).

[12] "South Africa, Settlers Index, 1820-1920" *FamilySearch* [online resource] https://familysearch.org (accessed 18 July 2022).

[13] WCARS, Colonial Office, CO 3987, Ref. 89 (18 December 1836).

on the second day, Haywood ordered him to go home and wait for the constable to fetch him. Bernard later recalled that the constable fetched him from home and he appeared before Matthew Gregory Blake who, in his capacity of Justice of the Peace, ordered that he receive twelve stripes on his back with the cat o'nine tails.[14] Although a complaint was laid, no action was taken against Blake.[15] This case is significant in that it shows that social vulnerability also extended to desperately poor Irish people who were brought to the Cape as indentured labour. In their home country the Irish were the "underclass" who were enserfed and often cruelly treated by British overlords.[16] While their descendants would benefit from socially constructed racial privilege within the South African context, during this historical period, they also struggled.

Japie of the Cape (2 November 1837)

Because Anna Keane was literate it is possible for us to get an insight into Bernard Keane's experience at the hands of Robert Haywood. Not so with Japie, who was indentured to Japloon of the Cape, also a shoemaker. Japloon cuts an interesting figure in that he was a shoemaker, described in Dutch as a "Baas schoemaker." However, during the year of this incident he was listed as the "slave" of "Mejufvrouw Johanna Frederica van Schoor." The seventeen year old Japie, whose father Loejoema (possibly Chinese) resided in Simon's Town, was bound as an apprentice to Japloon of the Cape. On his desertion a warrant was issued for his arrest.[17] The law pertaining to apprentices stated that they were obliged to work every day of the year except for Sundays and holidays. Deserting the workplace came with harsh penalties, as the following excerpt from the Abolition Act attests:

---

[14]WCARS, Records of the Magistrate of Simon's Town 1793-1985: 1/SMT 2/5, SMT 10/23 (1836) Ref. 42 and 42A (29 November 1836).

[15]WCARS. Records of the Magistrate of Simon's Town 1793-1985: 1/SMT 2/5, SMT 10/23 (1836) Ref. 45 (6 December 1836).

[16]For an insight into this history see Dean M Braa, "The Great Potato Famine and the Transformation of Irish Peasant Society" *Science & Society* 61, 2 (Summer, 1997): 193-215.

[17]WCARS, Records of the Magistrate of Simon's Town 1793 – 1985: 1/SMT 2/5, SMT 10/23 (1837) Ref. 62 (2 November 1837).

For every hour in which any labourer shall absent himself without reasonable cause he shall be adjudged to receive not exceeding ten stripes ... provided that such number of stripes shall not exceed thirty nine on the whole number of stripes.[18]

The story of Martha (April 1837)

On the morning of Saturday 29 April 1837, a four year old boy was forcibly removed from a house in Cape Town. His mother had left him there in the care of a woman described by the Special Justice Office in Cape Town as "the free woman Sophie" and "a respectable person."

The person who forcibly removed the child was Simon's Town resident William Rosseau Osmond, the man charged with assaulting Martha, the boy's mother. This fact alone would have heightened the tension in the household from where the child was taken, not to mention exacerbated the trauma of the child.

Martha had five children aged four, seven, ten, twelve and seventeen at the time. However, Martha would have been right to be particularly concerned about protecting her youngest child as he was under the age of six. Though there was one year to go before enslaved apprentices were due to be emancipated, this little boy fell into the age range of children at risk of being separated from their families post-emancipation.[19]

As Colonel John Bell explained to the Special Justice in Simon's Town, in terms of a clause in the British Slavery Abolition Act 1833:

> Inquiry having been made relative to the Apprenticing of children, under the Slave Abolition Act, the attention of the Law Officer of the Crown has been called to the subject; and I have now to acquaint you that it is the opinion of that gentleman,
>
> 1st that by the 1st section of the Act, all Slaves, who were on the 1st December 1834, above the age of 6 years,

---

[18]WCARS, Abolition of Slavery Ordinance No. 1, 1835.
[19]WCARS, Records of the Magistrate of Simon's Town 1793-1985: 1/SMT 2/5, SMT 10/23 (1837) Ref. 29 (1 May 1837).

became apprenticed laborers by virtue of that act so that of course no Indenture is necessary, nor can any be made in such cases.

Fig. 7-1. Untitled portrait
Artist: Lionel Davis

2d That by the 13th Section of the Act the Children therein described born of Slaves and being on the 1st of December 1834 under the age of six, may provided they are not at the time of Apprenticeship of the age of 12 years be apprenticed in manner therein mentioned, for any time not exceeding the completion of their 21st year but no such child if about 12 years of age can be apprenticed under the Act.

3d By the same Section 13 the Children therein described born of female Apprenticed Laborers after the 1st December 1834 may within the same age and for the same period be apprenticed in the like manner. Children therein described born of Slaves and being on the 1st of December 1834 under the age of six, may provided they are not at the time of Apprenticeship of the age of 12 years be apprenticed in manner therein mentioned, for any time not exceeding the completion of their 21st year.[20]

A story unfolds that illustrates the difficulties for enslaved people, indentured people and in fact all vulnerable people in this society, to access justice when the scales of power were weighted against them. The case of the child's removal was reported by Sophie to the Special Justice Office in Cape Town on Monday 1 May 1837, who in turn reported the matter to William Blake, the Special Justice Officer in Simon's Town. Blake was not only a social contemporary of William Osmond, but was himself guilty of a similar offence in respect of the Khoe child Valentyn.[21] In the letter, the Special Justice Officer in Cape Town stated:

> I think you will agree with me that Mr Wm Osmond was guilty of a gross infringement of the law in so doing and as he resides in your District, I beg to report the circumstances to you that you may take such cognizance of it as you may deem necessary and proper.[22]

In the time between the removal of the child and the report of the child's removal, it transpired that Osmond had separated Martha from her remaining children at his home, indenturing her to Mr Albertyn in Simon's Town. Research also shows that Martha and these four of her five children, namely

---

[20]Colonel John Bell cited in WCARS, Records of the Magistrate of Simon's Town 1793-1985: 1/SMT 2/5, SMT 10/23 (1835) Ref. 34 (29 May 1835).

[21]WCARS, Colonial Office, Memorials (1827), CO 3933, Ref. 6 (2 January 1827).

[22]WCARS, Records of the Magistrate of Simon's Town 1793-1985: 1/SMT 2/5, SMT 10/23 (1837) Ref. 29 (1 May 1837).

Spasie, aged seven at this time, Hennetjie aged ten, Jochon aged twelve and John aged seventeen were listed in the debt register as Osmond had taken out loans against them. Furthermore, in correspondence from the Cape Town Justice Office, it emerged that Osmond had badly assaulted Martha, to the extent that she had experienced "lameness in her arm," despite Osmond sending a letter to Major Blake on 1 May 1837 assuring him that he would not cause any ill-treatment to Martha.

As was the law at the time, when an enslaved person laid a charge of abuse against the "slave-holder," the enslaved person was incarcerated until the matter was settled. In Martha's case, her place of incarceration was the Simon's Town jail, the site of the Simon's Town museum today. However, in a second letter written on 1 May 1837, Osmond requested that Martha be sent to "Mr Thusman of Kalk Bay to whom I have hired her." Her stay there was not extended, as Martha's lame arm impeded her ability to work to Thusman's expectations and Martha was returned to the Simon's Town jail. However, Osmond claimed that during the time that Martha was sent to work at the Thusman household, he had visited the Thusman's and that Martha had gone down "on her knees to both Mrs Osmond & myself kissing our feet & praying us to take her home again." In a counter statement taken from Martha while she was in the Simon's Town jail, she stated that "she requested of Mr Osmond on her knees to let her have her children, but that she did not ask him to take her into his house, as stated in his letter."

Imhoff's Gift at the Close of the Apprenticeship Period

It is ironic that the date in 1837 that Pierre Rocher first sent a letter of complaint to the magistrate in Simon's Town about Leentje was 16 June, which is the date that South Africans commemorate the 16 June 1976 uprisings against apartheid.[23] Rocher was the largest "slave-holder" in the Simon's Town district, but this seemed to matter little to Leentje who was preparing herself for early freedom by any means. Rocher was a Frenchman who was born in Maubeuge, France on 8 March 1776 and arrived in Cape Town in 1803.[24] Like Osmond, Rocher also married into the wealthy Roussouw family, tying the knot with Aletta Margaretha Rossouw on 15 July 1810. On the

---

[23] WCARS, Records of the Magistrate of Simon's Town 1793-1985: 1/SMT 2/5. SMT 10/23 (1837) Ref. 41 (16 June 1837).

death of Francois Rossouw, Rocher purchased the Imhoff's Gift estate, at the time measuring some 6,000 acres, on perpetual quitrent.[25] This land was added to when, on 13 November 1818 he requested 100 morgen of land adjacent to Imhoff's Farm.[26]

Fig. 7-2. Imhoff's Farm, Kommetjie, 1925
Artist: Oil painting by Edward Roworth (in private hands)

He was also appointed Heemraad in Simon's Town (despite being a Roman Catholic at a time when this was initially thought to constitute an

---

[24]*South African Genealogies*, edited by Johannes August Heese and Roelof Theunis Johannes Lombard, (Stellenbosch: Genealogical Institute of South Africa, 2003) volume 9, Ra-Ron: 482.
[25]WCARS, Records of the Magistrate of Simon's Town 1793-1985: 1/SMT 2/5 (Inkomende briewe 1820), 1/SMT 10/12 [not numbered and dated 1814, but in this file].
[26]WCARS, Records of the Magistrate of Simon's Town 1793-1985: 1/SMT 2/5, Letters received by Resident Magistrate Simonstown 1818), 1/SMT 10/10, Ref. 247 (13 November 1818).

impediment).[27] Rocher was fortuitous in being granted exclusive use of the Slangekop Lake "upon the understanding that he constructs the Works proposed by him for the preservation of the Fish called Spruingers."[28]

The enslaved workforce on Imhoff's farm included eight labourers namely: Fortuin (1) and Fortuin (2) of the Cape; Galant of Madagascar; November of Malabar, Absalon of Mozambique, Demas of Mozambique, Nias of Mozambique and Salomon of Mozambique.[29] The shepherd who looked after Rocher's sizeable herd of sixty oxen, seventeen breeding cattle, six Spanish sheep and 133 goats was Anthony of Mozambique.[30] Rocher also owned twenty-four breeding horses and four pigs.[31] The wagoners who manned Rocher's nine wagons and saddle horses were Bastiaan and David from Malabar and Jack from Mozambique.

The household baking was done by Thomas from Mozambique while Dappat from Bougies was the household butcher. The large homestead at Imhoff's Gift was kept clean by Delphine of Mozambique, Philida of Madagascar and Sina from Bougies as well as Marietje, Leonora and Leentje of Cape. Three parentless enslaved children also worked on this estate. They were Pamela, Primo and Linder, who were bought at ages eleven, thirteen and eleven respectively. Of course, there were also enslaved children born on Imhoff's Farm. They were Marietje's children: Jacob, Lea and Altea; Delphina's children: August, Lys and Leblanc; Delphine's children: Carollus and Delphina; Leonora's children Spasie, Roselyn, Pamela, Apaloon and Hermanus and Leentje's children: Sara and Betje. Over time their numbers expanded further with the addition of November, "formerly of the property of Mr Lange"[32] and Fortuyn, who kept escaping until he was made to work in irons,[33] as well as "Dappat, who was bought from the Insolvent Estate of

---

[27] WCARS, Records of the Magistrate of Simon's Town 1793-1985: 1/SMT 2/5, SMT 10/19 (Letters Received from 3d January 1826 to 30 August 1826 & September) Ref. 17 (23 January 1826).

[28] "Spruingers" almost certainly refers to Springers (*Elops machnata*), a species of fish which frequent the waters of the south-western Cape. WCARS, Records of the Magistrate of Simon's Town 1793-1985: 1/SMT 2/5, SMT 10/19 (Letters Received from 3d January 1826 to 30 August 1826 & September) Ref. 30, (7 February 1826).

[29] WCARS, Colonial Office, CO 3932, Ref. 608 (29 May 1826).

[30] WCARS, CA SO 6/79, Slave Register M-W, 1824-1834.

[31] WCARS, *Opgaafrolle*, J131, 1826.

Gustavus Christoffel Greffrath on 13 January 1831."[34] There was also the "male negro" named Nakatinka who was indentured to Rocher and renamed Present, as well as Danatorcana who was re-named Joseph.[35]

At night all these enslaved people were cramped into the sparse "slave quarters" of Imhoff's Gift along with contract workers such as Leonora's partner Esau, who was Khoe and a contracted servant of Pierre Rocher. On 17 May 1826, Esau had appealed against his sentence to "be scourged with 100 lashes and to 3 years labour in Irons on the Public Works—for having taken Gin or Spirits from a cupboard in the hall of the Dwelling House of Pierre Rocher Esq of Slangkop."[36]

On 27 April 1837, as slavery was drawing to a close, Pierre Rocher tried to use the loophole in the Abolition Act to indenture the children of Martha, Delphine and Lentz. There were twelve children in total, whom Rocher insisted he was entitled to keep as unpaid indentured labour until they reached adulthood, stating that their parents had no means of supporting them other than what they received from him.[37]

Leentje

When Leentje packed her meagre belongings and left Imhoff's Farm for Simon's Town on 16 June 1837, Rocher wrote to Colonel Blake, the special magistrate at Simon's Town to request that she be "arrested and punished." At this stage Rocher appeared to be living between a home in Cape Town and Imhoff's Gift, where his son seemed to reside more permanently. In his letter Rocher wrote:

---

[32]WCARS, Records of the Magistrate of Simon's Town 1793-1985: 1/SMT 2/5, SMT 10/15 (Inkomende briewe 1823) Simon's Town, Ref. 65 (10 September 1823).

[33]WCARS, Records of the Magistrate of Simon's Town 1793-1985: 1/SMT 2/5, SMT 10/21 (Letters Received from December 1827 to December 1830) Ref. 60 (2 January 1828).

[34]WCARS, Memorials (Drafts) for the Remission of Fines, 1832-1824, SO 2/18 (1 September 1832).

[35]WCARS, Records of the Magistrate of Simon's Town 1793-1985: 1/SMT 2/5, SMT 10/15 (Inkomende briewe 1823) Simon's Town, Ref. 67 (21 July 1823).

[36]WCARS, Colonial Office CO 3932, Ref. 608 (29 May 1826).

[37]WCARS, Records of the Magistrate of Simon's Town 1793-1985: 1/SMT 2/5, SMT 10/23 (1837) Ref. 27 (24 April 1837).

> I had heard on history that Mr Bell intended to buy her for her freedom upon this, as I wished to get rit [sic] of her I offered her to Mr Bell, for a least sum that it should cost me to get another in her place, or to go the regular way, by arbitration. Mr Bell answered that it was not for him, that it was for the old Girl who she call her mama, but that this old Girl had no money, and that she wished only to hire her for the remaining time of apprenticeship and in this I do not agree.[38]

In further correspondence about Leentje in February 1838, Rocher wrote:

> You will remember Sir, that some time since, it was complained that Leentje refused to go to Cape Town when she was ordered to go, to attend her Mistress, whom was still in town. She objected in answer that she could not go with a wood wagon and you approved her objection, in pronouncing that a wagon with wood, was not a proper carriage. Some days after, she was ordered to [have] to go in a carriage on springs, with four horses, or in a oxwaggon [sic], where a proper plan should be left and fited [sic] up, on the botom [sic] upon this, having determined to depart with her I sold her, and eight or ten days since she was ordered to go to her nieuw [sic] master, with a wagon where a proper plan was fited [sic] up, on the botom [sic]. Instead of going, the Girl absented herself, and she has not been seen till the present, or since your letter was brought to me this morning about ten o'clock by a little girl, and having inquired, she answered that Leentje [gave] her, and that she must away immediately about her ration. Leentje can have no raison [sic] to complain, since she was ordered to go to her new master, and that she absented herself.
>
> Now Sir, I can but consider this girl as a deserter, and this is intended as an accusation against her on the purpose, praying that you will be pleased to comply her to go to Mrs Bis-

---

[38]WCARS, Records of the Magistrate of Simon's Town 1793-1985: 1/SMT 2/5. SMT 10/23 (1837) Ref. 41 (16 June 1837).

tardy at Cape Town, from whom she will be send [sic] to her new master.[39]

Pierre Rocher emerges in archival correspondence as a man who was not ready to let go of the institution of slavery and who did his best to block freedom for people on his "slave-holding." When the enslaved man Lindor offered six pounds for the purchase of his freedom, Rocher responded:

> I do not consent to Liberate Lindor for the sum of 6 pounds, as I do not think it a fair term for this Boy, being [a] good waggon driver, when common Boys are sold at public sale, at Rds 150 to more than Rds 200.[40]

This led to the case being sent for arbitration and on 15 May 1838 when the two arbitrators reached concession on the valuation, Rocher asserted his intention to apply for a new valuation.[41] When Rocher died in September 1838 there may have been a sense of relief felt by those enslaved people whose freedom, and the freedom of their children, were being thwarted by him.

Buying Freedom

Lindor was not the only enslaved person who tried to buy his freedom, even as 1838 was drawing to a close. When the Justice of the Peace set the purchase price of 4 months of "apprenticeship" for the enslaved man called Marthinus at £4.10, the "slave-holder" A A Bruyns refused this price, demanding that he be paid 120 Rixdollars for the remaining four months until Emancipation or that Marthinus continue in slavery at his household for this time.[42] However, Bruyns was summonsed to appear before the Chief Justice, after which he consented to accept the payment of £4.10. At this

---

[39]WCARS, Records of the Magistrate of Simon's Town 1793-1985: 1/SMT 2/5. SMT 10/24 (1838) (21 February 1838). A note at the left hand bottom of the page reads: "instead of going she absented two or three days."

[40]The exchange rate in 1825 was £1 per 0.075 Rixdollars. Pim de Zwart, "Real Wages at the Cape of Good Hope: a Long-Term Perspective, 1652-1912" *Tijdschrift Voor Sociale en Economische Geschiedenis* 10, 2 (2013): 54. WCARS, Records of the Magistrate of Simon's Town 1793-1985: 1/SMT 2/5, SMT 10/24 (1838) Ref. 9 (12 March 1838).

[41]WCARS, Archives, Records of the Magistrate of Simon's Town 1793-1985: 1/SMT 2/5, SMT 10/24 (1838) Ref. 9 (12 March 1838).

time it emerged that Marthinus had already taken matters into his own hands and left the Bruyns "slave-holding" on 1 August 1838. However, a warning was issued that unless the monies were paid over to Bruyns, Marthinus would have to return to this "slave-holding" for the remaining four months.[43]

Malagasy Community

By the 1830s a section of the people described as "prize negroes" in Simon's Town had grown into an established Malagasy community. When a visiting clergyman named Reverend John Canham visited Black Town in 1835 he found the entire Black Town community to be Madagascan and he addressed them in the Malagasy language, asking whether they were all Malagasy and requesting that they raised their hands if they were. He described how they all held up their hands, and said *"Malagash izahay rehetra* [We are all Malagasy]."[44] The Reverend John Canham also wrote:

> Before I left Simon's Town the following morning, a respectable Malagash female called at the house where I was breakfasting, and presented me in true Malagash stile some new laid eggs and pickled fish and thanked me for going over to see them.[45]

The spatially separate Madagascan community gives a hint to an interesting phenomenon that was developing in Simon's Town whereby the British Colonial Government segregated people by ethnicity. This theory is reinforced through comments made by Harriette Ashmore (the wife of Captain William Ashmore serving in India in the 16th (Bedfordshire) Regiment of Foot) visiting Simon's Town in 1835. Describing Simon's Town as "a pretty little fishing place, built much in the Dutch style" she observed:

---

[42]WCARS, Records of the Magistrate of Simon's Town 1793-1985: 1/SMT 2/ 5, SMT 10/24 (1838) Ref. 38 (1 August 1838).
[43]WCARS, Records of the Magistrate of Simon's Town 1793-1985: 1/SMT 2/ 5, SMT 10/24 (1838) Ref. 37 (23 August 1838).
[44]Pier M Larson, *Ocean of Letters, Language and Creolization in an Indian Ocean Diaspora* (Cambridge: Cambridge University Press, 2009), 238.
[45]Larson, *Ocean of Letters*, 239.

There are, on the side of one of the hills above Simon's Town, a few mud huts, which would apparently afford something like adequate shelter for the cattle, which are turned out to seek their food in their vicinity; but these, we were told, are inhabited by upwards of 150 Mozambique people, who were taken from a slave ship, and received together with their liberty, permission to inhabit that small portion of [g]round.[46]

---

[46]Harriette Ashmore, *Narrative of a Three Months' March in India; .... by the Wife of an Officer in the 16th Foot* (London: Hastings, 1841), 19-20.

PART 8

FROM EMANCIPATION TO WORKING CLASS COMMUNITY:

1838 TO 1843 AND BEYOND

Fig. 8-1. Admiralty House, entrance to Simon's Town, circa 1854
Source: Litho of painting by Thomas Bowler. Library of Parliament, 6544, 18546544

Between 1838 and 1843 Simon's Town saw the establishment of a subaltern community who eked out a living working for the Royal Navy or dockyard as cheap labour. The labour of indigenous people, who formed part of this community of diverse people, was consolidated through the Masters and

Servants Ordinance of 1841.[1] Some people in this community created independent livings, the men through fishing and the women as washerwomen, taking in laundry from sailors.

Fig. 8-2. Washerwomen at the Waterfall, Simon's Town, circa 1838
Source: Watercolour by Christopher Webb Smith. Library of Parliament, 19349 (vii)

It was also at this time that certificates were being issued for people whose pseudo-apprenticeship periods had reached completion. Seven such certificates were sent to the Resident Justice at the Simon's Town Magistrates Office by the Collector of Customs. He was told to let these "negroes" know that their apprenticeship period had expired and that they were "free and at liberty to hire themselves to any Master or Mistress." He was further to impress upon such "negro" that he or she is to "retain and carefully peruse

---

[1] Vertrees Candy Malherbe, "Colonial Justice and the Khoisan in the Immediate Aftermath of Ordinance 50 of 1828: Denouement at Uitenhage" *Kronos* 24 (November 1997): 77-90.

such certificate in token of his or her being so at liberty." Cruelly, their children's freedom was not included and the Collector of Customs requested information "where any Negress has given birth to a child during the period of her apprenticeship, whether such child be still living, and its sex and age."[2]

Many people lived in overcrowded conditions and they were forced to pool very limited resources in order to pay their rentals. In this way people depended on each other for their livelihoods and a strong sense of community formed out of communal living. However, symptoms of historical trauma and degradation were also rising to the surface.

It was at this time that there were complaints about the canteen run by T F Dreyers at which a resident complained of "actual indecencies" with "lewd Hottentot women who draw the troops, and their other associates thither, to the great annoyance of the neighbourhood."[3]

The freedom experienced post-slavery was a tenuous one. While Britain compensated "slave-holders" for the financial losses they incurred due to the emancipation of enslaved people in their "slave-holdings"; overwhelmingly, enslaved people were "freed" into a state of poverty. To this end, as the historians Hermann and Giliomee pointed out, "the habits of domination fostered under slavery" continued.[4] The anthropologist Michael Whisson wrote of the overcrowded conditions that marginalised people in Simon's Town were forced to live in, which left them particularly vulnerable to fatalities during the measles epidemic of 1839 and the smallpox epidemic of 1840.[5]

Because many enslaved children were traumatically sold off separately from their mothers while still very young, some had no idea of who their

---

[2]WCARS, Records of the Magistrate of Simon's Town 1793-1985: 1/SMT 2/5, SMT 10/25 (1843) Ref. 15 (17 February 1843).
[3]WCARS, Records of the Magistrate of Simon's Town 1793-1985: 1/SMT 2/5, SMT 10/25 (1843) Ref. 26 (19 April 1843).
[4]Richard Elphick and Hermann Giliomee, "The Origins and Entrenchment of European Dominance at the Cape, 1652-c.1840" in *The Shaping of South African Society, 1652-1840*; edited by Richard Elphick and Hermann Giliomee (Cape Town: Maskew Miller Longman, 1989), 556.
[5]Michael Whisson, *The Fairest Cape? An Account of the Coloured People in the District of Simonstown* (Johannesburg: South African Institute of Race Relations, 1972), 29.

parents were. Such was the case with Jan of the Cape married to Susanna of the Cape, their names suggesting very recent links to slavery. When Jan died at his residence in Simon's Bay on 10 April 1843, his parents were listed as "unknown" and his age was thought to have been about fifty. Such important identity and self-esteem enhancing details as lineage and age were details that were lost to Jan. What is interesting, or possibly predictable, is the way formerly enslaved people married people who stood within similar social hierarchies to themselves. Jan himself was a labourer and owned no immovable property.[6]

Notwithstanding the bleak conditions of the formerly-enslaved, they were still a step higher on the socio-economic ladder than the people referred to as "prize negroes" for whom pseudo-slavery in the form of fourteen year indentureships continued.

Traumatised Children and the Smallpox Epidemic of 1839

At dawn on Christmas Day 1839 the HMS *Modeste* anchored in Simon's Town with fifty children on board, most of whom were thought to be under ten years of age and who had been liberated off the Portuguese "slaver," the *Escorpião*.[7]

For many of the local residents "their distribution excited intense interest."[8] However, a journalist for the *South African Commercial Advertiser*, who was touched by their plight, reported:

> Set down upon our shores naked and, no interpreter having yet been found, speechless. A more helpless set of creatures, or more deserving of our sympathies, cannot be imagined. A large proportion of them are children, under ten years of age! We do not know where they came from …[9]

---

[6]Jan of the Cape, death certificate. Cape Province, Probate Records of the Master of the High Court, 1834-1989 *Family Search* [online resource] https://www.familysearch.org/ark:/61903/1:1: QGR7-RN1V (accessed 21 August 2023).

[7]Christopher Saunders, "Liberated Africans" and Labour at the Cape of Good Hope in the First Half of the 19th Century (Cape Town: Centre for African Studies, 1983), 11.

[8]Saunders, "Liberated Africans in Cape Colony in the first half of the Nineteenth Century," 231.

It soon unfolded that the consequences of the arrival of these children proved deadly for many in the colony, as by the time it was discovered that some of these children were infected with smallpox, a total of 973 people had already died through the spread of this disease. By this time the children were quarantined and further spread of the disease contained.[10]

On distribution of the remaining survivors, some were set to work "cleaning the streams that flowed through Cape Town."[11] From this time onwards all "prize negroes" arriving in the colony were placed into the quarantine system.[12] However, when "prize negro" children were placed in the infant school in Wynberg for treatment in 1840, this caused much consternation among the residents who, probably fearing another smallpox outbreak, petitioned the governor for their removal.[13]

The Arrival of the first Krumen

The Emancipation period was also a time when the British Royal Navy in Simon's Town started searching elsewhere for labour and started bringing male migrant workers in from Sierra Leone in West Africa, known to the Navy as Krumen or Kroomen [hereafter the author will use only Kru and Krumen except for "Kroomen" in direct quotations].

The first group of Krumen arrived in Simon's Town on the HMS *Melville* in 1838.[14] Their date of arrival was telling, having coincided with the emancipation of enslaved people at the Cape. At this time two distinct groups of people settled in Sierra Leone. The first group were the indigenous Kru people and the second group, the Settler-Liberians.[15] However, these two

---

[9] *South African Commercial Advertiser* (28 December 1839). Saunders, "'Liberated Africans' and Labour," 11.

[10] Saunders, "'Liberated Africans' and Labour," 11.

[11] Saunders, "'Liberated Africans' and Labour," 11.

[12] Saunders, "Liberated Africans in Cape Colony in the First Half of the Nineteenth Century," 231.

[13] Memorial to Sir George Napier, Governor and Commander in Chief, from residents of Wynberg (signed by twenty Wynberg residents): WCARS CO/4007 (9 January 1840), page 128.

[14] Arthur Davey, "Kroomen: Black Sailors at the Cape." Unpublished paper (1992), 9.

groups of men were employed collectively by the Navy as one group, under the blanket name of "Kroomen" i.e. Krumen.[16]

The Indigenous Kru people

Fishermen and canoeists by trade, the indigenous Kru people lived in little villages along the narrow strip of coast from the Sinoe River to Cape Palmas, amidst the lushness of palm trees and gentle streams.[17] There were five chief villages, namely the Kruber, Little Kru, Settra Kru, Nana Kru and King Williams Town. Their settlement here dates back to the early 1500's, where they formed "six *dake* [i.e. clans] of patrilineally-related people," i.e. the Jloh, Kabor, Gbeta, Sasstown, Grand Cess and Five Tribes or Krao.[18] Although they all shared a common language, the original Kru were in fact those of the Five Tribes or Krao *dake*.[19] The close interaction of the Krao with shore-living fishermen resulted in them becoming exceptionally skilled at canoeing on the treacherous seas of Liberia.[20] This activity was absorbed by the other *dake* and in time they were all generally referred to as Kru, a name which became synonymous with seafaring activities.[21] The village of Settra Kru in particular was described as being "superior to any other native settlement on the coast" with the people being "the best informed, most intelligent and finest in personal appearance."[22]

---

[15]Diane Frost, *Work and Community among West African Migrant Workers since the Nineteenth Century* (Liverpool: Liverpool University Press, 1999), 11.

[16]Michael Whisson, "Water and Workers: Meeting the Needs of the Royal Navy in Simon's Town" *Simon's Town Historical Society Bulletin* 13, 4 (July 1985): 152-153. "The term refers to the language spoken by the indigenous coastal peoples, although some of the men recruited by the Royal Navy were ex-slaves rather than true Kru speakers."

[17]"A large stream of sweet and clear water runs through a grove of palm-trees to the sea." Horatio Bridge, *Journal of an African Cruiser: Comprising Sketches of the Canaries, the Cape de Verds, Liberia, Madeira, Sierra Leone and other places of interest on the West Coast of Africa* (New York: George P Putnam, 1845), 117.

[18]Frost, *Work and Community*, 7.
[19]Frost, *Work and Community*, 7.
[20]Frost, *Work and Community*, 8.
[21]Frost, *Work and Community*, 10.
[22]Bridge, *Journal of an African Cruiser*, 74.

In 1847 the whole of this coastal area became absorbed into the State of Liberia, however, due to the distance between the Liberian Government based in Monrovia and these outlying areas, it was some time before the power of Monrovia was felt by the Kru people.[23]

Fig. 8-3. The Kru believed in Obeah (or fetish)
Source: Library of Parliament, 42697, 11

The Kru were easily identifiable by the adornment of a distinct broad blue streak from the forehead to the nose.[24] They also bore the mark of a trident, which was tattooed on either side of their temples and were known to mutilate their incisor teeth.[25] Although Isobel Gill, the wife of a missionary, wrote around 1878 that "the moral nature of the Krooman is undoubtedly

---

[23] Davey, "The Kroomen of Simon's Town" *Simon's Town Historical Society Bulletin* 16, 2 (July 1990): 51.
[24] "The Kroo Boys" *Christian Express* (1 September 1902): 139.
[25] Kenneth Douglas-Morris, *Naval Medals, 1793-1856* (London: K J Douglas-Morris, 1987), 15. See also *The Eastern Mail* 11, 3 (30 July 1857); J Cutler Tefft "Mendi Mission" *Dental Register* 7, 3 (April 1854): 214-215.

high, and one eminently fitted to receive Christianity," the Kru had a religion of their own.[26]

The Kru believed in *obeah* (or fetish), the belief in guardian spirits. The head fetish man was responsible for the spiritual welfare and protection of the clan and was tasked with sending the *obeah* (guardian spirit) into a *gre gre* (or *greegree*), which was a charm worn around the neck.[27] *Obeah* was also sent into larger objects, which were then believed to contain mystical powers that would assist their owners in achieving certain aims, like healing the sick or resolving disputes.[28] There was a certain karmic influence here as well in that people believed if they wronged others, the *obeah* or fetish of the person they had wronged would get them. This, along with the ingrained respect of elders and the stronghold of the chief, created a community of people who were hierarchical and moralistic.[29]

That they also believed in reincarnation is borne out in the extract of a diary of Assistant Surgeon Henry Tracey who served on the *HMS Melville* when he said "they conceive that the body remains only a short period in the grave and that they will soon return to their mammies in their own country and meet each other again."[30]

Clannish by nature, the underlying feature of the Kru was one of respect, especially towards the elders, who bore iron rings around their legs as insignia. The sight of a large number of Krumen canoeing along the coast, singing a chorus as they rowed, was a familiar one. Usually one member would lead in recitative and the others would follow in chorus.[31] According to Kenneth Douglas-Morris, "the Kroos not only controlled the shipment of palm-

---

[26] Isobel Gill, *Six Months in Ascension: An Unscientific Account of a Scientific Expedition* (London: Murray, 1880), 237.
[27] "I saw a native doctor making his "greegree" or charm, for rain." Alfred Burdon Ellis, *The Land of Fetish* (London: Chapman and Hall, 1883), 50. Bridge, *Journal of an African Cruiser,* 105.
[28] "It is about the golden axe. The axe belongs to the fetish: it is a sign of the fetish. The axe was sent ... to obtain our desires peaceably." Ellis, *Land of Fetish*, 308-309.
[29] "Age is more respected by the Africans than any other people." Bridge, *Journal of an African Cruiser,* 17.
[30] Henry Tracey, *A Visit to Cape Town in 1838* (Johannesburg: Friends of the Library, University of the Witwatersrand, 1980), 8.
[31] Bridge, *Journal of an African Cruiser,* 23.

oil but also the supervision and sailing of coastal vessels, mainly because they were the local tribe which would manage canoes in the surf."[32]

In fact their industry in utilising this resource took many forms. The oil from the palms formed part of a sauce served with rice, constituting a meal, the fibres were used to fashion ropes, looms and brooms and its leaves for roofing and fencing.[33]

Fig. 8-4. The Kru dominated the palm trade
Source: Library of Parliament, 42697, 02

Opportunities for contracting out their labour to passing ships arose with the formation of a British crown colony in Sierra Leone in 1807.[34] It was then that the indigenous Kru migrated down to Freetown, to barter their labour.[35] Prized for their strength and agility, seafaring ways and naviga-

---

[32]Douglas-Morris, *Naval Medals*, 14.
[33]Merran McCulloch, *The Peoples of Sierra Leone* (London: International African Institute, 1950), 10. Series: Western Africa Part II.
[34]Davey, "Kroomen: Black Sailors at the Cape," 2.
[35]Frost, *Work and Community*, 7.

tional expertise there was a demand for Kru labour by merchant ships. Horatio Bridge, a United States Naval officer of the 1840s, described the Kru thus:

> The Kroomen are indispensable in carrying on the commerce and maritime business of the African coast. When a Kroo-boat comes alongside, you may buy the canoe, hire the men at a moment's warning, and retain them in your service for months.[36]

For the Navy, the use of Kru labour had much to do with the high rate of mortality amongst white seamen, succumbing to malaria and fever in tropical West Africa. It is therefore no surprise that this area was referred to as a "white man's grave." With the use of Kru labour, the white seamen were exempted from all strenuous jobs, especially those requiring excessive exposure to the sun and "mosquito-ridden mangrove swamps."[37]

The Kru always undertook these journeys as a group, under the leadership of a Kru headman who was responsible for the return of the group. Acting as a mediator between the workers and their employers, the role of the headman was that of staff recruiter, manager, disciplinarian and carer.

He was answerable not only to the European employers of Kru labour, ensuring the strict management of the workforce, but also to the families of the men he recruited that they would return safely. In addition, he was the only person permitted to punish an erring Kruman for any transgression.[38]

One wonders why, in such a clannish community, the men were happy to leave their families for such long periods. It appears the main incentive was marriage, as a man's status was determined by the number of wives he could afford. On returning from their journeys these men would take a wife or many wives, depending on the wealth they had accumulated, and share the

---

[36] Bridge, *Journal of an African Cruiser*, 16.
[37] Frost, *Work and Community*, 35.
[38] Jane Martin, "Krumen 'down the Coast': Liberian Migrants on the West African Coast in the 19th Century" *The International Journal of African Historical Studies* 18, 3, (1985): 408.

remainder of earnings with their families.[39] One Jack Purser of Settra Kru had no fewer than twenty-nine wives![40]

For the younger men, some as young as fourteen, leaving their families to work abroad had become a rite of passage, carrying on in the tradition of their fathers, who had done so before them.[41] These young men, whose homecoming would spark days of festive celebrations, would give all their earnings to their fathers. Once home, even though they may have been away for a long period of time, they would place themselves once more under the authority of their parents.[42]

The habitat of the Kru family took the form of a cluster of bamboo houses, which was enclosed by a bamboo wall. Within this patriarchal family structure the man's authority in the hierarchical order was unquestioned, however, within these boundaries, the first wife held special status. It was she who managed the household affairs, controlled the finances and directed the labour of the other wives.[43] Therefore additional wives not only increased the husband's status, but also benefited him materially. While the husband worked away, the wives took care of his assets by cultivating the land, where yams, sweet potatoes and rice were grown.[44]

A common sight in the villages was women bearing clay pots of water on their heads, which they would collect from a stream. Collecting water was an integral part of the day as the Kru bathed at least twice a day.[45] It is no wonder that the Mayor of Simon's Town, in 1893, described the Krumen as being "cleanly in their habits".[46] Another common sight in the villages was the freedom of dress of the women, which suited the warm, tropical climate. In his journal, Horatio Bridge comments on one of the wives of a successful trader in Settra Kru, as follows:

---

[39] Bridge, *Journal of an African Cruiser*, 17.
[40] Bridge, *Journal of an African Cruiser*, 105.
[41] Martin, "Krumen 'Down the Coast," 407.
[42] Bridge, *Journal of an African Cruiser*, 17.
[43] Bridge, *Journal of an African Cruiser*, 19.
[44] Davey, "The Kroomen of Simon's Town," 51.
[45] Bridge, *Journal of an African Cruiser*, 106.
[46] Davey, *The Kroomen of Simon's Town*, 52.

A cloth around her loins, dyed with gay colors, composed her whole drapery, leaving her figure as fully exposed as the most classic sculptor could have wished. It is to be observed, however, that the sable hue is in itself a kind of veil.[47]

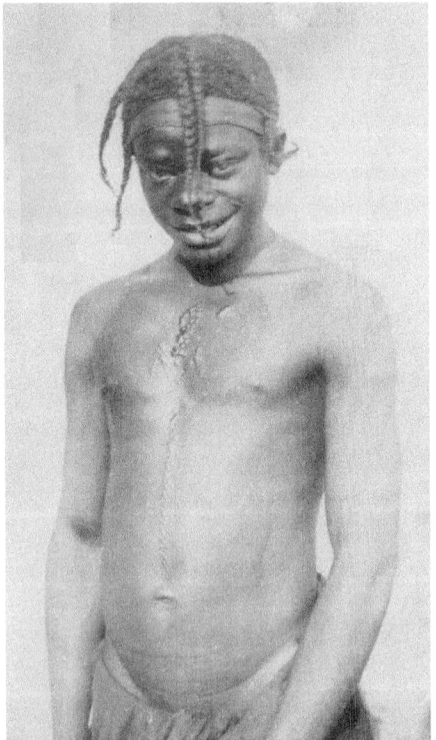

Fig. 8-5. A young Kru boy
Source: Library of Parliament

Besides her freedom of dress, life for the Kru woman carried little other choices, especially in terms of marriage. According to Horatio Bridge, girls as young as fourteen were sometimes married to men as old as sixty.[48]

---
[47]Bridge, *Journal of an African Cruiser*, 116.
[48]Bridge, *Journal of an African Cruiser*, 19.

It was because of this that the missionary schools took in mostly boys, who were said to "show a considerable aptitude for learning." As for the girls it was said that

> it is an obstacle in the way of educating girls, as many of them are betrothed before entering school, and, just when their progress begins to be satisfactory, their husbands claim them and take them away.[49]

The Kru were almost the only people of that time who voluntarily engaged in migrant labour, a practice that in later years became a way of life for the majority of black South Africans.[50] While the Kru prided themselves in being free agents to contract out their labour as they pleased, they were strongly opposed to being enslaved. In cases where Krumen were faced with enslavement, they opted to die instead. Thus a number of Krumen took their lives by drowning or starving themselves to death when placed in this predicament.[51] Unfortunately this repulsion of slavery did not deter them from being involved in the enslavement of others. Their involvement in the "slave-trade" as interpreters and middlemen is well documented by Diane Frost in her study of West African migrant workers. In fact, with the decline of the pepper trade in the eighteenth century, this involvement was heightened.[52] Paradoxically, in the 1860s they were employed by the Royal Navy to take part in anti-slavery patrols on the East Coast of Africa![53]

The Settler-Liberians

The Settler-Liberians were a composition of Black Loyalists and formerly enslaved people liberated off "slave" ships by the British anti-slavery patrols. While the Black Loyalists were the pioneers in the formation of Freetown, over time the "liberated slaves" became absorbed into their community.

---

[49]Bridge, *Journal of an African Cruiser,* 105.
[50]Frost, *Work and Community,* 37.
[51]"The Kroo Boys" *Christian Express* (1 September 1902): 139.
[52]Frost, *Work and Community,* 9.
[53]Arthur Davey, "Tindals, Seedies and Kroomen" (*Simon's Town Historical Society Bulletin* 17, 4 (July 1993): 157.

The Black Loyalists

During the War of American Independence from 1775-1783, a large number of African Americans, most of whom had escaped from their American enslavers, fought on the side of the British forces in return for their freedom. This they were encouraged to do through two proclamations sent out, four years apart, which called on enslaved African Americans to desert their "masters" and serve on the side of the British, in return for their freedom.

The first proclamation issued by Lord Dunmore in November 1775, declared:

> To the end that peace and order may be restored ... I do require every person capable of bearing arms to resort to his Majesty's standard ... and I do hereby further declare all indentured servants, Negroes or others (appertaining to Rebels) free, that are able and willing to bear arms, they joining His Majesty's Troops, as soon as may be, for the more speedily reducing this Colony to a proper sense of their duty to his Majesty's crown and dignity.[54]

Whereas the first proclamation made it clear that the British were only seeking people who were able to take up arms, the second proclamation issued by Sir Henry Clinton in 1779, was more inclusive. In it the promise of "full security" to "any Negro who shall desert the Rebel Standard," was offered not only to those who could take up arms, but also to those who could assist behind the lines as cooks, laundresses, nurses and labourers.[55] For the British this strategy was devised to bolster their strength against the Americans, and for the enslaved African people in America, this was their precious opportunity to break free of the shackles of slavery.

After the colonists defeated the British, there were fears that the British would renege on their promises, but through the efforts of Sir Guy Carlton, the promises were kept.[56] This offered a spark of hope for many as, in return for their loyalty, their names were recorded in a ledger titled "The Book of Negroes," with which came the promise of a better life. It was thus with

---

[54]Lawrence Hill, "Freedom Bound" *The Beaver* (February-March 2007): 18.
[55]Hill, "Freedom Bound," 18.
[56]Hill, "Freedom Bound," 22.

hopeful hearts that some of the three thousand men, women and children of African ancestry, sailed away from New York between April and November 1783. However, not all these people received their liberty. Only those, the so-called Black Loyalists, who could prove that they assisted the British during the war, left New York as free people, i.e. the ones who held the coveted status of having their names recorded in The Book of Negroes. For the others, enslaved and indentured workers of the United Empire Loyalists, their status as "slaves" remained unchanged. The only difference for them would be the new environment that they found themselves in.[57]

Some African Americans returned with the military personnel to England and others took up the promise of free land in Nova Scotia, the easternmost province of Canada.[58] However, each group encountered a different set of problems. In England, slavery had been declared illegal by Lord Chief Justice Mansfield back in 1772, in a ground-breaking case brought by the abolitionist Granville Sharpe.[59] Unfortunately, many of these Black Loyalists were unable to find employment there.[60] With minimal chances of improving their lives economically, they added to the ranks of Britain's poor.

Meanwhile, for the Black Loyalists who arrived in Nova Scotia, it was a case of Paradise Lost. Not only were the promises of free land not kept, but they found themselves in a society where racism was rife and they were made to feel unwelcome. This was displayed in no small measure when those living in Birchtown were driven out of their homes by white soldiers.[61]

These were the factors that prompted Thomas Peters, a former sergeant with the Loyalist forces, to journey from Nova Scotia to England, to seek an audience with Granville Sharpe. He informed Sharpe of the frustration of himself and other formerly enslaved people back in Nova Scotia as the prom-

---

[57] Hill, "Freedom Bound," 18 and 22.
[58] James W St G Walker, *The Black Loyalists: The Search for a Promised Land in Nova Scotia and Sierra Leone, 1783-1870* (Toronto: University of Toronto Press, 1992), 7.
[59] Walker, *The Black Loyalists*, 95.
[60] Julia Bibko, "The American Revolution and the Black Loyalist Exodus" *#History: A Journal of Student Research* 1 (1 December 2016): 64. *SUNY Open Access Repository* [online resource] http://hdl.handle.net/20.500.12648/2669 (accessed 29 September 2023).
[61] Hill, "Freedom Bound," 22.

ises of land had not been honoured. Peters and his fellow Nova Scotians were then offered asylum in West Africa.

Thus in 1786 Sharpe and his supporters devised a plan to transport about 400 formerly enslaved people and "some sixty 'shanghaied' Plymouth street walkers"[62] to a small strip of land on Africa's West Coast. Although this area had been used as a base by Portuguese traders for several centuries, Sharpe visualised it becoming a self-governing colony, which he called the Province of Freedom.[63]

The casualties on this expedition were high. The sea journey and conditions of travel took their toll and many died before reaching the "promised land." Sick and weary, still more died a short time after their arrival in the new settlement, named Granville Town. For those who survived there were many hardships to overcome, but they were determined to re-build their lives back on the continent from which their forefathers were taken. Two years later, just as they were starting to lay down roots, their security was once again threatened when their settlement was destroyed by fire. Homeless and displaced, they collected what they could salvage and moved a small distance away. Here the settlement was rebuilt, over a period of two years, and by 1790 Freetown was established.[64]

Between 26 February and 9 March 1792, a total of 1,190 people arrived in Sierra Leone from Nova Scotia, aboard fifteen ships. This was the largest free migration to Africa of formerly enslaved people of African descent ever recorded in history.[65] In 1800 their numbers were augmented by five hundred "maroons or outlawed negroes" who arrived from Jamaica.[66]

Life at Freetown was challenging and hardships plenty, with the result that in the first twenty years from its inception, many settlers had died.[67] How-

---

[62]Whisson, "Water and Workers," 151.

[63]John Peterson, *Province of Freedom: A History of Sierra Leone, 1787-1870* (Evanston: Northwestern University Press, 1969), 103.

[64]"The continued migration of Kru to Freetown for seafaring work can be explained in part by the greater opportunities in ship work Freetown offered, but also because of increased harassment of Kru migrants endured from the Liberian government when recruited for work on European steamers." Frost, *Work and Community*, 13 and 34.

[65]Peterson, *Province of Freedom*, 106 and 140.

[66]Bridge, *Journal of an African Cruiser*, 168.

ever, because of the abolition of the "slave-trade" by Britain in 1807 (effective 1808),[68] and through the efforts of the British anti-slavery patrols set up at Freetown, their numbers became augmented by "liberated Africans."[69]

The "Liberated Slaves"

In his journal Horatio Bridge expressed his sentiments about the "liberated slaves" as follows:

> The fate of the rescued slaves is scarcely better than that of the crews of the captured slave-vessels. The latter are landed on the nearest point of the African Coast, where death by starvation or fever almost certainly awaits them.[70]

From 1808 many formerly enslaved people who had been "liberated" from "slave" ships by the British anti-slavery patrols arrived in Sierra Leone.[71] Those landed at Freetown by the British anti-slavery troops were placed in the "Queen's Yard" where they were offered as apprentices for periods of five to nine years to applicants able to pay the government a fee for their services. However, if no applicants were forthcoming, they were "turned adrift, to be supported as they may, or, unless Providence takes all the better care of them, to starve."[72]

Many of these formerly enslaved people in fact died, but notwithstanding the many deaths that occurred, more and more human cargoes were offloaded at Freetown by the British anti-slavery patrols. It was for this reason that the population increased and by 1870 reached a total of 70 000 people. This number was bolstered by local members of the Kru clan who were encouraged to join the settlement and offered various monetary rewards for settling there. By 1816 there was sufficient Kru settlement into Sierra Leone, for there to be a quarter named "Krootown."[73]

---

[67] Peterson, *Province of Freedom*, 121.
[68] Peterson, *Province of Freedom*, 256.
[69] Peterson, *Province of Freedom*, 274.
[70] Bridge, *Journal of an African Cruiser*, 51-52.
[71] Bridge, *Journal of an African Cruiser*, 168.
[72] Bridge, *Journal of an African Cruiser*, 170.
[73] Frost, *Work and Community*, 8.

The people of Sierra Leone were thus a mixture of indigenous Kru people, Black Loyalists from America and "liberated slaves," who came from nearly every ethnic group along the Atlantic Coast of Africa. For example, a young "Kruman" on board a ship who spoke "better English," eventually admitted that he was a native of North Carolina, but had resided in Liberia for many years.[74]

The differences between the indigenous Kru people and the "liberated slaves" were vast. While the latter had experienced the brutality of slavery, the former had partaken in its perpetuation. This fact alone was breeding ground for resentment, contributing towards a rift between these two groups of people. Religious differences were also difficult to reconcile. Whereas to the indigenous Kru people, their religion was a legacy inherited from their ancestors, with the underlying element being respect; the anglicised African Americans clung to Christianity, which they had embraced as a lifeline, offering them hope at the time of their deepest suffering.

In addition to the above, there were other areas of conflict. For the Kru who had previously had the monopoly over trade and commerce, the Settler-Liberians "under the auspices of the American Colonisation Society" became an economic threat.[75] Further resentment simmered when, during the 1840s, the Settler establishment expanded onto Kru land.[76]

These conflicted interests, i.e. the one group struggling for survival in a new land and the other fighting to maintain what they had, resulted in "intermittent warfare" between the two groups during the nineteenth century.[77] However, in 1845, a Treaty of Peace and Friendship was struck between the Krus and the Settler-Liberians. A significant overture from the Kru in this Treaty was renouncement of their involvement in the "slave-trade."[78] Thus by the middle of the nineteenth century a single creolised society began to form, who identified themselves as Sierra Leoneans, with the common language being Krio, a mixture of English and various African languages.[79]

---

[74] Bridge, *Journal of an African Cruiser*, 60.
[75] Frost, *Work and Community*, 10-11.
[76] Frost, *Work and Community*, 11.
[77] Frost, *Work and Community*, 13.
[78] Frost, *Work and Community*, 32-33.

The Simon's Town link

In the run up to 1838, business and the farming sector were in a state of panic as they feared the loss of labour. The Navy was no different. For the Navy, the Krumen provided a cheap, yet powerful labour force.[80] Their ability to do strenuous manual work in extreme heat, their strong athletic build, sobriety and law-abiding natures made them all the more appealing.

Brought to Simon's Town as contract workers, they performed several arduous tasks such as mooring, clearing coal from lighters and watering and coaling of ships. On board they fulfilled various job descriptions, as stewards, cooks, carpenters-mates and deck-hands.[81]

As an aside, joining the Navy also meant a new identity for indigenous Kru people in that their African names were replaced with names given to them by Navy personnel. Some of these names were overtly British, such as Johnson, Waintop, Andrew, Baker or Brown and others were downright degrading such as Black Whale, Jim Crow, Bottle of Beer, Tom Cockroach and Dick Deadeye.[82] Significantly, although they came from three different streams, they were collectively referred to as "Kroomen" by the Navy.

The Navy tried to insulate the Krumen from the local community, telling them not to mix with the local people on their arrival. The local people, whom the Krumen were to avoid, were people whose ancestors were indigenous "San" and Khoe people or people whose ancestors were enslaved in the town.[83]

However, the Krumen soon attracted the interest of some of the local women, and vice versa. This resulted in a number of liaisons taking place, some resulting in marriage. These men now adopted Simon's Town as their new home and did not wish to return to Sierra Leone when their contracts expired.[84] One such example, in 1893, was a Kruman by the curious name of "Flying Jib Number 2", who appeared before the Cape Labour Commis-

---

[79] Peterson, *Province of Freedom*, xxi.
[80] Whisson, "Water and Workers," 153.
[81] Davey, "The Kroomen of Simon's Town," 52.
[82] Davey, "The Kroomen of Simon's Town," 52-53.
[83] Whisson, *The Fairest Cape*, 4.
[84] Davey, "The Kroomen of Simon's Town," 11.

sion saying that he had been living in Simon's Town since 1887, was married to a local woman and wanted to stay in the country.[85]

Another Kruman who married a local woman was Jack Savage, whose Certificate of Service in the Royal Navy shows that he first entered their service on the *Penelope* on 1 October 1893. He and his wife Sabinea lived in Davis Cottage, Simon's Town. Thrice decorated by the Navy, his last medal was the British War Medal that he received on 31 August 1925. Jack was pensioned off in 1919, however, it was only in 1923 that his naval pension was approved, at thirty two pounds and six shillings per year, back-dated to 1919.[86]

In 2009 I had the pleasure of visiting Jack Savage's last surviving son, Peter James Savage, aged eighty, at his home in Ocean View. Mr Savage, who was the youngest of his eleven siblings, had little memory of his father who died when he was four. He recalled a happy childhood in Simon's Town, but a strict Calvinistic upbringing by his mother, where the rod was very rarely spared. Mr Savage could not give me any information about his parent's ages except to say that his mother was much younger than his father. By the time of his father's death, many of his siblings were already adults, working as labourers at the Simon's Town Dockyard to support the family. Mr Savage had no knowledge of his father's history in Sierra Leone, saying that in those days the adults never discussed anything with the children. However, certain of his mannerisms, especially his very entertaining and amusing way of questioning me with riddles, is a mannerism that I have been told by another Simon's Town resident, was very typical of the Krumen.

A sprinkling of other Krumen also married local women and as the Krumen were such highly valued workers, this state of affairs was accepted in individual cases, though not encouraged. By now Krumen were employed in many other spheres of Cape society. Some worked at Admiralty House, two were horse-riding companions to the Admiral's daughters, others worked as cooks in private homes, and one enterprising Kruman ran a cab service in Cape Town. The Dockyard also absorbed a number of Krumen, having taken in their first Krumen apprentices in 1859. These men were also served

---

[85]Davey, "The Kroomen of Simon's Town," 15.
[86]Jack Savage's Certificate of Service with the Royal Navy, Simon's Town Museum.

with an order to "stay away from the evil examples of liberty men and Hottentots."[87] This order was reinforced by Rear Admiral Salmon in 1883, when he decreed that Krumen should not leave the Dockyard area, where they resided, without permission.[88]

When Edwin John Harvey Pinkham became master of the Admiralty coal hulk, *The Nubian* in 1901, his staff of nine included seven Krumen. Being a decidedly unusual man, Pinkham made *The Nubian* home to his family and staff along with an assortment of animals, including pigs, chickens, ducks, pigeons, cats and a monkey! A regular church-goer, he and his family were transported to St Frances church every Sunday in a gig pulled by "four smartly dressed Kroomen."

When Pinkham was attacked by one of the Krumen, "due to discontent among the Kroomen," this man was court-martialled and found guilty of attempted murder, to which he was sentenced to be flogged by the Head Kruman.[89] This occurrence was out of character for the Krumen who were lauded by the Mayor of Simon's Town, Frederick Hermanus Schumdorf Hugo to the Cape Government Commission in 1893 as being "well behaved, non drinkers and cleanly in their habits." James Pigott of the Royal Navy described the Krumen as "intelligent, well-behaved and sober."[90] Still others described them as "hard workers who rarely complained."[91]

Although the cause of the "discontent among the Kroomen" in the case of Edwin John Harvey Pinkham is not known, a meeting by the National Council of Glebo in Sierra Leone, attended by "chiefs and mission-educated men" reflected issues affecting Kru migrant workers generally. The recommendations of the Council were printed in the *African Times* of 30 April 1874, distributed in London, under the title "New Regulations in Hiring Kroomen at Cape Palmas" issued by Sear Nybar Weah, King of the Gedeboes or Kroo people at Cape Palmas and other parts adjacent."

---

[87]Davey, "Kroomen: Black Sailors at the Cape,"10.
[88]Whisson, "Water and Workers," 153.
[89]Bill Rice, "*Nubian* (C.370): The Admiralty Coal Hulk based at Simon's Town from 1901-1912" *Simon's Town Historical Society Bulletin*, 23, 2 (July 2004): 76.
[90]Davey, "The Kroomen of Simon's Town," 52.
[91]Frost, *Work and Community*, 35.

Although these regulations never became effective, it gave an illuminating picture of how the Kru migrant workers were treated in certain quarters. This was also the first time that the Kru migrant workers were given a "voice." The regulations proposed were as follows:

- Krumen were only to be shipped if money was paid to them in advance

- No-one mistreating Krumen or detaining them for over twelve months would be allowed to recruit [Krumen] again

- There was to be no collective punishment for one man's theft

- Sick men were to be sent home

- Merchants down the coast were to ensure that the Krumen would have secure passage directly to their homes.[92]

Apart from the "Pinkham story," there is no other recorded evidence to suggest discontent amongst, or ill-treatment of, Kru people in Simon's Town. In an article about the opening of the Simon's Town Railway Station in 1890, the reporter described the crowd on the platform as "staid-looking Europeans, gorgeously attired Malays, ... and Kroomen from Sierra Leone dressed in sailor clothes and with merry good-humoured faces."[93]

By 1901 the accommodation at West Dockyard must have become stretched, as a sizeable "Kroo Town" had developed near the railway station, consisting of tents. Of this settlement, the historian Arthur Davey remarked that, although the living conditions were deplorable, the crime rate amongst the Krumen was very low and consisted mostly of petty fines, i.e. one Krumen was fined for letting his pigs run into the street! In these cases they always paid their fines promptly.[94]

---

[92]Martin, "Krumen 'Down the Coast,'" 415.
[93]David M Rhind, "The Simon's Town Railway Line" *Simon's Town Historical Society Bulletin* 16, 2 (July 1990): 60.
[94]Davey, "Kroomen: Black Sailors at the Cape," 12.

While the first Kruman to be buried in Simon's Town was nameless and, as a "pagan," was buried in the bush outside the walls of the burial grounds; many Krumen became assimilated into the society in which they found themselves. They attended St George's Naval Church at the Dockyard, where a number of them were baptised. The burial records of St Francis Church also document the burial of two women who were wives of Krumen in 1859 and 1861.[95]

Most Krumen worked for the Navy for their contract period of three years and were eager to return home, but a few served for more than twenty years, earning Petty Officer rates, parchment certificates, good conduct badges, naval pensions and long service and conduct medals. These were invariably men who had married and settled in Simon's Town.[96]

Whereas some Krumen came to Simon's Town to serve out their contracts and return home and others came here to start new lives, some unwittingly came here to die. Such was the case of L T Dow, who was fatally wounded while serving in the First Anglo-Boer War (1880-1881).

Francis Gibson, a shipwright apprentice of HMS *Boscawen* who was educated at the Missionary School in Sierra Leone, was only sixteen when he died in Simon's Town in 1858.[97]

In all, the number of Krumen commemorated individually in the Garden of Remembrance at Seaforth, Simon's Town and in the Commonwealth Cemetery in Dido Valley totals eighty-nine. Evidence of twenty-six more burials surfaced in Naval Hospital and Burial records.[98]

In 1903 the Vice Admiral reported difficulty in recruiting Kru labour from Sierra Leone. This was put down to these men preferring shorter trips on merchant ships and disliking the weather conditions of the Cape.[99] The poor remuneration by the Navy was given as another likely reason.[100] While these reasons were all valid, the political tensions in Liberia were an even

---

[95] Davey, "The Kroomen of Simon's Town," 51.
[96] Douglas-Morris, *Naval Medals*, 13.
[97] Davey, "The Kroomen of Simon's Town," 52.
[98] Davey, "The Kroomen of Simon's Town," 51.
[99] Whisson, "Water and Workers," 153.
[100] Whisson, "Water and Workers," 153.

stronger factor, as the Liberian government began to cast its net over the outlying areas under its control.

With the implementation of the Port of Entry Act of 1864, the Liberian government sought to remedy its economic problems by gaining control over, and exacting an income through, the Kru migrant workers. This Act limited the return of Krumen to five points of entry, i.e. the Cape Mount, Monrovia, Buchanan, Sino and Cape Palmas, where customs were collected from returning migrant workers.[101] In addition to this, employers were also ordered to pay a fee to the Liberian government for departing Kru workers, i.e. $1.00 for a labourer and $2.00 for a stevedore. While this Act (and a later one in 1873) were not effectively executed, it was the beginning of the end of free movement for the Krumen, as further more stringent legislation followed.[102]

Kru descendants from Simon's Town include the late Ronald Roberts of Retreat, whose grandfather, Joseph Roberts, was a Kruman from Sierra Leone who had married Louise Summers from Simon's Town. Joseph worked as a cook for a Mrs King Salters in Simon's Town. Another well known former Simon's Town resident and Kru descendant is the late Peter Clarke, who was a poet, artist and writer. A further illustrious descendant of the Krumen is artist and writer Lionel Davis, whose ancestry can be linked to Tom Davis of Sierra Leone. Tom Davis died in Simon's Town in 1896, at the age of twenty-three years.

The late Joan Swain, who worked at the Simon's Town Museum for many years, was the granddaughter of Jack Savage, mentioned earlier in this chapter.

Some records of Krumen in the latter part of the 1800s are listed below

On 5 January 1880 the Kruman Benjamin Andrews married Spasie Isaacs at St Francis Church in Simon's Town.[103] Their marriage was witnessed by

---

[101] Martin, "Krumen 'Down the Coast,'" 416.
[102] Martin, "Krumen 'Down the Coast,'" 416.
[103] This record, and the birth, marriage and death records that follow, may be found in the registers of St Francis Church, Simonstown, accessible online via *Family Search* [online resource] https://familysearch.org.

Thomas Bestman and Sarah James. Neither the couple nor their witnesses were literate.

Thomas Peter married Amelia May at St Francis Church on 25 May 1884. Though Thomas Peter was not literate, having signed his marriage certificate with an X, his wife signed her name in full. On 12 March 1895 the Kruman Thomas Freeman, who was employed by the Royal Navy, married Sarah Williams at St Francis Church in Simon's Town. They were married by John Eedes, in the presence of Sarah Coffee and both Thomas and Sarah signed their marriage certificate with an X. Sadly their marriage was short-lived as Thomas died just four years later on 2 March 1898, at the Royal Naval Hospital in Simon's Town. He was only twenty-four years old.

The Sierra Leonean Thomas Dowling who worked in Simon's Town as a cook died at the age of twenty-eight, on 29 April 1896. On 11 August 1899, the six day old child of Royal Navy Kruman John Robert Coffee, died of "pneumonia exhaustion." His father signed his death notice with an X.

When two cottages were demolished for the building of the Simons Town School (later the Simon's Town Municipality) in 1896, the third cottage was shared by America Morrison, Thomas Davis and John Davis.

The Residents of Black's Cottages

In later years residents from Black's Cottages, Simon's Town included the washerwoman Maria Laguma (born in 1864), whose parents were Isaac and Dinah Payne. From her home in Black's Cottages she raised her five children, taking in washing while her fisherman husband Daniel Laguma eked out a living from the sea. Daniel's death from consumption on 26 December 1900 was a precursor to thirty-six year old Maria Laguma's death just weeks later on 11 February 1901. With Maria's death their five children Louisa aged twenty, Maria aged fifteen, Pearlie aged thirteen, Willie aged eleven and Daisy aged ten were left as orphans in Black Town. Maria left an insurance policy valued at £14.00, but the long-term survival of her children would have depended on Louisa and Maria's ability to continue to serve their mother's customers as washerwomen, and also the kindness of neighbours.

Many children as young as nine were sent out to work to supplement meagre incomes, the girls as cleaners and the boys as helpers to the fishermen.

Among the struggling fishing communities of Simon's Town it was also customary to share and help one's neighbours, especially when the fishermen made a "catch."

Some years ago this custom of reciprocal sharing was explained to me by Mrs Sybil Roberts, a former Cole Point Road, Simon's Town resident, as follows:

> If you had more than your share you know, you just um, gathered together whatever [you] could share and *"vat maar oor vir Aunty Mariam, Uncle Taggie het nie uitgegaan"* i.e. take some food over to Aunty Mariam, Uncle Taggie didn't have a catch [of fish today]. That is why Uncle Taggie could always bring us *'n stukkie vis* [a piece of fish].[104]

Today there is no tangible evidence of Black Town, which has been replaced by the Simon's Town Municipal buildings and the original Simon's Town High School building, which over time became utilised as the Simon's Town Library. However, the memory of the people of Black Town is honoured through the living monuments: their descendants.[105]

The "Liberated Africans"

During the post Emancipation period, the British anti-slavery squadron intercepted a number of ships carrying enslaved people on "slavers," who were meant for plantation slavery in the Americas and Brazil. Most were Mozambican and many were young children. After being removed from these "slavers" they were brought to Cape Town.[106] At the Cape they were referred to as "Liberated Africans" or "prize negroes."

The experience of the so-called "Liberated Africans" or "prize negroes" as they were registered in the census, differed vastly from the experiences of the Krumen, who were migrant workers hired by the Navy for a set period and

---

[104] Interview/conversation between the author and Mrs Roberts.

[105] Part of this chapter was previously published under Joline Young, "The West African Kroomen and their links to Simon's Town" *Quarterly Bulletin of the National Library of South Africa* 64, 2 (April-June 2010): 62-75.

[106] Jaqueline Lalou Meltzer, "Liberated Africans and the Barracks at Papendorp" *Bulletin of the National Library of South Africa* 74, 1 (June 2020): 49.

received payment for their services. There was a certain bearing in the Krumen who could be seen in the town wearing their smart naval uniforms and who had money to pay their way. Notwithstanding racial barriers, the Krumen still had the dignity of free movement and choice in a way that the indentured "Liberated Africans" did not. This set the Krumen apart from the indentured "Liberated Africans" to whom these markers of dignity were denied.

On landing, their journey to the so-called Negro Barracks in Papendorp (today's Woodstock) would have depended on whether they were landed in Table Bay or Simon's Bay. If landed in Table Bay the "Liberated Africans" (also referred to as "negroes" or "prize negroes") were unceremoniously marched along the beach on a route that would not pass along roads or past houses. For those landed in Simon's Bay, they were transported by wagon out of sight of the actual town, "off the High Road and by the Flats."[107]

Lalou Meltzer describes their trauma thus:

> People from the ships arrived after weeks of capture, usually in the company of dozens of very small children (often under the age of 10) having been marched to the East African coast, boarded on Portuguese slave ships, recaptured by the British naval ships, confined in suffocating holds and after further delays brought to port in Simon's Town—all the while surrounded by death and disease.[108]

Certainly the Reverend Pascoe Grenfell Hill commented on what were evident signs of trauma among the "captured Africans" who arrived in Simon's Bay after being taken off the Portuguese "slaver" *Progresso*. He made particular mention of their visible "anxiety and apprehension" and sombre countenances.[109]

In addition to the psychological trauma, there were also the physical health issues to contend with. Such was the case when the Portuguese "slaver," the *Amizade Constante* was captured off the Zambezi River mouth by the HMS *Modeste*. After arriving in Simon's Bay with 568 enslaved persons on board it

---
[107]Meltzer, "Liberated Africans," 50.
[108]Meltzer, "Liberated Africans," 52.
[109]Meltzer, "Liberated Africans," 55-56.

became evident that there was an outbreak of smallpox on board "in the hold" which had already claimed the lives of fifty-two of the original number of 620 people. Some of the sick were cared for at the hospital in Simon's Town while the more seriously ill were transported for hospitalisation at the old Military Hospital. However, by 1 October 1840, ninety-one of the total of 568 "liberated Africans" had already died.[110] Those who survived would of course be indentured in the town after a period of quarantine.

By 1840, new regulations pertaining to indentureship periods of adult people "liberated" off "slave" ships effectively reduced their indentureship periods to one year for males aged seventeen years and upwards and one year for females aged fifteen years and upwards. However, the regulations stipulated that children could be indentured until the age of eighteen for males and sixteen for females.

This is pertinent when one considers that the groups of "liberated Africans" who arrived on these shores included "a large number of very small and teenage children."[111] Indeed this would have also been the case for the three children born on Cape soil to pregnant mothers taken off the "slaver" *Josephine* captured by *Thunderbolt* on 29 January 1844.

On arrival in Papendorp they were quarantined before being assigned to take up indentureships in private homes or on farms. Some were assigned to residents in Simon's Bay. While we will never know the names of all the people who were indentured here, surviving records give us a glimpse of at least some of the people who arrived in Simon's Bay after being taken off "slavers" during this historical period.

These records are derived from a ledger titled "Negroes" covering the period 1843 to 1846, which pertinently records the ethnic names of the persons so indentured and their estimated ages. They had all undergone the particularly painful process of branding and the symbols with which they were branded were also recorded.[112]

The first entry pertaining to Simon's Bay concerns a nine year old boy named Gambo, who had been taken off an unnamed brig that had been captured by HM ketch *Aurora* and landed in Table Bay on 24 October 1843.

---

[110]Meltzer, "Liberated Africans," 54.
[111]Meltzer, "Liberated Africans," 49.

Gambo was indentured as an apprentice to Richard Black, the shipwright carpenter in Simon's Bay, on 30 November 1843. Gambo had been branded with an "S" on his left breast.[113]

By 5 December 1843 five more children, who had been taken off the aforementioned unnamed brig captured by HM ketch *Aurora* and landed in Table Bay on 24 October 1843, commenced indentureships in Simon's Bay. Their names were Gongo, Kapemba, Leeko, Jepoola and Jarra. With the exception of Kapemba, they were all indentured as house-servants to residents in the town, some of whom were naval employees.

The seven year old boy Gongo, branded with an X within a diamond shape on his right breast, was indentured as a house-servant to Thomas Sam White who worked as a superannuated clerk in the Naval Dockyard in Simon's Town and was married to Petronella Wikboom.

The eight year old boy Leeko, was branded with an S between his shoulder blades. He was indentured as a house-servant to Jerome Gustave Requier.

The six year old girl named Jepoola was indentured as a house-servant to Johs [Johannes?] F de Wet, the Navy Contractor in Simons Town. The eleven year old girl named Jarra, branded with a diamond shape on her right breast, was indentured as a house-servant to the storekeeper Jos Pearson. However, on 5 January she was "transferred" to William Cornelis Kings of George (Officer of the Peace).

By contrast, the eleven year old boy named Kapemba was apprenticed to I Chapman, a carpenter from Simon's Bay. Kapemba was described as having a distinctive large scar on the right side of his belly and a speck in his right eye. Some seven years later, on 5 January 1850, Kapemba would leave Simon's

---

[112] Branding people was characteristic of the Atlantic "slave-trade." This took place during what was referred to as their first passage, that is, the period of the journey from capture to the coast. "Judging from the Customs records at the Cape, CCT 382, the same practice appears to have taken place in the Portuguese slave trade on the southeast African coast, as it was brought into the orbit of the Atlantic slave trade. This may be a difference with the Indian Ocean slave trade for it seems there is no record of branding of slaves at the Cape during the VOC period." Meltzer, "Liberated Africans," 60. See also Katrina H B Keefer, "Marked by Fire: Brands, Slavery, and Identity" *Slavery & Abolition* 40, 4 (May 2019): 2, 6-8, 18-19 referring to the practice on the West coast of Africa.

[113] WCARS, CCT 382 (30 November 1843).

Bay and travel to Swellendam where he was "transferred" to the Reverend James Baker. By this time he would have been eighteen years of age.[114]

When the "slaver" *Josephine* was captured by HMS *Thunderbolt* on 29 January 1844, Jatha, Nongongo, Mangoola, Meloogee, Langaivae, Chornbac and Maria Tomassa were among the people "liberated" off the "slaver." By the time of their arrival, they would have witnessed the deaths of fifteen of the unwilling passengers on board with them who had fatally succumbed to the ravages of the middle passage. Having survived, these children would continue their lives under changed circumstances, commencing indentureships in Simon's Bay.

Jatha, aged twelve, who was branded with an inverted capital G on his right breast, was indentured to a local merchant in the town. However, by 14 September 1845 his circumstances would change once more as he was taken by wagon to Cape Town, having been "transferred" to a family in "Cape Gardens."[115]

Nongongo, aged nine, was branded with the letters "AB in a triangle" on his right breast and the letters "MC" on his left breast. On 14 March 1844 he was indentured as a household servant to a naval officer in Simon's Town, namely W[illia]m Deas Thomson.[116]

For Mangoola, Meloogee and Langaivae, there was at least some comfort in being indentured together. On 14 March 1844 they were all indentured to Isaac de Villiers, a farmer from Hoop Noordhoek.

Mangoola aged nineteen, was branded with a Z on her right shoulder blade.[117] Meloogee, aged twenty-five, was also branded with a Z on his right shoulder blade.[118] They were joined by Langaivae on 24 April 1844. He was aged 35 and was similarly branded with a Z on his right shoulder blade. While Mangoola was indentured as a house servant, Meloogee and Langaivae were indentured as farm servants.[119]

---

[114]WCARS, CCT 382 (5 December 1843) and (5 January 1850).
[115]WCARS, CCT 382 (14 March 1844) and (14 September 1844).
[116]WCARS, CCT 382 (14 March 1844).
[117]WCARS, CCT 382 (14 March 1844).
[118]WCARS, CCT 382 (14 March 1844).
[119]WCARS, CCT 382 (24 April 1844).

Further indentureships in Simon's Bay on 14 March, 1844 relate to the following children:

The thirteen year old boy named Chornbac was indentured as a house servant to Stephen Lamb of Simon's Bay. He was branded with a square-shaped symbol on his left breast.[120]

Maria Tomassa, also aged thirteen, was noted to have a scar under her right eye and was branded with the number 14 on her left arm. She was indentured as a house servant to Lieutenant William Papillon Jamison of the British Royal Navy in Simon's Town on 14 March 1844.[121]

There were also the ten year old boys named Joakee and Kambaleeree who were on the slaver *Enriquetta,* which was intercepted by HMS *Thunderbolt* and landed on 2 February 1844. Joakee was branded with an S and inverted G on his right breast and an S on his right arm. Kambaleeree was branded with inverted GS on his right breast and an S on his right arm. They were both indentured as house servants to William Anderson, who was recorded as being a "wine merchant" in this listing.[122]

Two children who were indentured to Matthew George Blake, the Resident Justice in Simon's Bay on 5 November 1845, were an eleven year old boy named Guahaiataika who was branded with two half moons on his forehead and a twelve year old girl named Monashia, branded with "000" on her forehead as well as marks on her temples. They were among the people landed from the HMS *Helena* and *Mutine* in Simon's Bay on 15 June 1845. The pair were noted to each have a sibling who had also arrived on the ship, a sister and brother respectively. We are left to speculate as to whether they ever saw one another again.[123]

The six year old boy named Wasawaanoo who was landed from HMS *Mutine* in Simon's Bay on 26 March 1845 and quarantined at the Negro Buildings, was indentured to John Breaks, who worked as a naval officer in Simon's Town. However, his stay there ended three years later when he was

---

[120] WCARS, CCT 382 (14 March 1844).
[121] WCARS, CCT 382 (14 March 1844).
[122] WCARS, CCT 382 (14 March 1844).
[123] WCARS, CCT 382 (5 November 1845).

"transferred" to a Mr van Breda in Malmesbury on 17 June 1848. Wasawaanoo was branded on his forehead and temples with three lines.[124]

By 1847 the regulations pertaining to "Liberated Africans" were revised to ensure that children under eleven years of age could be apprenticed until the age of eighteen years for males and seventeen years for females. Most commonly they were apprenticed as "household servants" however, some were apprenticed in husbandry, gardening or skilled trades. It was also stated that in the cases of persons aged sixteen years and upwards, *if they consented* they could be apprenticed for up to five years.[125] However, for displaced young people with few alternatives, the veracity of their consent is open to conjecture.[126]

For those of us from my generation who grew up in descendant communities, it was common for our parents to tell us that they only knew their family histories up until their grandparents. They would say that the elders did not discuss anything with them and that children were not allowed to sit in adult company. One wonders now whether this was the elders' way of protecting their offspring from this traumatic legacy.[127]

John Osmond and Agia of the Cape

When John Osmond died at the age of seventy-seven on 9 May 1847 his occupation was described as "proprietor of sundry houses, lands."[128] His death notice mentioned two children: Agnes Osmond married to Thomas Pownall Pellew Barrow[129] and William Osmond (deceased) who had left "five minor children orphans."[130] Significantly, there was no mention of his

---

[124] WCARS, CCT 382 (17 June 1848).
[125] WCARS, CCT 382 (14 March 1844).
[126] Meltzer, "Liberated Africans," 57.
[127] Yvette Abrahams, Colonialism, Dysfunction and Disjuncture: The Historiography of Sarah Bartmann. Thesis (PhD) University of Cape Town, 2000, 240. Abrahams states "My elders chose, often, not to tell me of my history because the pain, anger …. were considered not suitable for children."
[128] WCARS, MOOC, 6/9/42, Ref. 8968 (1847), John Osmond, Death Notice.
[129] Marriage, Agnes Osmond to Thomas Pownall Pellew Barrow (19 November 1833). South Africa, Church of the Province of South Africa, Parish Registers, 1801-2004 [online resource] *Family Search* https://www.familysearch.org/ (accessed 22 August 2023).

daughter, Fatima. Fatima was born to John Osmond and Agia of the Cape on 13 January 1834. As this year was the beginning of the Emancipation period of Apprenticeship, it would be fair to say that Fatima was born at a time when enslaved people were caught between slavery and working class freedom.

Fig. 8-6. Smith's Lane, Simon's Town, 1975
Source: Watercolour by John Hall

Agia of the Cape lived with her children Henry Johnson, Sarah Christian and Fatima in a property owned by John Osmond in Smith's Lane. His patronage of Agia and her children evidently came at a price. On 1 February 1847 Agnes Barrow, "in her capacity as executrix testamentary" of the Estate of her father, ceded and transferred a certain property in Smith's Lane,

---

[130] WCARS, MOOC, 6/9/19, Ref. 4081 (1840). William Rasseau [sic=Rossouw] Osmond, Death Notice.

Simon's Town to Agia of the Cape. This was on the condition that after the demise of Agia, the property would be passed on to her children in equal shares: namely Henry, Sarah and Fatima. It is important to note that this property was not given to Agia as a gift. She had to purchase the property from the Estate for a sum of one hundred and twenty five pounds.

Fig. 8-7. Rectory Lane, Simonstown
Source: Oil on canvas by Terence McCaw

Fatima would have just become a teenager when her father died. It may well be that, had he lived, he would have done more to protect Fatima from life's blows, particularly within the dominated society into which she was born. However, life was not kind to Fatima. She lost both her husband and her only child, named Moridien, while still very young. Her own life was short-lived and, in contrast to her half-sister Agnes Barrow, was one of hardship and heavy toil.

From her abode in Rectory Lane, Simon's Town, Fatima would walk to the houses of the various Simon's Town residents from whom she earned her living as a charlady and at night her tired feet would trudge the steps of Rectory Lane until she reached her home from where one hopes she found some respite from her daily toil. On 25 August 1875, forty-one year old Fatima died at the home in Rectory Lane, which until her death she shared with her mother Agia and widowed sister Sarah. According to her death certificate, Fatima died penniless. Neither Agia nor her daughters left wills.

However, in 1902 her brother Henry Johnson put in a claim for the property in Smith's Lane. At this time Agia, Sarah and Fatima had already died. Fatima was the youngest of Agia's children and, as already mentioned, was born on 13 January 1834. Her two other children, namely Sarah Christian and Henry Johnson, were born on the 19 March 1832 and 29 September, 1830 respectively.[131]

Agia died on 18 June 1877, just two years after the death of her daughter Fatima. As there was a special condition in the transfer of this property that after the death of Agia transfer would pass to her three children in equal shares; Henry Johnson made an application to the Master of the Supreme Court to have the property transferred to his name.[132] This application was made two years after the death of his sister Sarah Christian, who died on 9 May 1900.[133]

Henry Johnson seemed to have fared better than his sisters in that he was a shoemaker by trade whereas they were both charwomen, although as we have learnt shoemaker's apprentices were often very badly treated. Sadly, his marriage to Hester Hendricka Germans was short-lived as she died in 1863 at the age of twenty four years, just seven years after their marriage at St Francis Church in 1856. He did not marry again.

---

[131]Agia, Death Notice, WCARS, MOOC 6/9/455, Ref. 2480 (26 July 1902). (Date filed).
[132]WCARS, MOOC 6/9/455, Ref. 2478, 11 December, 1903.
[133]WCARS, MOOC 6/9/455, Ref. 2470, 21 July, 1902.

Henry Johnson's attempts to have the property described as "Lot No. 1 of the divided upper part of the property belonging to the late John Osmond"[134] passed into his name bore fruit and, on 19 August 1903, the property was transferred to him. When Henry Johnson died on 10 June 1909, he was also registered as living in the house in Rectory Lane, Simon's Town and was survived by his two sons from this marriage, John and William Johnson. Although one document states that both Fatima and Henry were "the illegitimate children of John Osmond," the death certificate of Henry Johnson, completed by his son, John Henry Johnson, does not mention Osmond and names his parents as Henry Johnson and Agia Johnson.[135] The reason for this is open to conjecture.

How do we understand the dynamics between Agia of the Cape and John Osmond? Osmond was a powerful "slave-holder" who held high office in the town[136] whereas Agia of the Cape was born into slavery circa 1803, denied more than the most rudimentary education and inducted into a life of labour as a washerwoman.[137] Certainly this interaction was not equal and I question whether Agia had agency and choice. This view is strengthened by the fact that a month after Osmond's death Agia married Paul Christians, the father of her daughter Sarah Christians.[138] The couple married according to "Malay [i.e. Muslim] rites." That they were married for twenty-eight years until Paul Christians died circa 1875, suggests that he was her true love. Two years after his passing, Agia herself took leave of this world.

---

[134]Simon's Town Museum, Deeds Registry No. 542.
[135]Death certificate of Henry Johnson dated 29 October 1909. Probate Records of the Master of the High Court, 1834-1989[online resource] *Family Search* https://www.familysearch.org/ark:/61903/1:1:QP4B-SGB6.
[136]WCARS, Records of the Magistrate of Simon's Town 1793-1985: 1/SMT 2/5, SMT 10/22 (1831-1833) Ref. 6 (19 January 1831).
[137]WCARS, MOOC 6/9/455, Ref. 2480 (26 July 1902).
[138]WCARS, MOOC 6/9/455, Ref. 2480 (26 July 1902).

Closing Words

This book honours the memory of a diverse and socially vulnerable people, who lived in Simon's Town at a time when Simon's Town was a remote place that was easier to access by sea than by land. The book also honours their descendants, most of whom were forcibly removed to Ocean View during the era of apartheid forced removals.

The vulnerable people mentioned in this book lived through some of the most historically poignant moments in South Africa's history; however, it is likely that they were unaware of them. They were a subjugated people who lived in a remote corner of the False Bay Coast. Theirs was a world where poverty and trauma was commonplace and where access to education and information was sparse. They lived at a certain time in history when the Cape was a colony like the other colonised areas known as Natal, the Transvaal Republic and the Orange Free State, which would eventually be joined into one country known as the Union of South Africa in 1910.

However, for the vulnerable people mentioned in this book, this was a far away time and a different world to the world they knew. They lived in a secluded area, which was hidden between the seaside and the mountains. Though they came from diverse ancestral backgrounds, their often brutal historical experiences solidified a sense of community, which would grow from these turbulent beginnings. Although they and their descendants were eventually styled into a single colonial identity construction referred to as "Coloured," the indications are that they rejected this identity as privately they identified themselves and each other as "Simonites."

> O ye who pass by this way
> I will not pass you without looking you in the eye
> For we both come from the town that was yours and mine
> We may differ in culture and ways
> As Simonites we'll stay.

—*the late Ronald Roberts, former Simon's Town resident and Kru descendant*

Message to my enslaved mother

Who are you, nameless, faceless woman? I encountered you in an advertisement in the *Cape Gazette*. The year was 1820 and you and your four children were advertised as goods for sale at an auction along with livestock and household furniture. No mention is given of your name, or the slave name that had been allocated to you, nor is there any mention of where you came from or how old your children were. The only information that seemed pertinent to the auctioneer, J Snell, was that you were 27 years old and a good washerwoman. But I wonder about you. Did you know, on that day, that you and your children were going to be auctioned off, or were you just called away from your work and taken to the spot in front of the Old Admiral's House when your number was called? Was it a quick five minute transaction? Was it over before you even realised what was happening? And your children; were they sold to the same enslavers who bought you or were they sold separately? If they were sold separately, did they cry to come with you or did they also simply not realise what was happening? Would you have tried to protest, and if you did, were you whipped and forced away? If your children were sold off separately to you, did you ever see each other again? And if you did not, what were the nightmares that plagued you during those lonely hours when the world was sleeping? Did you have more children after this, and if you did, did you form a comfortable psychological barrier from them, knowing that they too might be taken from you on any day, at any time?

I imagine that at night, you awoke from your sleep only to be haunted by their cries. Maybe sometimes you woke up in the morning expecting them to be there and then reality would dawn and you would realise that you were in a different environment and they were gone. If you felt outrage at what had happened, did you keep it to yourself, living as you were in a society where what was happening to you was quite acceptable? Was it acceptable to YOU? Did you hate the people who did this to you or was your sense of self so diminished that you accepted any abuse meted out to you?

And sometimes, when even your acceptance got the better of you and you felt that painful yearning that any mother feels when she is parted from her children, no matter whether those children were born of love or forced into your womb by your enslaver's lust, how did you deaden the pain? Did you steal some wine to drink to help numb the constant ache in your heart, to help you sleep, to help you forget? And in the end, did you forget? Did you even forget who you yourself were? And if you did, what did it matter to the people who enslaved you, as long as the washing was clean. Even if you sometimes smelt a little bit of alcohol, would they not have just said "these people are all like that, that is why we have to treat them as children, because that is what they are, they have the minds of children. They don't even have feelings for their own."

I think about you a lot, nameless, faceless woman. Standing there, outside the Old Admiral's house where you were a nothing, a mere chattel, a washerwoman, a body to serve and to be abused. You were not allowed an opinion, you were not allowed to protest, you were not allowed to feel; so whatever you felt was to be hidden deep within the crevices of your tormented soul. But you did feel, nameless, faceless woman. I sense your feelings so strong within me now. Your tears cry out to be heard, from beneath these official words, and I catch them in my heart.

So now you know that we are connected, nameless, faceless woman. So now that we have met each other in this transitory space, you can finally see who I am. I am the bloodline that exists between the past and the present.

I am the inheritor of your broken dreams and the offspring of your pain. But allow me also to be the caretaker of a new dawn, where the chains of slavery and despair will be loosened from our minds as well as our bodies.

So now I reach out to you, over centuries past, for you, nameless, faceless woman, you are my past and I, nameless, faceless woman, am your future.

© *Joline Young 2009*

Acknowledgements

Researching and writing this book has been a labour of love, and I dedicate this work to Blanche, Nicole, Colin, Kyle, Ocean, Nick and Charlie as well as the descendants of the people mentioned in this book, with love.

Thank you to ANFASA (The Academic and Non Fiction Authors Association) from whom I received a small author's grant in 2009 towards this work as well as the David and Elaine Potter Foundation who funded my Master's research on "The Enslaved People of Simons Town 1743-1843." I am grateful for their support and enthusiasm for this project.

My gratitude goes to the late Professor Robert Shell who suggested the title for this book. I am profoundly grateful for his unwavering support of my research into slavery and valued guidance over the years. I can still hear him saying "secondary sources are Fool's Gold."

My sincere thanks also go to Prof Nigel Worden who supervised my Masters thesis on slavery and who taught me the finer aspects of research methodology.

Thank you to all the staff of the UCT African Studies, Rare Books and the Chancellor Oppenheimer Library who were always so helpful and efficient and to all the wonderful lecturers in the UCT Department of Historical Studies.

My profound thanks also go to Yvette Abrahams and Shamiela Abrahams of the UCT San and Khoi Centre from whom I have learnt the intricacies of Deep Listening, as well as June Bam-Hutchison who formerly headed up the Centre. Thanks also to the staff at the Department of Cultural Affairs and Sport (DCAS), particularly Jaline de Villiers. It has been a pleasure to work with you all on a range of interesting projects.

I would also like to thank the Western Cape Archives and Records Services team for providing an outstanding service to all researchers in such a welcoming and efficient space. Thanks particularly to Erika le Roux and Maxine Khan.

While most of the research material that informed this book comes from the Western Cape Archives, I initially also accessed the archives of the Heritage and Simon's Town Museums for which I am no less grateful. Thank you to all for their kind assistance.

Thanks in particular to Mr and Mrs Davidson of the Heritage Museum for welcoming me into their hearts and home. Thanks also to the Khan family of Simon's Town.

The late Maureen Rall and also Helene Everad from the Netherlands offered me a vital translation service, which has added great value to my research.

I am grateful to Lila Komnick (now retired) and Robert Dolby of the Library of Parliament who were most generous in helping me to source images for this book from their collections. Other artworks and photographs are printed here through the generosity of Lionel Davis, Muriel Rubin, Koos Bekker and Mary Kindo. Laura Mitchell kindly gave me permission to use the map drawn for her by Susan Reese, which has added context.

The book cover was designed by Denise Rowland and Elize Potgieter who really took this project to heart. Their design is a beautiful rendition of the story of slavery in Simon's Town.

I am particularly grateful to all the fascinating former Simon's Town residents whom I met as I embarked on my oral history research of Simon's Town during 2008 and 2009, some of whom have sadly since passed away. It has been an honour to meet you all.

My immense thanks go to my publisher and dear friend Dr Sandra Rowoldt Shell for her tireless and dedicated labour of love as she brought this manuscript into publication. Thank you Sandy. What an unforgettable journey we have been on together over these last few months.

Thank you also to my lovely family, and amazing friends and colleagues in the heritage sector, as well as all the wonderful people I have met through my historical walking tours of Simon's Town and Cape Town: you all make life beautiful.

Selected Sources

Archival Sources

Western Cape Archives and Records Service (WCARS)

Colonial Office (CO)

Council of Justice (CJ)

Master of the Orphan Chamber (MOOC)

Notarial Deeds of the Cape District (NCD)

Opgaafrolle

Records of the Magistrate of Simon's Town:
  Letters Received, 1/SMT 2/5, 1793-1932.

Slave Office:
  Slave Office SO 17/1 "Notes collected from the Colonial Placcards since 1652 upon the subject of Slavery and Indian Statutes 1652-1818,
  Confidential Reports of the Protector of Slaves, SO 3/20.
  SO 4/12 Book of Complaints, Guardian of Slaves 1826-1830.
  SO 2/16 Slave Registry Department, Correspondence.
  SO 6/79 Slave Register M-W 1824-1834.

Verbatim Copies (VC)

Elliot Collection of Photographs

Accessions

Samuel Eusebius Hudson, Essay on "Improvements," 1807 to 1814, WCARS, A 602/9.

Simon's Town Museum,

The Willis Files:

Cape Freeholds, Volume 2 Part 3, 13.04.1717-10.08.1746.

Cape Old Freeholds, Volume 3, 06.10.1746-27.08.1782

Slave Registry files, Simonstown

Slavery files

The Heritage Museum, Simon's Town

Kitaabs, newspaper cuttings and photographs.

Cape Transcripts 1673-1834;

Cape Transcripts, 1673-1834: Transcriptions of Manuscripts from the Cape Archives about People at the Cape of Good Hope. *Genealogical Society of South Africa* [online resource] https://www.eggsa.org/sales/pop-tanap2.htm.

Published books

Printed Primary Sources:

Heese, Johannes August and Roelof Theunis Johannes Lombard. *South African Genealogies*. Volumes 1-17. Stellenbosch: Genealogical Institute of South Africa, 1986-2008.

Hoge, John. *Personalia of the Germans at the Cape, 1652-1806.* Cape Town: Cape Times, 1946. Archives Year Book, 1941.

Kaapse Argiefstukke. *Kaapse Plakkaatboek*: deel I-VI (1652-1806). Cape Town: *Cape Times*, 1944-1951.

Leibbrandt, Hendrik Carel Vos. *Precis of the Archives of the Cape of Good Hope, Requesten (Memorials)*, Volumes 1-4, A-E; F-O; P-S; T-Z. Cape Town: South African Library, vols 1-2, 1905-1906; reprints vols 3-4, 1988-1989.

Theal, George McCall. *Records of the Cape Colony* Volumes 1-36. Cape Town: William Clowes & Sons for the Cape Government: 1897-1905.

PRINTED SECONDARY SOURCES

Adhikari, Mohamed. *The Anatomy of a South African Genocide: The Extermination of the Cape San Peoples.* Claremont: UCT Press, 2010.

Ashmore, Harriette. *Narrative of a Three Months' March in India*; …. by the Wife of an Officer in the 16th Foot. London: Hastings, 1841.

Australian Dictionary of Biography [online resource] https://adb.anu.edu.au/biography/bigge-john-thomas-1779/text1999.

Bam, June. *Ausi Told Me, Why Cape Herstoriographies Matter.* Auckland Park: Fanele, 2021.

Barnard, Lady Anne. *South Africa a Century Ago: Letters Written from the Cape of Good Hope (1797-1801).* London: Smith Elder, 1901.

Bekker, Anton Ettienne. *The History of False Bay up to 1795.* Simon's Town: Simon's Town Historical Society, 1990.

Boezak, Willa. "The Cultural Heritage of South Africa's Khoisan" in *Indigenous Peoples' Cultural Heritage: Rights, Debates and Challenges*; edited by Alexandra Xanthaki, Sanna Valkonen, Leena Heinämäki, and Piia Kristiina Nuorgam. Leiden: Brill/Nijhoff, 2017, 253-272.

Bolsmann, Eric H. T*he Mount Nelson.* Pretoria: HAUM, 1978.

Bradlow, Frank Rosslyn and Margaret Cairns, *The Early Cape Muslims: A Study of their Mosques, Genealogy and Origins.* Cape Town: Balkema, 1978.

Bridge, Horatio. *Journal of an African Cruiser: Comprising Sketches of the Canaries, the Cape de Verds, Liberia, Madeira, Sierra Leone and other places of interest on the West Coast of Africa*. New York: George P Putnam, 1845.

Cape Melting Pot; translated by Delia Robertson from Hans F Heese, *Groep Sonder Grense*, … Bellville: University of the Western Cape, 1985. Downloadable from *Cape Melting Pot* [online resource] http://www.e-family.co.za/ffy/RemarkableWriting/CapeMeltingPot-FFY.pdf

Dapper, Olfert, Willem ten Rhijne and Johannes Gulielmus de Grevenbroek. *The Early Cape Hottentots*; edited by Isaac Schapera and B. Farrington. Cape Town: Van Riebeeck Society, 1933. VRS Series I: 14.

Diemont, Marius. *Rogues to Riches, The Fortunes of Olof Bergh and the Van der Stels*. Hermanus: Penstock Publishing, 2012.

Dommisse, Boet. *Admiralty House, Simon's Town*. Cape Town: CTP Book Printers, 2005.

Ellis, Alfred Burdon. *The Land of Fetish*. London: Chapman and Hall, 1883.

Elphick, Richard. *Kraal and Castle: Khoikhoi and the Founding of White South Africa*. New Haven and London: Yale University Press, 1977.

Elphick, Richard and Hermann Giliomee, *The Shaping of South African Society, 1652- 1840*. Cape Town: Maskew Miller Longman, 1989.

Encyclopedia of Antislavery and Abolition Volume 2: J-Z. Britain: Greenwood, 2007.

Forster, George, *A Voyage Round the World: In his Britannic Majesty's Sloop, Resolution, ... and 5*. London: printed for B White, 1777: Volume 2.

Frost, Diane. *Work and Community among West African Migrant Workers since the Nineteenth Century*. Liverpool: Liverpool University Press, 1999.

Geyser, Ockert. *The History of the Old Supreme Court Building*. Cape Town: Africana Press, 1982.

Gill, Isobel. *Six Months in Ascension: An Unscientific Account of a Scientific Expedition*. London: Murray, 1880.

Gorelik, Boris (editor). *"An Entirely Different World": Russian Visitors to the Cape 1797-1870.* Cape Town: Van Riebeeck Society, 2015. VRS Series 2: 46.

Holman, James. *A Voyage Round the World, Including Travels in Africa, Asia, Australasia ...* London: Smith, Elder, 1834, volume 2.

International Handbook of Multigenerational Legacies of Trauma; edited by Yael Danieli. New York: Plenum Press, 1998.

Larson, Pier Martin. *Ocean of Letters: Language and Creolization in an Indian Ocean Diaspora.* Cambridge: Cambridge University Press, 2009.

Linder, Adolphe. *The Swiss at the Cape of Good Hope, 1652-1971.* Basle: Basler Afrika Bibliogaphien, 1997.

Linder, Adolphe. *The Swiss Regiment Meuron at the Cape and Afterwards, 1781-1816.* Cape Town: Castle Military Museum, 2000.

Lloyd, Christopher. *The Navy and the Slave Trade: The Suppression of the African Slave Trade in the Nineteenth Century.* London: Routledge, 2012.

Loos, Jackie. *Echoes of Slavery, Voices from South Africa's Past.* Cape Town: New Africa Books, 2004.

Mavór, William. *An Historical Account of the Most Celebrated Voyages ...* Volume 12. Philadelphia: Samuel F. Bradford, 1802.

McCulloch, Merran. *The Peoples of Sierra Leone.* London: International African Institute, 1950.

McKenzie, Kirsten. *The Making of an English Slave-Owner: Samuel Eusebius Hudson at the Cape of Good Hope 1796-1807.* Rondebosch: UCT Press, 1993.

Menakem, Resmaa. *My Grandmother's Hands: Racialized Trauma and the Pathways to Mending Our Hearts and Bodies.* Las Vegas, NV: Central Recovery Press, 2017.

Nair, Adoor KK Ramachandran. *Slavery in Kerala.* Delhi: Mittel Publications, 1986.

Penn, Nigel. *The Forgotten Frontier, Colonist and Khoisan on the Cape's Northern Frontier in the 18th Century.* Claremont: Juta, 2005.

Percival, Robert. *An Account of the Cape of Good Hope...* London: Baldwin, 1804.

Peterson, John. *Province of Freedom: A History of Sierra Leone, 1787-1870.* Evanston: Northwestern University Press, 1969.

Philip, Peter. *British Residents at the Cape 1795-1819.* Claremont: David Philip, 1981.

Pryce-Lewis, Owen. *When First We Practice: or the Life of Jean Michiel Endres.* Simon's Town: The Simon's Town Historical Society, 1989.

Raikes, Henry. *Sir Jahleel Brenton, Memoir of the Life and Services of vice-Admiral Sir Jahleel Brenton* ...; edited by Henry Raikes. London: Hatchard and Son, Piccadilly, 1846.

Rice, Bill. "*Nubian* (C.370): The Admiralty Coal Hulk based at Simon's Town from 1901-1912" *Simon's Town Historical Society Bulletin* 23, 2 (July 2004): 74-78.

Ross, Robert. *Cape of Torments: Slavery and Resistance in South Africa.* London, etc.: Routledge & Kegan Paul, 1983.

Ross, Robert. *Status & Respectability in the Cape Colony, 1750-1870: A Tragedy of Manners.* Cambridge: Cambridge University Press, 1999.

Rowe, Judy. *The Story of Rocklands Farm Simon's Town, South Africa 1815 – 2010.* Simonstown: Judy Rowe, 2010.

Shell, Robert Carl-Heinz. *Children of Bondage, A Social History of the Slave Society at the Cape of Good Hope, 1652-1838.* Johannesburg: Witwatersrand University Press, 1994.

Shell, Robert Carl-Heinz. *From Diaspora to Diorama: The Old Slave Lodge in Cape Town.* Cape Town: NagsPro MultiMedia, 2012.

Shell, Sandra Rowoldt. *Children of Hope: The Odyssey of the Oromo Slaves from Ethiopia to South Africa.* Ohio: Ohio University Press, 2018.

Sidanius, Jim and Felicia Pratto. *Social Dominance.* Cambridge: Cambridge University Press, 2001.

Sleigh, Dan, *Die Buiteposte: VOC-Buiteposte onder Kaapse Bestuur, 1652-1795.* Pretoria: HAUM, 1993.

Simon's Town. Municipal and Naval Regatta Committee. *Souvenir of Simon's Town: Van Riebeeck Tercentenary Souvenir.* Simon's Town: Committee of the Simon's Town Municipal and Naval Regatta, 1952.

Spilhaus, Margaret Whiting. *Company's Men.* Cape Town: John Malherbe, 1973.

Taylor, Stephen. *Defiance: The Extraordinary life of Lady Anne Barnard* New York: W.W. Norton, 2017.

Theal, George McCall. *History of South Africa since September 1795.* London: Swan Sonnenschein, 1908.

Thurston, Henry Winfred. *The Dependent Child: A Story of Changing Aims and Methods in the Care of Dependent Children.* New York: Columbia University Press, 1930.

Tracey, Henry. *A Visit to Cape Town in 1838.* Johannesburg: Friends of the Library, University of the Witwatersrand, 1980.

Tuckey, James Kingston. *An Account of a Voyage to Establish a Colony at Port Phillip … in the Years 1802-3-4.* London: Longman, Hurst, Rees and Orme, 1805.

Ulrich, Nicole. "Abolition from Below, The 1808 Revolt in the Cape Colony" in *Humanitarian Intervention and Changing Labor Relations: The Long-term Consequences of the Abolition of the Slave Trade.* Leiden: Brill, 2011, 193-222.

Walker, James W St G. *The Black Loyalists: The Search for a Promised Land in Nova Scotia and Sierra Leone, 1783-1870.* Toronto: University of Toronto Press, 1992.

Whisson, Michael. *The Fairest Cape?* Johannesburg: South African Institute of Race Relations, 1972.

Worden, Nigel. *The Chains That Bind Us.* Cape Town: Juta, 1996.

Worden, Nigel, Elizabeth van Heyningen and Vivian Bickford-Smith, *Cape Town: The Making of a City.* Cape Town: David Philip Publishers: 1998.

Worden, Nigel. *Slavery in Dutch South Africa*. Cambridge: Cambridge University Press, 1985.

JOURNAL ARTICLES

Anti-Slavery Reporter and Aborigines' Friend 2, 20 (2 August 1847): 119. (Evidence of premature births among "slave" women in consequence of the brutality of enslavement).

Bibko, Julia. "The American Revolution and the Black Loyalist Exodus" *#History: A Journal of Student Research* (1 December 2016): 64. SUNY Open Access Repository [online resource] http://hdl.handle.net/20.500.12648/2669 (accessed 29 September 2023).

Davey, Arthur. "The Kroomen of Simon's Town" *Simon's Town Historical Society Bulletin* 16, 2 (July 1990): 51.

Davey, Arthur. "Tindals, Seedies and Kroomen" *Simon's Town Historical Society Bulletin* 17, 4 (July 1993): 157-158.

Dooling, Wayne. "The Origins and Aftermath of the Cape Colony's 'Hottentot Code' of 1809" *Kronos* 31 (November 2005): 50-61.

Guelke, Leonard and Robert Carl-Heinz Shell, "Landscape of Conquest: Frontier Water Alienation and Khoikhoi Strategies of Survival, 1652-1780" *Journal of Southern African Studies* 18, 4 (December 1992): 803-824.

Havemann, Roy and Johan Fourie, "The Cape of Perfect Storms: Colonial Africa's First Financial Crash, 1788-1793" *Economic Research Southern Africa (ERSA)* Working Paper 511 (March 2015).

Hill, Lawrence. "Freedom Bound" *The Beaver* (February-March 2007): 18.

Keefer, Katrina H B. "Marked by Fire: Brands, Slavery, and Identity" *Slavery & Abolition: A Journal of Slave and Post-Slave Studies* 40, 4 (May 2019): 659-681.

Laidlaw, Zoe. "Investigating Empire: Humanitarians, Reform and the Commission of Eastern Inquiry" *Journal of Imperial and Commonwealth History* 40, 5 (December 2012): 749-768.

Laidler, Percy Ward. "Medical Establishments and Institutions at the Cape During the Opening Years of the Nineteenth Century" *History of Medicine* (10 July 1937): 484-485.

Langham-Carter, Reginald Robert. "George Sturt, Colonial Chaplain" *Simon's Town Historical Society Bulletin* 10, 1 (January 1978): 12-17.

Malherbe, Vertrees Candy. "Colonial Justice and the Khoisan in the Immediate Aftermath of Ordinance 50 of 1828: Denouement at Uitenhage" *Kronos* 24 (November 1997): 77-90.

Malherbe, Vertrees Candy. "The Khoekhoe Soldier at the Cape of Good Hope: How the Khoekhoen were drawn into the Dutch and British Defensive Systems, to circa 1809" *South African Military History* Journal 12, 3 (June 2002).

Marks, Shula. "Khoisan Resistance to the Dutch in the Seventeenth and Eighteenth Centuries" *Journal of African History* 13, 1 (1972): 55-80.

Martin, Jane. "Krumen 'down the Coast': Liberian Migrants on the West African Coast in the 19th Century" *The International Journal of African Historical Studies* 18, 3, (1985): 401-423.

Mason, John Edwin. "The Slaves and Their Protectors: Reforming Resistance in a Slave Society, the Cape Colony, 1826-1834" *Journal of Southern African Studies* 17, 1 (March 1991): 103-128.

Meltzer, Jaqueline Lalou. "Liberated Africans and the Barracks at Papendorp" *Bulletin of the National Library of South Africa* 74, 1 (June 2020): 45-66.

Philip, Peter H. "The Vicissitudes of the Early British Settlers at the Cape" *Quarterly Bulletin of the South African Library* 40, 4 (June 1986): 159-170.

Read, Audrey. "Black Town in Simon's Town" *Simon's Town Historical Society Bulletin* 20, 4 (July 1999): 139-142.

Rhind, David M. "The Simon's Town Railway Line" *Simon's Town Historical Society Bulletin* 16, 2 (July 1990): 54-61.

Rugarli, Anna Maria. "Eyes on the Prize: The Story of the Prize Slave Present" *Quarterly Bulletin of The National Library of South Africa* 62, 4, (October-December 2008): 161-172.

Saunders, Christopher. "'Liberated Africans' and Labour at the Cape of Good Hope in the First half of the 19th Century" in *Africa Seminar: Collected Papers*. Cape Town: University of Cape Town. Centre for African Studies, Volume 3 (March 1983).

Saunders, Christopher. "Liberated Africans in Cape Colony in the First Half of the Nineteenth Century" *The International Journal of African Historical Studies* 18, 2 (1985): 223-239.

Shell, Sandra Rowoldt. "Trauma and Slavery: Gilo and the Soft, Subtle Shackles of Lovedale" *Bulletin of the National Library of South Africa* 71, 2 (December 2017): 141-156.

"Some Facts in the History of the Parish of St France's Simon's Town" Claremont: *Peninsula Herald*, 1903.

Warden, Robert. "Extracts from the Journal of Robert Warden ..." *Quarterly Bulletin of the South African Library* 7, 3 & 4 (March/June) 1953: 68-79.

Whisson, Michael. "Water and Workers: Meeting the Needs of the Royal Navy in Simon's Town" *Simon's Town Historical Society Bulletin* 13, 4 (July 1985): 152-153.

Young, Joline. "The West African Kroomen and their links to Simon's Town" *Quarterly Bulletin of the National Library of South Africa* 64, 2 (April-June 2010): 62-75.

Zwart, Pim de. "Real Wages at the Cape of Good Hope: a Long-Term Perspective, 1652-1912" *Tijdschrift voor Sociale en Economische Geschiedenis* 10, 2 (2013): 28-58.

NEWSPAPERS

Cape Town Gazette [and African Advertiser]

Christian Express

South African Commercial Advertiser.

Theses

Abrahams, Yvette. Colonialism, Dysfunction and Disjuncture: The Historiography of Sarah Bartmann. Thesis (PhD) University of Cape Town, 2000.

Brenner, Ashley. The "Dutch Have Made Slaves of Them All, and… They Are Called Free": Slavery and Khoisan Indentured Servitude in the Eighteenth-Century Dutch Cape Colony. Thesis (MA), Emory University, 2009.

Cladingbowl, Janet-Anne. A Study in the Development of Simon's Town 1898-1910. Thesis (BA Honours), University of Cape Town, 1984.

Corns, Donna. Offended Shadows: Marronage in the Cape Hanglip 1720s-1730s. Thesis (BA Honours), University of Cape Town, 2011.

Guler, Jessica. The Relationship among Previous Exposure to War and Conflict, Acculturation, and Identity Formation among Adolescent Refugees. Thesis (BA Hons), University of Central Florida, 2014.

Muller, Merle. Aspects of Social Composition of Twelve Malay Households in Simonstown. Thesis (Social Anthropology Honours), University of Cape Town, 1969.

Reidy, Michael Charles. The Admission of Slaves and "Prize Slaves" into the Cape Colony, 1797-1818. Thesis (MA), University of Cape Town, 1997.

Robinson, Enid Helen, Beyond the City Limits, People and Property at Wynberg, 1795 to 1927. Thesis (PhD), University of Cape Town, 1995.

Twidle, Hedley. Prison and Garden: Cape Town, Natural History and the Literary Imagination. Thesis (PhD), University of York, 2010.

Young, Joline. The Enslaved People of Simon's Town. Thesis (MA), University of Cape Town, 2013.

Unpublished Manuscripts

Davey, Arthur. "Kroomen: Black Sailors at the Cape." Unpublished paper (1992).

"Out of Livery: the Papers of Samuel Eusebius Hudson, 1764-1828" edited by Robert Carl-Heinz Shell. Unpublished manuscript, 2013.

Shell, Robert Carl-Heinz. Saledeed dataset (unpublished).

Whisson, Michael. "Group Areas: The Case of Simon's Town." Unpublished paper.

Whisson, Michael. "Group Areas: The End of the Hottentot Tradition in the Simon's Town District." Unpublished paper.

Young, Joline. Database of enslaved children in Simon's Town during the Dutch colonial era (unpublished, December 2013).